Higher Education and the Lifecourse

SRHE and Open University Press Imprint
General Editor: Heather Eggins

Current titles include:

Catherine Bargh *et al.*: *University Leadership*
Ronald Barnett: *Beyond all Reason*
Ronald Barnett: *The Limits of Competence*
Ronald Barnett: *Higher Education*
Ronald Barnett: *Realizing the University in an Age of Supercomplexity*
Tony Becher and Paul R. Trowler: *Academic Tribes and Territories (2nd edn)*
Neville Bennett *et al.*: *Skills Development in Higher Education and Employment*
John Biggs: *Teaching for Quality Learning at University (2nd edn)*
David Boud *et al.* (eds): *Using Experience for Learning*
David Boud and Nicky Solomon (eds): *Work-based Learning*
Tom Bourner *et al.* (eds): *New Directions in Professional Higher Education*
John Brennan *et al.* (eds): *What Kind of University?*
Anne Brockbank and Ian McGill: *Facilitating Reflective Learning in Higher Education*
Ann Brooks and Alison Mackinnon (eds): *Gender and the Restructured University*
Sally Brown and Angela Glasner (eds): *Assessment Matters in Higher Education*
James Cornford and Neil Pollock: *Putting the University Online*
John Cowan: *On Becoming an Innovative University Teacher*
Gerard Delanty: *Challenging Knowledge*
Chris Duke: *Managing the Learning University*
Heather Eggins and Ranald Macdonald (eds): *The Scholarship of Academic Development*
Gillian Evans: *Academics and the Real World*
Andrew Hannan and Harold Silver: *Innovating in Higher Education*
David Istance, Hans Schuetze and Tom Schuller (eds): *International Perspectives on Lifelong Learning*
Norman Jackson and Helen Lund (eds): *Benchmarking for Higher Education*
Merle Jacob and Tomas Hellström (eds): *The Future of Knowledge Production in the Academy*
Peter Knight: *Being a Teacher in Higher Education*
Peter Knight and Paul Trowler: *Departmental Leadership in Higher Education*
Peter Knight and Mantz Yorke: *Assessment, Learning and Employability*
Mary Lea and Barry Stierer (eds): *Student Writing in Higher Education*
Ian McNay (ed.): *Higher Education and its Communities*
Elaine Martin: *Changing Academic Work*
Louise Morley: *Quality and Power in Higher Education*
Moira Peelo and Terry Wareham (eds): *Failing Students in Higher Education*
Craig Prichard: *Making Managers in Universities and Colleges*
Michael Prosser and Keith Trigwell: *Understanding Learning and Teaching*
John Richardson: *Researching Student Learning*
Stephen Rowland: *The Enquiring University Teacher*
Maggi Savin-Baden: *Problem-based Learning in Higher Education*
Peter Scott (ed.): *The Globalization of Higher Education*
Peter Scott: *The Meanings of Mass Higher Education*
Maria Slowey and David Watson: *Higher Education and the Lifecourse*
Anthony Smith and Frank Webster (eds): *The Postmodern University?*
Colin Symes and John McIntyre (eds): *Working Knowledge*
Peter G. Taylor: *Making Sense of Academic Life*
Richard Taylor, Jean Barr and Tom Steele: *For a Radical Higher Education*
Susan Toohey: *Designing Courses for Higher Education*
Paul R. Trowler (ed.): *Higher Education Policy and Institutional Change*
Melanie Walker (ed.): *Reconstructing Professionalism in University Teaching*
David Warner and David Palfreyman (eds): *The State of UK Higher Education*
Gareth Williams (ed.): *The Enterprising University*
Diana Woodward and Karen Ross: *Managing Equal Opportunities in Higher Education*

Higher Education and the Lifecourse

Maria Slowey and David Watson

Society for Research into Higher Education
& Open University Press

Published by SRHE and
Open University Press
McGraw-Hill Education
McGraw-Hill House
Shoppenhangers Road
Maidenhead
Berkshire
England
SL6 2QL

email: enquiries@openup.co.uk
world wide web: www.openup.co.uk

First published 2003

Copyright © Maria Slowey and David Watson 2003

A catalogue record of this book is availabe from the British Library

ISBN 0 335 21377 4 (pb)   0 335 21378 2 (hb)

Library of Congress Cataloging-in-Publication Data
CIP data has been applied for

Typeset by RefineCatch Limited, Bungay, Suffolk
Printed in the UK by Bell & Bain Ltd., Glasgow

Contents

Foreword

By Lord Moser KCB CBE FBA

This book is extremely timely with higher education, rightly, back on our front pages and as a government priority. Moreover, it is widely accepted that universities and colleges have a role 'at the heart of the country's well-being' – the words in the Report of the National Commission on Education (*Learning to Succeed* 1992) on which Sir David Watson played a crucial part.

Maria Slowey, Sir David Watson and their fellow authors have produced a worthy successor to the Commission's Report. They correctly treat education as a seamless web from cradle to grave, focusing throughout on lifelong learning. They pay due attention to the basics of literacy and numeracy, without which the pyramid of learning too easily crumbles.

The book also shows how remarkably the universities have developed over the years. They have coped with the vast increase in student numbers and with the welcome growth in the proportion of mature and part-time students. And they have come to contribute more and more to the understanding of the nation's social, economic, communication and cultural problems. The processes of learning and teaching have undergone vast changes, another area where the universities have shown themselves helpful.

All told, the book illustrates how the obligations of the modern universities have become ever more diverse and challenging. They combine their response to these challenges with the central task of ensuring that they enrich our individual lives. Our universities and colleges are indeed a source of pride.

All this emerges from a challenging book which I commend to all who are interested in higher education.

Acknowledgements

All editors of multi-authored volumes will tell their friends at some stage what a nightmare the job is. Editors, authors and publishers can all develop differing ideas about content, style and relevance as well as different answers to that profound metaphysical question of when a deadline is really a deadline. What is more, such difficulties seem to be compounded when there is a determination – as here – for the totality of the book to tell a story.

This time we feel we have been blessed. *Higher Education and the Lifecourse* began as an idea sketched by the two of us on a beermat at a Teaching and Learning Research Programme (TLRP) seminar in London in June 2002. By the time of the Society for Research into Higher Education (SRHE) Conference in Glasgow in December, and with the benefit of an excellent set of conference abstracts, it had expanded to a full provisional outline on two pages. At that stage Shona Mullen of the Open University Press had taken over from John Skelton and become a valued co-conspirator. It then expanded to a suitcase as we negotiated with selected authors (some from the conference, some directly commissioned) about their contributions. With their remarkable forbearance, and willingness to respond quickly to suggestions and ideas, we were able to make a book out of the suitcase by March 2003 and are now able to go to press in July. We thank our fellow-authors most sincerely.

We also have other personal obligations to record. Gabrielle Lee and Irene McLaren of the University of Glasgow and Rachel Bowden of the University of Brighton made contributions that went far beyond their famed administrative and technical efficiency. Other thanks, for advice and encouragement, go to Elizabeth Maddison, Tom Bourner, Betty Skolnick and Richard Taylor. We trust that they, and others across the fast-moving field of research into higher education, will enjoy the story.

Maria Slowey and David Watson
Glasgow and Brighton
16 June 2003

Notes on contributors

Kepa Artaraz was born in Bilbao, Spain, but completed his higher education in the UK, having recently gained a Doctorate in Cuban Studies at the University of Wolverhampton. He has worked at the Universities of Nottingham and Wolverhampton and has become interested and involved in public policy research, especially in the areas of widening participation in education and social inclusion. He is currently employed as a researcher at the Centre for Guidance Studies, University of Derby.

John Brennan is professor of higher education and director of the Centre for Higher Education Research and Information at the Open University. He has directed many national and international projects on topics such as graduate employment and quality assurance in higher education, and has written books, articles and reports on these and other higher education themes. His most recent book (with Tarla Shah) is *Managing Quality in Higher Education* (2000).

Philip Candy is the Director of Learning Strategy and Standards with the newly established National Health Services University (NHSU) in the UK. Among his responsibilities are the development and launch of an e-learning platform to serve the needs of the entire workforce of the National Health Service, potentially as many as 1.2 million people. He was previously a National Research Fellow with the Australian Department of Education, Science and Training, where he examined on-line and technologically assisted learning across the lifespan. Prior to this, for five years, he was the Deputy Vice-Chancellor (Scholarship) at the University of Ballarat.

Joyce Chamberlain is currently the Manager of the Rural Opportunities Project in the rural West Midlands, England. In the previous few years Joyce was a Director of a London-based change management consultancy, operating in the fields of senior executive development and organizational change management at home and abroad. An Associate Lecturer with the Open

University Business School, she was formerly Head of Personnel and Administration for the Council for National Academic Awards and earlier Training Officer for the City of Birmingham Education Authority. She has a research degree in Organizational Psychology, University of Lancaster, and an MBA (OUBS) specializing in knowledge management and SMEs.

John Field is Deputy Principal of the University of Stirling, where he works as Director of the Division of Academic Innovation and Continuing Education. Previously he worked at the University of Warwick, where he was Professor of Lifelong Learning. He has also worked in the School of Education, University of Ulster, following a career in further education in Barnsley. He has advised a number of government bodies in Britain and elsewhere, and was a member of the National Advisory Group on Continuing Education and Lifelong Learning, whose report influenced the Green Paper *The Learning Age*. His most recent books include *Lifelong Learning and the New Educational Order*, which has just appeared in a Japanese translation, and *Social Capital*.

Brenda Gourley joined The Open University as Vice-Chancellor in January 2002 from the University of Natal, where she had been Vice-Chancellor since 1994. She is a member of the British Council's Education and Training Advisory Committee and on the Board of the International Association of Universities. Professor Gourley has continuing academic interests in Strategic and Systems Thinking, Leadership and Ethics and was awarded an honorary degree by the University of Nottingham in 1997 for her contribution to higher education.

Dai Hounsell is Professor of Higher Education at the University of Edinburgh, where he co-directs the Enhancing Teaching-Learning Environments in Undergraduate Courses project. The project is funded by the Economic and Social Research Council as part of its Teaching and Learning Research Programme. He was founding director of the Centre for Teaching, Learning and Assessment at Edinburgh, and is an editor of the international journal *Higher Education*.

Neil Moreland began his working life as a graduate librarian in a rural area of England before becoming a teacher. He worked in three colleges of further education before joining the School of Education at the University of Wolverhampton, where he became Associate Dean. All his higher degrees were completed part-time, including a Doctorate from the University of Warwick. He left full-time work at the School of Education in 2000 to devote himself to research and consultancy activities in education and health.

Louise Morley is a Reader in Higher Education Studies at the University of London Institute of Education, UK. She is Director of the Centre for Higher Education Studies (CHES). She is also Director for a DFID/Carnegie-funded research project on gender equity in Commonwealth higher education. Her previous posts were at the University of Sussex, the University of Reading and the Inner London Education Authority. Her research and publication interests focus on quality, equity, gender, power and empowerment in higher education. Recent publications include *Quality and Power in Higher Education* (2003), *Organising Feminisms* (1999), *School Effectiveness* (1999), *Breaking Boundaries* (1996) and *Feminist Academics* (1995).

Andrew Pollard is Professor of Education at the University of Cambridge and previously worked at Oxford Brookes University, University of the West of England and University of Bristol. He has conducted educational research at the interface of psychology and sociology for many years, and is currently Director of the ESRC Teaching and Learning Research Programme (TLRP).

Brian Ramsden is currently Professor Associate in the Department of Information Systems and Computing at Brunel University, and acts as a consultant about higher education data to a number of public bodies and higher education institutions. He retired from the post of founding Chief Executive of the Higher Education Statistics Agency in 2001, having previously been the Head of Planning at the Open University. His research interests include institutional differentiation and performance and higher education participation.

Sheila Riddell worked as a teacher of English in a comprehensive school for seven years before undertaking a PhD at Bristol University in the sociology of education. She is currently Director of the Strathclyde Centre for Disability Research, University of Glasgow. She has researched and written extensively on the implications of many aspects of social policy for disabled people.

Tarla Shah is the projects and development officer at the Centre for Higher Education Research and Information, Open University. Her research interests are in the area of quality assurance and higher education and work. Her recent project work includes an international study undertaken for OECD on the impact of quality management and assessment on higher education, which led to a co-authored book (with John Brennan) entitled *Managing Quality in Higher Education*, a 12-country European project on graduate employment, and a study for DfES on employment prospects of part-time students. She is managing editor of the *Higher Education Digest*. She is a member of the Consortium of Higher Education Researchers.

Maria Slowey is Professor and Director of Adult and Continuing Education at the University of Glasgow, where she has been Head of Department, Head of the Planning Unit and Vice-Dean (Research). She is engaged in research and policy development at national and international levels on issues of participation in lifelong learning. She was a member of the Cubie

Independent Inquiry on Student Finance and an advisor to the Scottish Parliamentary Inquiry on lifelong learning. She is currently a member of the ESRC Research Priorities Board, the Steering Committee for the ESRC TLRP and is Chair of the Research Committee of the SRHE. Recent Publications include *Higher Education and Lifelong Learners: International Perspectives on Change* (2000) with Hans Schuetze, published in Japanese translation in 2002.

Teresa Tinklin has been a Research Fellow at the Centre for Educational Sociology, University of Edinburgh, since 1998. Before that she was a researcher at the Scottish Council for Research in Education. Her research focuses on inequalities in education, including studies of the experiences of disabled students in higher education, gender differences in school performance and social class differences in access to higher education.

Professor Sir David Watson is an historian, and has been Vice-Chancellor of the University of Brighton since 1990. His academic interests are in the history of ideas and in higher education policy. His most recent books are *Lifelong Learning and the University* (1998), *Managing Strategy* (2000) and *New Directions in Professional Higher Education* (2000). He was a member of the CNAA, the PCFC, the HEFCE, the Paul Hamlyn Foundation's National Commission on Education, and the Dearing Committee of Inquiry into Higher Education. He was a member of the HEFCE Learning and Teaching Committee between 1998–2003. He was the chair of the Universities Association for Continuing Education between 1994 and 1998, and currently chairs the Steering Committee for the ESRC's research programme into teaching and learning as well as UUK's Longer Term Strategy Group.

Alastair Wilson is currently a Research Fellow at the Strathclyde Centre for Disability Research, University of Glasgow. He has worked on a number of different research projects looking at education, training and employment opportunities for disabled people. His current research interests are the experiences of disabled students in higher education and the mental health needs of young people with learning difficulties.

List of acronyms

ACE	American Council on Education
ACU	Association of Commonwealth Universities
AGCAS	Association of Graduate Careers Advisory Services
ANTA	Australian National Training Authority
API	Age Participation Index
CHERI	Centre for Higher Education Research and Information
CSU	Higher Education Careers Service Unit
DDA	Disability Discrimination Act 1995
DEFRA	Department for Environment, Food and Rural Affairs
DEST	Department of Education Science and Training
DfEE	Department for Education and Employment (now DfES)
DfES	Department for Education and Skills
DSA	Disabled Students Allowance
DTI	Department of Trade and Industry
ECStA	European Council for Student Affairs
ELLC	Enterprise and Lifelong Learning Committee
ESRC	Economic and Social Research Council
EUA	European University Association
FEC	Further Education College
FTE	Full-time Equivalent
GATS	General Agreement on Trade in Services
GCSE	General Certificate of Secondary Education
HE	Higher Education
HEFCE	Higher Education Funding Council for England
HEI	Higher Education Institution
HERDA	Higher Education Research Development Association
HEROBAC	Higher Education Reach Out to Business and the Community
HESA	Higher Education Statistics Agency
ICSED	International Standard Classification of Education
ICT	Information and Communication Technologies

IER	Institute of Employment Research
ISCED	International Standard Classification of Education
LSDA	Learning and Skills Development Agency
LSC	Learning and Skills Council
LSRC	Learning and Skills Research Centre
NAO	National Audit Office
NCIHE	National Committee of Inquiry into Higher Education
NIACE	National Institute of Adult Continuing Education
NHSU	National Health Service University
NUS	National Union of Students
NVQ	National Vocational Qualification
OECD	Organisation for Economic Co-operation and Development
OFTE	Office of Training and Further Education
ONS	Office for National Statistics
QAA	Quality Assurance Agency for Higher Education
QUANGO	Quasi-Autonomous Non-Governmental Organization
PFI	Private Finance Initiative
R & D	Research and Development
RAE	Research Assessment Exercise
RTC	Regional Technical College
SAT	Scholastic Aptitude Test
SCOP	Standing Conference of Principals
SCUTREA	Standing Conference on University Teaching and Research in the Education of Adults
SHEFC	Scottish Higher Education Funding Council
SME	Small and Medium-sized Enterprises
SOIED	Scottish Office Education and Industry Department (now part of Scottish Executive)
SRHE	Society for Research in Higher Education
TLRP	Teaching and Learning Research Programme
TQA	Teaching Quality Assessment
TQM	Total Quality Management
UACE	Universities Association for Continuing Education
UCoSDA	Universities' and Colleges' Staff Development Agency
ULOLN	UK Open Libraries Network
UNESCO	United Nations Educational Scientific and Cultural Organization
UUK	Universities UK
WTO	World Trade Organisation

List of figures and tables

Tables

Editors' introduction

Maria Slowey and David Watson

As we enter the twenty-first century it is increasingly clear to professionals at all levels of the formal and informal education system that we need to refresh the concept of lifelong learning (see, for example, Field and Leicester 2000: xviii). It is no longer exclusively, or even mainly, about heroic second-chancers, isolated autodidacts, climbers of the ladder of professional qualifications, or the lifestyle choices of the relatively affluent retired. Instead, educational opportunity has become critical to social cohesion, to economic security, to personal well-being: in short, to life-chances.

Most importantly, the concept needs to be expanded so that it is both lifelong and lifewide, concerned not just with the serial requirements of those already engaged, but also with the links to equity and the creation of opportunities for those who have not found the process so easy, frequently through no fault of their own.

Such voices are not often heard. However, in early 2001 the Steering Committee for the ESRC's Teaching and Learning Research Programme (TLRP) undertook a wide consultation on the potential for a specific phase of research focused particularly on post-compulsory education. Part of this exercise involved thirteen focus groups, including two self-identified as 'non-participants in learning'. The biggest problem identified by this latter group was prejudice, and a sense of disengagement from a process dominated by the immediately and easily successful. As one participant put it: 'bring people together and let them listen, so that people who think they are up here (lifts hand high) listen to people who are down here (hand on floor)' (TLRP 2001).

Summing up the whole exercise (which encompassed over 500 respondents to questionnaires as well as the participants in structured discussion), the Director of the Programme emerged with a clear message:

It was persistently suggested that *research to promote inclusion* [emphasis in original] was the key issue. Excellence was mentioned only once. Inclusion focused on learners 'at risk' or 'the casualties of schooling' or learners not well served (e.g. the great majority of workers in SMEs). If a choice were to be made then the clear advice was to focus on 'non-participant' or 'inactive' learners, those least well served by current provision and those most limited in achievements relevant to the learning society.

(DesForges and Kanefsky 2001)

A strong foundation in basic skills is an essential prerequisite for education over the lifecourse. The 'casulties of schooling' represented by the seven million adults in the UK who do not succeed in basic literacy and numeracy tests pose a challenge to all parts of all compulsory and part-compulsory education system (Moser, 1999).

This volume is structured around some of the key resulting arguments for policy and practice in the specific arena of higher education. We do not wish to overstate the importance of higher education; it is simply one feature in the expanding and complex landscape of post-compulsory education and training. We do believe, however, that, despite widespread analyses pointing to growing commodification in the UK and internationally, universities continue to have a very distinctive role to play in the social, economic and political sphere. What is more, this role should continue to combine innovative and traditional elements. In this volume we employ the idea of *learning over the lifecourse* as a contribution to achieving a better understanding of what such distinctiveness might mean for lifelong learners and higher education in the early stages of the new century.

In Section I, we take up the issue of higher education and lifelong learning, addressing in particular the changing nature of the student population. This section sets the scene for the rest of the volume. The convergent and divergent patterns of change in the UK and Europe are mapped by Brian Ramsden in chapter one. The complexities underlying this overall picture are then traced in chapter two by John Field, looking in particular at expansion from the perspectives of access and equity. These chapters thus seek to address one of the key questions in any discussion of higher education and the lifecourse: 'who are today's students?'

This question is further explored in chapters three and four through two contrasting case studies. One powerful way of exploring the extent to which expansion is or is not addressing lifelong learning needs (in the 'refreshed' sense espoused here) is through an investigation of the experience of 'outsiders'; that is, through the experience of particular groups of non-traditional learners. We could have chosen from a wide range of possible populations: for example, women taking technological subjects, adults and younger students from working-class backgrounds, or those taking part-time undergraduate degrees in universities other than the Open University. The two specific examples selected here are students with disabilities (analysed by Sheila Riddell, Teresa Tinklin and Alastair Wilson) and those living in rural areas (using a new conceptual tool devised by Neil Moreland and Joyce Chamberlain).

This is not to suggest a prioritization of these sections of the population over others. They are simply illustrative of groups of learners who are relatively newly recognized by the system and whose needs are inadequately understood both empirically and theoretically. The intention is that the exploration of the nature of the 'reasonable adjustments' which might be required to support equity objectives and the learning needs of such students should help to throw light on the more general challenges facing higher education.

Having established this broadly demographic context we move on in Section II to a consideration of some of the key 'lifewide' implications for the culture of higher education and the nature of the student experience. A crucial part of the learning experience in higher education relates to assessment and feedback. Dai Hounsell's chapter five shows how the active engagement of learners in the assessment process, drawing on wide-ranging knowledge and life skills, can potentially enhance the learning outcomes. This issue of student engagement is explored from a somewhat different perspective in chapter six. Here, the complex question of new power relations between learners and universities (which are accentuated by new economic arrangements) is 'reconstructed' by Louise Morley in the context of the growth of 'consumer culture'.

If students are being redefined in certain respects as customers, clients or investors, and if higher education is now only one of many players in the post-compulsory field, might such trends imply a potential diminution of the role of universities in relation to the needs of lifelong learners? The thrust of our argument in this volume is that, on the contrary, the need for the strengthening of core values and functions of universities has never been greater. (For example, Barnett 1990, 2003; Scott 1995; Watson and Taylor 1998). This is the 'traditional' point of reference alluded to above. However, this is certainly not to suggest that higher education should simply provide more of the same. There are crucial questions to be asked about what kinds of higher education innovation are needed to support new learners, new forms of learning and new career and employment options. These issues are taken up in chapters seven and eight, respectively.

The potential for harnessing new technologies to support new ways of learning necessitates change on the part of universities as some traditional boundaries become blurred. What responsibility, if any, do they have currently to support independent and on-line learners who may not be enrolled on formal programmes but who look to the university as a learning resource over their lifecourse? What new partnerships might universities need to forge, not only with other educational providers but also with the state, the private sector and civil society? Approaching these topics from the two quite different perspectives of on-line learning and the impact of higher education on employment, and taking into consideration broader social and economic inequalities, Philip Candy's chapter seven and John Brennan and Tarla Shah's chapter eight carry implications for new partnerships, and ways in which they might help the universities enhance the contribution they can make to learning and employment opportunities for *all* their current and past students.

Several of the resulting strands are drawn together in Section III, which addresses the question of higher education and the lifecourse from four different perspectives. These are closely inter-related but distinctive, and progress – Russian doll-style – from the macro level of the international community, through the nation state and civil society, to the institutional perspectives of colleges and universities, finishing at the micro level of the individual.

In chapter nine, Brenda Gourley presents the case for revisiting the broader purposes of higher education in the context of the powerful forces associated in different ways with globalization. This discussion is taken forward by Maria Slowey in chapter ten through an exploration of aspects of contemporary connections between universities and civil society. To what extent does the articulation of these links through the notion of the 'third mission' or 'third arm' of higher education appear likely to assist in positioning universities to meet the broad challenges of learning over the lifecourse? The options at an institutional level of adopting an actively engaged, rather than a passive or responsive, stance in relation to the enhancement of learners' life-chances are taken up by David Watson in chapter eleven. Here a critique of higher education – and aspects of university practice – is counterposed by an analysis of the distinctive contribution which universities can make, actually and potentially.

Andrew Pollard's concluding chapter brings the discussion back to the level of the individual learner. Here, a theoretical framework is developed which traces the learning connections of the individual over the course of his or her lifecourse and proposes a model for the ways in which higher education might be called upon to respond to these diverse and changing needs. The book thus ends by reaffirming its core methodological commitment: to the concept of the educational lifecourse as a significant way in which issues of equity, inclusion and civil engagement can be brought to the fore to the mutual (re)energizing benefit of higher education and society.

There are two influential sources for the research and commentary included here. Several of the chapters began life as presentations and papers to the Society for Research in Higher Education (SRHE) Annual Conference held in Glasgow in December 2002. This conference focused in particular on 'understanding student learning', on 'new students and new learning', on 'supporting student success', and on issues of 'participation and equity'. At the same time, the editors and several of the contributors are closely involved with the TLRP programme introduced above. This programme – the largest ever managed by the ESRC, with a planned £25m of expenditure over eight years – has the ambitious aim of 'improving outcomes for learners in a very wide range of UK contexts across the lifecourse'.

Partly as a result, the centre of gravity of the volume is in the UK, although several of the chapters look outwards from UK experience to the rest of the world, or in the opposite direction. As in many countries across the world, the UK system has experienced very rapid growth (see figure 0.1).

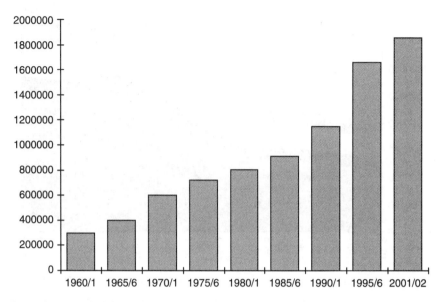

Figure 0.1   Total higher education student numbers, UK, 1960–2002

Source: DES 1969; HESA 1999, 2002

However, as figure 0.2 illustrates, such growth has emphatically not been a question of 'more of the same'. A comfortable majority of students in the UK system are now not on full-time first degrees. Easily the fastest-growing element across the sector has been in part-time postgraduate education, while there has also been substantial development of full and part-time sub-degree work (listed here as 'other'). The latter is primarily the result of the Department of Health moving professional courses into universities and colleges from the NHS. Part-time study in general is becoming more popular; it is significant that the fastest-growing group joining the Open University is the under-25s. In effect, a case could be made that the UK system delivered a framework for lifelong learning before it became a policy.

In this respect, UK higher education appears to be becoming more like North America and less like its continental European neighbours. A recent comparative survey has explored this polarity between a highly traditional continental European model (with interesting echoes in Japan, as well as in a number of other regions, not covered by the OECD – for example the Middle East) and a more flexible and relatively responsive approach in the newly 'mass' English-speaking systems. This, in turn, raises questions about potential contrasts beyond the OECD group: for example, with the Latin American countries now attempting to compete with North America, or the

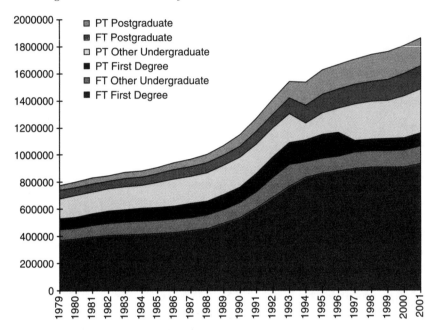

Figure 0.2   Number of students by mode of study and level of course, 1979–2001

Source: DES 1991, 1992; DfE 1994; HESA 1996, 1997, 1998, 1999, 2000, 2001, 2002

African universities seeking to break free from colonial models (see Schuetze and Slowey 2000).

However, the authors' final conclusion is a depressing one. They draw out some almost universal features: the failure of even the most 'diverse' and 'democratic' of systems to deal effectively with class and socioeconomic background; a lack of 'fit' between analyses of deficit at the basic skills or adult literacy levels and ambitious higher education targets; the challenges posed by the increasing necessity of paid work by students; and the reinforcement rather than the dissolution of institutional hierarchies as high status is conveyed and confirmed by traditional approaches to recruitment and to pedagogy and research. On this last issue they outline a model ('a framework of change') whereby axes of structure (formal or 'closed' to non-formal or 'open') and nature of the student body ('homogeneous' to 'heterogeneous') converge on elite institutions in the former case, and much lower status provision – through general colleges, workplace learning and the like – in the latter. Their final assessment is that 'rather than challenging existing social and economic inequalities, the increasing marketisation and differentiation of higher education actually works to allow the tertiary system to expand without questioning, let alone altering existing hierarchies' (Scheutze and Slowey 2000: 23). In this sense a vision held by higher educational developers within the OECD for a widespread social democratic role for 'recurrent education', based in the work of Jarl Bengtsson, is still far from realization (see Istance et al. 2002: 2–6).

At the heart of the lifecourse analysis is the concept of fairness, or social justice. In certain respects higher education has become 'fairer' as it has expanded. In terms of participation (notably in the United Kingdom), higher education is significantly fairer to women, to members of several ethnic minorities, to certain categories of older student, and to those with disabilities. Their success has, however, come at the price of others on the other side of the divide that separates those with access to knowledge and information, to skills and to influence from those who do not have such access. One of our most severe problems in the UK is that of improving the circumstances, the motivation and the opportunities available to new 'minorities' emerging as a consequence of growing social and economic polarizations between different sections of the population.

There are, we believe, two main morals to be drawn from the analysis in this volume in so far as it relates to the UK. The first is for our political and funding masters, and it centres on the need for greater patience, calm and cooperation with the professional community in tackling what are long-haul issues at least as complex and deep-seated as New Labour's concern to defeat child poverty. The second is for that professional community itself. The concept of higher education and the lifecourse demands a much greater sensitivity to and trust in the preferences, goals and ambitions of our actual and potential learners than our current structures and attitudes accommodate.

We also think that many of the issues raised carry international resonance. Evidently, global social, economic and political forces impact very differently on the higher education systems of different countries – in particular those which start with relatively rich or painfully poor legacies of human and infra-structural resources. However, factors such as the changing nature of the student body, the particular needs of under-represented groups, the poten-tial for on-line learning, the opportunities to connect – and in some cases help to rebuild – civil society are important for each national system in its own way. In our view, investigating higher education from the perspective of learning over the lifecourse begins the process of identifying the right ques-tions to be posed by any system which seeks to develop a socially constructive role for its universities and colleges.

Glasgow and Brighton
March 2003

Section I

Higher education and lifelong learning

1

Euro Student 2000: comparisons with the United Kingdom

Brian Ramsden

Discussions of participation and the demographic development of UK higher education frequently lack a sound comparative dimension. What studies there are on lifelong learning in an international context normally fight shy of assessing comparative performance in an accessible way (including, for example, Schuetze and Slowey 2000).

In the year 2000, eight European countries carried out a collaborative exercise in order to compare information about higher education students. The exercise was called *Euro Student 2000* (HIS 2002).

Euro Student 2000 was initiated as a joint European project at the Conference of Directors General for Higher Education in the EU Member States held in Weimar, Germany, in 1999. The conference recommended that a European social survey be carried out among students enrolled in tertiary education. A feasibility study carried out in response to a suggestion made by the European Council for Student Affairs (ECStA) formed a basis for this recommendation.

The *Euro Student 2000* project involved an international survey in order to generate quantitative information about the student experience in eight European countries. In particular, it aimed to generate and present internationally comparable indicators on the social and economic conditions of student life in higher education. The following eight European countries participated in the project:

- Austria
- Belgium (Flemish and Wallonia-Brussels communities, separately)
- Finland
- France
- Germany
- Ireland
- Italy
- The Netherlands.

National surveys were undertaken in the participating countries, which, in the year 2000, were responsible for carrying out their own empirical surveys among students enrolled at their higher education institutions.

The United Kingdom did not participate in the project. However, the UK does have a comprehensive system of data collection, on an annual census basis, about students in Higher Education (HE) through its Higher Education Statistics Agency (HESA).

The aim of this chapter is to relate the findings of the *Euro Student 2000* project to the statistical data available about higher education study within the United Kingdom, and so to generate some comparative information about the UK, as compared with the countries which participated in the *Euro Student 2000* project.

This chapter thus compares and contrasts data about the UK higher education student experience with some of the findings of the *Euro Student 2000* project. It does not attempt a simplistic one-to-one mapping, however, since the data are not susceptible to this. Indeed, the *Euro Student 2000* project found the same problem of mapping across countries, and there are many examples of data not being available in specific countries under the *Euro Student 2000* project.

The chapter concentrates on a limited number of data items for which there is a robust basis for comparison with the UK. It also notes respects in which the data collected for *Euro Student 2000* could not be collected in respect of the UK, for example because the definitions are considered to be socially unacceptable or irrelevant.

What is meant by higher education?

For the purposes of the *Euro Student 2000* exercise the participating countries adopted a convention of using the ISCED 97 definitions (UNESCO 1997) relating to ISCED stages 5 and 6. The definitions are as follows:

• ISCED stage 5: First stage of tertiary education (not leading directly to an advanced research qualification)
• ISCED stage 6: Second stage of tertiary education (leading to an advanced research qualification)

In UK terms, this definition includes all students following undergraduate courses, both for first degrees (ISCED 5A) and for other undergraduate qualifications (ISCED 5B) and those following postgraduate programmes (ISCED 6).

Pragmatically, this chapter is limited to data about students in higher education institutions within the UK, using data drawn from the publications of the Higher Education Statistics Agency (HESA). It is recognized that this definition excludes students following higher education courses in further education colleges and private providers of higher education within the UK.

Items covered in the *Euro Student 2000* report and which will be studied in this chapter are student characteristics (gender profile, age profile, and physically disabled students), as well as the nature of study programmes, as follows:

- Non-traditional routes to higher education
- Type of institution students attend
- Duration of study programmes by field of study
- Students' social background – occupational status of students' fathers
- Student type of residence
- Higher education catchment area

Student status – full-time and part-time

Before examining any of the other specific statistics generated by the *Euro Student 2000* project, we should look at one area in which the UK situation differs radically from that of the countries surveyed under *Euro Student 2000*, and where that difference has a major impact on statistical comparisons under other headings, that is, the distinction between full-time and part-time study.

The *Euro Student 2000* report observes that:

Officially, formal part-time studies only exist at the higher education institutions of a few countries, namely in Ireland and the Netherlands. However, even in these countries most of the students studying for a higher education degree are enrolled as full-time students. ... Officially, there is no part-time study format for regular university or college students in Austria, Finland, Germany or Italy, where students are expected to be full-time learners. However, the time budgets [a method of estimating the time commitment of students in higher education, adopted for the Euro Student survey] ... show that a significant proportion of students in these countries take up employment besides their studies during term/semester or care for children, and so spend much less time on their studies than those who do not take up secondary employment and therefore can spend more hours per week on their studies. The extent of unofficial part-time studies is substantial.

In more detail, the Report's accompanying CD-Rom notes that:

- In formal terms, only full-time students are enrolled at Germany's higher education institutions. This means that the status of part-time students is officially unknown. Nevertheless, part-time students do exist in actuality. They are enrolled as full students, but spend much less time on study-related activities than do their full-time fellow students. 'Academic freedom' means that students are able to decide the intensity of their studies for themselves.
- Only full-time students are acknowledged by Italian universities.
- [In Austria] at universities there is no part-time status ... [but]

because of the increasing number of working students, there are a lot of *de facto* part-time students.

The situation in the UK is radically different. Part-time study is a major and recognized mode of involvement in higher education, at both undergraduate and postgraduate levels. Different funding and student support régimes exist for full-time and part-time study. Some institutions of higher education, notably the Open University and Birkbeck College University of London, cater solely for part-time students; at the undergraduate level many others have a large minority of part-time students.

This clear differentiation between full-time and part-time study within the UK provides opportunities for individual students to plan the relationship of paid employment and study, although it does not perhaps provide the flexibility which exists in some other European countries to undertake a 'full-time' course of study over a flexible period of time, while undertaking work or family commitments. Full-time programmes in the UK are of clearly delineated length, and variations from that length generally require formal approval.

Published statistics show that 39 per cent of students following higher education programmes in the UK are formally enrolled on part-time courses (HESA 2002a). It is difficult to plot comparative figures for the countries which participated in the *Euro Student 2000* project, for reasons given above. However, the report usefully describes the situation in the individual countries, and identifies the few instances in which there are formal part-time registrations, and also, for most other countries, the percentage of 'full-time' students who pursue study-related activities for less than 20 hours per week – a proxy for part-time study. (For comparison, within the UK a full-time course of less than 24 weeks is regarded as 'part-time'.) In some instances countries did not report data under a particular head: they are shown as having no data in the relevant figures. The students following structured part-time studies in Ireland and the Netherlands should be noted also.

From these statistics it is possible, in most cases, to derive a 'quasi-part-time' percentage. In Ireland, for example, this can be derived from the 12 per cent following formal part-time programmes, plus the 12 per cent of full-time students who pursue study-related activities for less than 20 hours per week. Comparative figures on this basis are shown in figure 1.1.

It cannot be over-emphasized that the existence of the distinct formal part-time route to higher education qualifications in the UK significantly affects many of the other statistics which are referred to in this chapter. For example, the part-time route to higher education qualifications is, predictably, followed by students who are generally older than those entering full-time higher education. Part-time programmes, especially by distance learning, also offer particular opportunities to students with disabilities. These and other statistical comparisons are influenced by the substantial proportion of students following a formal part-time route in the UK. This is one of three major areas of difference between the UK and most of the countries surveyed under *Euro Student 2000*.

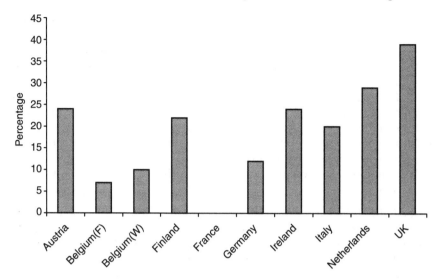

Figure 1.1   'Part-time' students as a percentage of total

Note: In some instances countries did not report data under a particular head: they are shown as having no data in the relevant figures.

Age profile of students

There is obviously no area of comparison which is more likely to be influenced by the UK's substantial part-time higher education provision than the age profile of students. The *Euro Student 2000* report sets out the age differences between students in the nine participating communities. The report further observes that: '[t]he average age of students varies substantially in the countries surveyed and is influenced by various factors, including the respective ways in which degree courses are organised, which differ from one country to the next'. In particular:

• At almost 26, the highest average age is found among Finnish students. This high age is caused by various factors, including the large proportion of students enrolled at higher education institutions for a large number of years, because they pursue their studies alongside a full-time job. Admissions restrictions in Finland also mean that studies often only commence after completion of a waiting period. A further reason is that a noticeably high proportion of students in Finland only gain entry to higher education at an older age, namely via non-traditional access routes.
• The high age of students in Austria and Germany (around 25) can also be explained, among other reasons, by the fact that, essentially, the first degree is awarded after completion of long or very long degree courses. And studies also commence at a later stage, namely after a gap between leaving school and entering higher education.

- The situation in France is different (average age of 22.4), where the transition from school to higher education generally occurs without any gaps.
- At 23, the average age of students in Ireland is low. Ireland offers students the opportunity to complete their higher education in shorter education courses.
- By far the lowest average age of students is found among students in Flanders, namely 21. This is the result of the 'year-system', which encourages students to complete their studies quickly.
- Meanwhile, students in the Wallonia-Brussels Community are only marginally older (21.5 on average).
- Italy and the Netherlands have values which lie in between the two extremes.

In the light of the earlier observation about the significance of the part-time route into higher education within the UK, it is challenging to identify a basis for expressing comparative figures. Ongoing and unpublished work by the current author has identified significant differences in the average ages of students within the UK dependent on their mode of study, level of study and country of origin. Even within the UK itself, there are significant differences in age among full-time undergraduate students from Scotland, as compared with the rest of the UK. These differences arise from the traditionally earlier age at which Scottish students enter higher education.

The overall average age of students in higher education institutions in the UK is 29.8 years, which is far higher than that reported in the communities surveyed under *Euro Student 2000*. However, it is clear from the individual country commentaries on their statistics that these are predominantly limited to undergraduate students (ISCED 5). In respect of undergraduate students, irrespective of mode of study, the average age in the UK is 27.9 years (26.9 in Scotland).

A comparative graph is shown in figure 1.2.

On the other hand, it should be noted that the average age of full-time and sandwich students studying for a first degree is 21.9 years (21.6 in Scotland).

Gender profile

The *Euro Student 2000* report notes that:

> [h]igher education has long ceased to be a male privilege in the surveyed countries. Study entrant figures have developed in favour of women, while women have meanwhile overtaken the men in the student body in most countries . . .

However, the report identifies considerable differences in the gender profiles of the nine participating communities, with substantial majorities of female students in, for example, Ireland and Finland, while noting that women are still in a minority in the Netherlands, Austria and Germany.

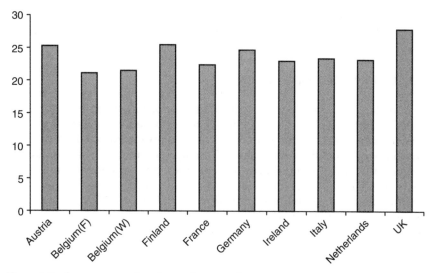

Figure 1.2 Average age of undergraduate students

In the UK, as in most of the communities surveyed under *Euro Student 2000*, women are in a majority among the higher education student population: comparative figures are shown in figure 1.3.

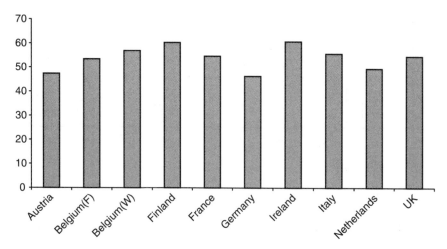

Figure 1.3 Females as a percentage of all students

It will be noted that only Ireland and Finland have a significantly higher proportion of female students than the UK, while Belgium, France and Italy have a broadly similar proportion. However, we should note that the number of students from outside Europe studying within each country has an effect on the overall gender balance. It is, for example, the case that the large number of students from outside the EU studying in the United Kingdom are predominantly male, and these students have an effect on the overall proportion.

Students with disabilities

The *Euro Student 2000* report describes the proportion of students in higher education with a physical disability. The information is based on self-assessment by the students concerned. The report acknowledges that the definitions of disability within the different communities will vary, and it does not attempt to standardize the outcomes. Several participating countries in the *Euro Student 2000* project had no data in this area.

Within the UK, disability information provided to HESA was similarly derived on a self-assessment basis.

Comparative data is shown in figure 1.4.

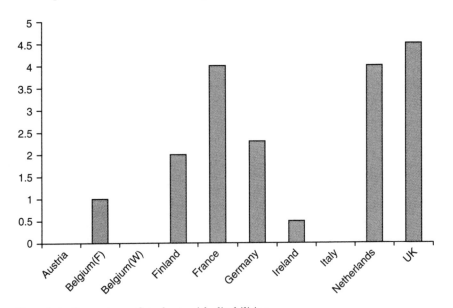

Figure 1.4 Percentage of students with disabilities

On this basis, it appears that the UK has a higher proportion of students with disabilities than other European countries for which data is available, although the figures should be treated with caution because of differences in definitions. We should also note that, as indicated above, the existence of a part-time route to higher education qualifications within the UK serves to facilitate access by students with disabilities. (This is especially true in respect of distance learning programmes, such as those offered by the Open University, which is by far the largest single UK provider of HE programmes for students with disabilities.)

Non-traditional entry routes

The *Euro Student 2000* report observes that:

[t]he paths along which prospective students gained their higher education entrance qualification differed to varying degrees in the participating countries. Besides the classical access routes to higher education via
the general schooling system, additional access opportunities, so-called
'non-traditional routes' are now being offered. The proportion of students deciding in favour of the non-traditional routes varies from one
country to the next.

The wide variation between the countries participating in the *Euro Student
2000* project is noted. At one extreme, Finland has 17 per cent of students
entering through 'non-traditional routes'. At the other extreme, there is no
recognized alternative entry route to higher education in Italy, and less than
1 per cent enter through unconventional routes in the Flemish community
of Belgium.

Within the UK, it is difficult to establish a comparable statistic, partly
because entry to higher education is less formally circumscribed than in
some other European countries, and is also evolving rapidly.

At a simplistic level, it might be regarded that the 'traditional' qualifications for entry to full-time higher education in the UK are at least two GCE A
levels, or equivalent qualifications in Scotland. In 2000–2001, 32 per cent of
entrants to full-time courses in higher education institutions in the United
Kingdom held other qualifications, as illustrated in table 1.1.

Table 1.1 Percentage of entrants to full-time undergraduate
programmes in the UK with 'non-traditional' qualifications

Qualification	Percentage
Advanced GNVQ	7.85
BTEC/SCOTVEC Higher Award	2.88
BTEC/SCOTVEC Lower Award	4.67
Access/Foundation	4.85
Other qualifications	5.92
No recorded qualifications	5.86

Source: HESA 2002b

However, in many respects, the evolving nature of entry to HE courses in
the UK should lead us to exercise caution in considering some of these
entrants as being 'non-traditional'. In addition to complexities in relation to
full-time entry to higher education, we should be aware of the substantial
number and proportion entering part-time programmes.

HESA data shows over 200,000 students commencing study on part-time
undergraduate programmes in the year 2000–2001. These students may be

following programmes leading directly to a first degree, programmes which do not have a sole specified outcome (such as those offered by the Open University) or programmes which have an objective related to the personal or professional needs of the individual. In addition over 100,000 people commenced part-time programmes leading to postgraduate qualifications (ISCED 6), either through research or through taught programmes.

These very large numbers of part-time entrants, amounting to more than 35 per cent of the total entry to higher education within the UK, together with the observations above about entry to full-time HE courses, make it difficult to derive comparisons with the figures published in the *Euro Student 2000* report. It is perhaps best to summarize the situation as being that the concept of 'non-traditional' entry to higher education does not carry the same clear and formalized meaning as in other EU countries. This is the second major area of difference between the UK and the *Euro Student 2000* communities.

Types of institution attended

The *Euro Student 2000* report observes that: '[I]n order to meet the changing social and economic (financial) demands which higher education faces, most member countries are pursuing policies of differentiating their higher education system.'

- Germany, with its practice-oriented universities of applied sciences (Fachhochschulen, FH), and the Netherlands, with its similar institutions (Hoger Beroepsonderwijs, HBO) are pressing ahead with a process of institutional differentiation . . .
- Corresponding measures have also been initiated and carried out in Austria, where it is expected that the number of FH students will continue to rise. Experience shows that there is a great demand for this type of higher education institution with its strong emphasis on an applied and practical education and training.
- In Finland, a number of polytechnics (amk-institutions) were established in the 1990s alongside the traditional universities.

The report notes, however, a rather different pattern in France and Italy (with the latter showing only 1 per cent of students engaged in higher education outside the traditional university model).

A very different situation exists in the UK and one which is unique among the communities under consideration. Far from identifying a clear distinction between academically and vocationally oriented institutions, the pattern of HE institutions in the UK is based on an inclusive 'diversity' model, introduced following the passage of the Further and Higher Education Act of 1992. This gave university status to the former Polytechnics and Scottish Central Institutions, and provided for common funding methodologies for all of the institutions of higher education within the UK.

This is the third major difference between the UK situation and that of the countries surveyed under *Euro Student 2000*. However, at the time of writing, there is uncertainty about whether, as a result of the publication of the White Paper *The Future of Higher Education* (DfES 2003: Col. 5735), a new differentiation of institutions might be introduced, involving significant differences in research funding alongside a general redefinition of universities.

While the restructuring of higher education in the UK in order to differentiate an elite cadre of institutions is opposed by many of those involved in higher education (Warwick 2002), it appears to be possible at the time of writing that, at least in terms of central funding, some greater differentiation may be introduced, which would reflect the position in some other EU countries.

Length of study programmes

The *Euro Student 2000* report describes the very different lengths of study for first degree programmes in the nine communities.

Overall, lengths of study programmes in those countries for which data is available range from 3.1 years in Ireland to 7.5 years in Italy. Equivalent figures for the UK can be derived from figures produced by HESA showing the expected length of study programme of new undergraduates. These figures are limited to full-time students, and as we have noted, there is a substantial proportion of UK students who study on a part-time basis.

The comparative figures for the *Euro Student 2000* participants and for the UK are shown in figure 1.5.

It will be seen that the United Kingdom, in common with Ireland, has a very much shorter duration of study than other participating communities. To some extent this difference must be regarded as being structural. However, this is not entirely the case. For example, in respect of some specific countries within the *Euro Student 2000* constituency, the report observes that:

- [in **Germany**] The standard duration of a degree course (Diplom degree) at a university of applied sciences (Fachhochschule) averages out at four years. At the 'traditional' universities, the standard duration for Diplom and Magister degree courses is set at 4.5 years. However, students often take much longer than the standard duration to complete their studies.
- [in **Ireland**] 57.1 per cent of students are in courses lasting three years or less; 38.5 per cent are in courses taking four years to complete; while 4.4 per cent are in courses of five years or more duration.
- [in **Finland**] The average time of study in universities is 6.5 years. It varies according to field of study from 5 (education) to 10 years (architecture).

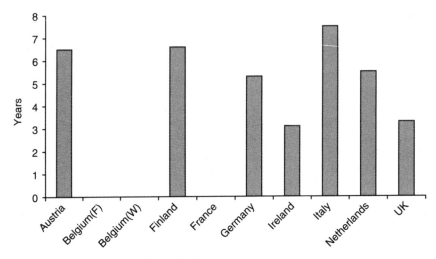

Figure 1.5   Duration of study for first degree

These average times are measured from the starting point to graduation. These numbers tell how long taking the exam takes on average. . . . From those who started their studies in 1991 only 52 per cent had graduated by the end of 1998. Twenty-three per cent of those who started graduated in five years . . . The average time was 7 years and 49 per cent of those started had graduated in seven years' time. Twenty-four per cent used more than seven years to graduate and 27 per cent had not graduated. The theoretical time for studies is five years in most fields of study. This is only a political and administrative goal. It has not much to do with reality. Student grants from the state can be obtained for fifty-five months which means six years of study.

Students' social background

The *Euro Student 2000* project examined the social class of students, as determined by the occupational status of the student's father.

This is not a measure that is recognized within the UK, and the limitation to the father's occupational status would certainly be regarded as inappropriate and misleading in the context of the general economic family circumstances within the UK. However, the UK does identify social class of entrants to full-time undergraduate courses, using a measure which is based on the occupational classification of the parent, step-parent or guardian who has or had the highest income in the household in which the student was brought up, in the case of students aged under 21 on entry to higher education.

The *Euro Student 2000* report notes that: '[t]he proportion of students from working-class (bluecollar worker) families among the total student body differs substantially from country to country', and it proceeds to identify these differences.

Comparative figures for the *Euro Student 2000* participants and the UK are shown in figure 1.6.

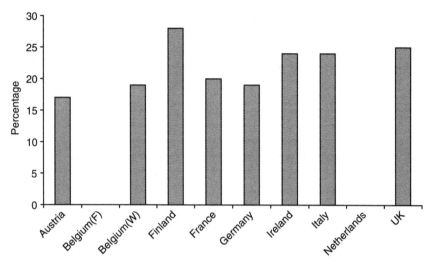

Figure 1.6   Percentage of students from lower socio-economic groups

Notes: The UK figures are sourced from Performance Indicators in Higher Education Institutions (HEFCE 2001). Possibly the figures for Finland should be treated with some caution, since they appear to be out of line with other European countries in relation to social class; definitional issues may be relevant here.

On the basis of the figures underlying this chart, it appears to be the case that the UK has a higher proportion of its students coming from manual occupational backgrounds than any *Euro Student 2000* country apart from Finland.

Student accommodation

The *Euro Student 2000* report describes the accommodation arrangements for students in each of the communities surveyed, and compares institutional and parental accommodation. By definition, this leaves an unallocated component of the overall accommodation arrangements of students, which is their own owned or rented accommodation.

Comparable figures for the UK can be derived from work undertaken by HESA in respect of the publication *Insight 2000* (HESA 1999), which is also confirmed by relevant surveys.

Comparative figures are shown in figure 1.7.

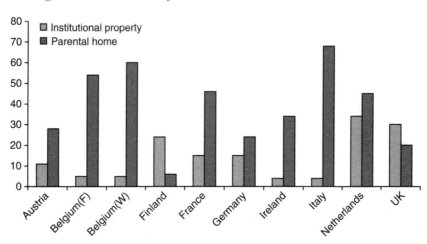

Figure 1.7   Percentage of students occupying institutional and parental accommodation

With the exception of Finland, the UK has the highest ratio of students in institutional accommodation to those in parental accommodation. And, in absolute terms, it has the second-highest percentage in institutional accommodation, after the Netherlands.

Higher education catchment area

The *Euro Student 2000* report discusses the concept of 'catchment areas' and the extent of regionalization of student enrolments. It measures this by identifying the proportion of students who grew up within a 100-km radius of the university or college they are attending. At 47 per cent, the lowest value comes from Finland, with the other end of the scale being taken by the small area of Flanders, at 96 per cent.

Precisely comparable figures could be derived for the UK, using the postcode of students' residence before entering higher education. However, such comparisons should be treated with caution. The figures used for *Euro Student 2000* include all students, and as we have noted the concept of a separate part-time mode of study is not recognized in many countries: by definition, part-time students, who are highly represented in the UK, are more likely to study near to their homes.

It is possible, however, to make some approximate comparisons, using data analysed by HESA for its publications. I have drawn in particular on work undertaken for the publication *Insight 2000* (HESA 1999) and further analysis by Perry (2000), some of which is further analysed in a report on patterns of higher education institutions in the UK (Ramsden 2001).

On the basis of this work it is possible to estimate the proportion of *full-time* students in the UK studying within proximity to their place of residence. Figure 1.8 shows comparative figures on the basis of these estimates.

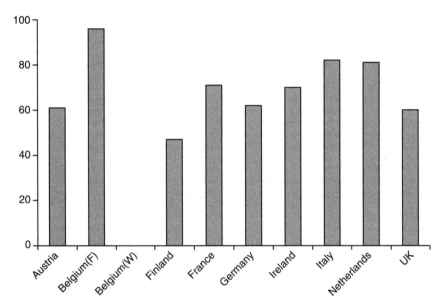

Figure 1.8   Estimated regionalization rate (catchment area up to 100 km), as a percentage

We may see here that the UK appears to have a lower rate of attendance at 'local' institutions than most other countries surveyed. Some of the differences arise from obvious geographical or structural factors: the high figures in Flanders and the Netherlands arise from the comparatively small geographical areas of those communities. However, as the *Euro Student 2000* report notes, '[a]n overall examination across all participating countries shows that a generally high degree of regionalisation cannot be overlooked.'

Within the UK the figure of 60 per cent, being based on full-time students, is an underestimate of the overall position, because it ignores all the students who study on a part-time basis. It is also somewhat out of date, and we should be aware that Perry noted a small but significant trend in students electing to study closer to their homes (2000).

Areas where comparisons cannot easily be derived

The issues covered above relate to only a minority of the data items described within the *Euro Student 2000* report. Much of the report is concerned with analysis derived from data items collected through the common survey instruments used in the project: these are concerned to a considerable extent with the economic and social circumstances of students, and by definition they relate to issues that are not easily captured through a census data collection such as that which is adopted in the UK.

Prima facie, it would be possible to derive comparable information for the UK from the several surveys which are carried out either under government auspices or by other bodies. I have, however, concluded that such comparisons would be invalid because of the different definitions and consistencies involved. Comparisons are always dangerous, but comparisons based on different assumptions and definitions are a hindrance to understanding, not a help. I have therefore eschewed such comparisons.

The *Euro Student 2000* report notes that:

> efforts . . . need to be made to ensure that further EU member countries are included in the project in the future, since only such an approach will allow the social dimensions within the European Education Area to be depicted across the whole of Europe, with all its peaks and troughs.

Whether or not that objective is accepted, the absence of the UK from the *Euro Student 2000* project has resulted in one of the major providers of higher education in Europe being excluded from an interesting piece of research. Its absence may perhaps reflect a limited interest within the UK about some of the international issues raised by the *Euro Student 2000* project, for example language competence, although it should also be seen in the context that the UK is a major provider of higher education to students from other European countries.

Further *Euro Student 2000* exercises are likely to be carried out, and it may be the case that a broader constituency of countries, including the UK, would facilitate a better understanding of many of the policy issues which face all countries today.

Conclusions

This necessarily brief comparative survey has compared statistical information which is readily available within the UK with the findings of the *Euro Student 2000* project. In addition to the detailed comparisons which have been outlined above, major differences have been noted:

- The formal structured part-time route to higher education qualifications within the UK is not paralleled in most other European countries, although in many of those the concept of 'full-time' study is much diluted by students who chose an informal part-time route. This major structural difference hinders statistical comparisons under several other heads.
- Whereas the countries surveyed under *Euro Student 2000* show a clear distinction between academically and vocationally oriented institutions,

the pattern of higher education institutions in the UK is based on an inclusive 'diversity' model.

- While the UK has a high proportion of students who enter without 'conventional' qualifications, the concept of 'non-traditional' entry to higher education does not carry the same clear and formalized meaning as in other EU countries.

In the meantime, it should be of significant interest to policy-makers in the UK that in this wider context and *inter alia*, their student body exhibits: the highest proportion of part-time students; the oldest average age; the highest percentage with declared disabilities; the second highest percentage of students from lower socio-economic backgrounds (after Finland); and the second lowest rate of 'local' attendance (including the proportion living in the parental home – also after Finland).

[Acknowledgement: This chapter could not have been written without the help and cooperation of Dr Klaus Schnitzer of the Hochschul-Informations-System in Hanover, whose work on the *Euro Student 2000* project has provided the context and stimulus for this analysis.]

2

Getting real: evidence on access and achievement?

John Field

Higher education is in a process of transition, even of transformation. We hear this statement so often that it has become a cliché, yet it is equally axiomatic that higher education institutions are deeply conservative. This tension between continuity and change, stagnation and revolution, is at the heart of our present dilemma. I am reminded of the words of Giuseppe Tomasi di Lampedusa's *Leopard*, in which the fictional Sicilian noble reflects on what the landed aristocracy must do to accommodate itself within a capitalist democracy: 'If we want things to stay as they are, things will have to change.' The challenge of widening participation in higher education is at the heart of this dual process of continuity and change. It poses enormous questions about the future of higher education. And it is an area where the higher education research community has been particularly productive; no matter what other gaps and uncertainties in our knowledge, we can be reasonably confident in describing this as a topic where the evidence base has considerable breadth and depth.

Students and learning: just what *is* changing? What is staying the same? And what is changing only so that things stay as they are? I want to divide these questions into two groups. First, and centrally, there is a group of questions to do with new learners. Are universities really taking in new learners? If so, who are these new learners, just what is particularly new about them, and how are they faring in comparison with the more established learners? The first part of this paper attempts to answer these questions, with reference to recent research evidence from the UK and, to a lesser extent, elsewhere in Western Europe. Second, there are questions about learning. How are universities and other higher education institutions (HEIs) changing? To what extent do the changes represent a response to new types of learner? And is change more talked-about than achieved? Is the discourse of change providing a cloak behind which the main actors in higher education are seeking to conceal their deep conservatism? Or on the contrary, are HEIs steadily becoming learning organizations that are able to adapt to a more turbulent and unpredictable environment while maintaining a stable core?

Changing students?

Globally, the higher education system is in the throes of a remarkable expansion. Conventionally, higher education participation is measured in terms of the age participation index (API), or the ratio of higher education students to the number of 18-year-olds in the population. For much of the twentieth century, the API was in single figures; indeed, for most of the century, in European countries it was below 5 per cent. Globally, the API is now reportedly around 16 per cent, and it is said that students account for 1 per cent of the world's population of 6.2 billion people (Blight et al. 2000: 95). Here in Britain, the API currently stands at roughly 33 per cent, and the government proposes a target of 50 per cent participation among the 30-year-olds and younger by 2010. Participation is said to have already reached this level in Scotland, and it is not far behind in Northern Ireland and some English regions. Peter Scott has pointed out that 350,000 new students are required to meet this target, which he calculates as the equivalent of 20 average-sized British universities (2002).

There has, then, been considerable expansion of participation, and much more is planned. Yet are we really able to describe these students as new learners? So we might assume, on the basis of much of the policy literature. In England, for example, the Green Paper on lifelong learning announced that the Government's plans for growth 'in higher education, which will increase participation by mature students and young people, will allow us both to meet the expected demand from young people and widen access to higher education' (DfEE 1998: 32). In Scotland, an age participation rate that has already reached 50 per cent is held to have created 'both access and quality' (ELLC 2002: para. 127). Indeed, the Scottish Executive believes that with a 50 per cent baseline already achieved, there is no further need for expansion in higher education (Scottish Executive 2003b: 29). Because 'much of the increase amongst socially disadvantaged groups has been through the expansion of take up of higher education opportunities at FE colleges' (Scottish Executive 2003b: 33), the Executive believes that it can best promote equity by improving the potential for articulation and progression between the two sectors (Scottish Executive 2003a: 55–6).

First, the social class mixture has changed relatively little despite expansion. Broadly, the evidence shows a general rise in the age participation index across all social classes. Figures 2.1 and 2.2 trace this development for higher education entrants in Britain in 1991 and 2000, categorized by parental occupation. Figure 2.1 shows that 55 per cent of children from professional backgrounds entered higher education in 1991, as against 36 per cent from the intermediate group, 22 per cent from skilled non-manual backgrounds, and 11 per cent from skilled manual worker families. All of these had risen by 2000: among professionals, it had reached 76 per cent, and 48 per cent for the intermediate strata; among skilled non-manual worker families the API was 33 per cent, and among skilled worker families only

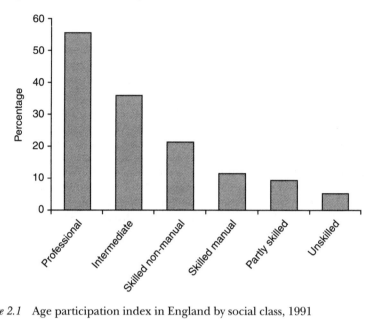

Figure 2.1   Age participation index in England by social class, 1991

Source: Margaret Hodge, Parliamentary Reply, *Hansard*, 8 July 2002, Column 722W

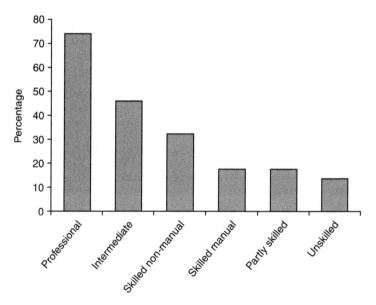

Figure 2.2   Age participation index in England by social class, 2000

Source: Margaret Hodge, Parliamentary Reply, *Hansard*, 8 July 2002, Column 722W

19 per cent. The broadly even nature of this rise is particularly surprising, given that each of the different social categories started from a very different base. However, future expansion plans cannot be achieved by relying on the same sources of new recruits. It has been persuasively suggested by one team of researchers that the professional category has more or less reached saturation point, and that no further expansion can be expected from this source; increases must depend on raising the demand in other social strata (Gilchrist et al. 2003).

Figure 2.3 allows us to trace the evolution of growth across broad social categories over the last decade. If we simply follow the broad trends, it shows that in England participation rose for all groups during the early 1990s, reaching a plateau in 1997, and then falling back slightly before more or less recovering the previous position by 2000. What this suggests is firstly that the bulk of expansion occurred entirely before 1997, which means that it took place under the Conservative Government. While the plateau of the mid-1990s was initially a consequence of the Conservatives' policy of consolidation, figure 2.3 also confirms that participation stagnated in the early years under New Labour. Indeed, in the short term the API fell slightly, probably reflecting the negative impact of changes in student funding in 1998, and at 33 per cent overall was no higher in 2000 than in 1996.

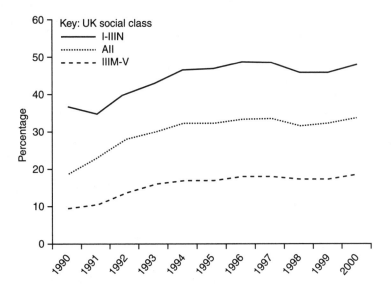

Figure 2.3 Changes in the age participation index in England, 1990–2000

Source: Margaret Hodge, Parliamentary Reply, *Hansard,* 8 July 2002, Column 722W.
Office for National Statistics (2000) Standard occupational classification 2000. London: The Stationery Office.

At the level of the system as a whole, socioeconomic inequality has persisted through the 1990s with very little perceptible change. Rather crudely, it might be said that the main impact upon equity of the post-Robbins period has been the extension of higher education to women. From being a predominantly male preserve in the 1950s, almost all European higher education systems recruit at least as many females as males. Although part of this shift may be due to administrative factors (for example, the reclassification in Britain of nurse training as higher education), the extent of this transformation should not be understated. It encompasses a number of traditionally elite subjects such as law, medicine and dentistry and is by no means confined to low-status subjects and those where HEIs face recruitment difficulties. As much as with men, though, the access of women into higher education is largely a reflection of socioeconomic situation, and it therefore confirms the persistence of this particularly deep-rooted form of inequality within the higher education system.

Systems, though, are differentiated. In many countries, there is a more or less formalized classification of higher education institutions, and this can have significant consequences for students from different backgrounds. In a detailed study of race and institutional differentiation in the USA, Lorenzo Morris showed in the late 1970s that black American undergraduates tend to be systematically over-represented in non-elite institutions and on two-year programmes, and systematically under-represented in elite institutions and four-year programmes (Morris 1979). More recent work has confirmed that although the US undergraduate population has steadily become more ethnically diverse, minority students are clustered in particular levels and fields of third-level education (Nettles 1988). The obvious question is whether similarly differentiated patterns exist elsewhere.

Comparable evidence is harder to come by in respect of social class in European higher education systems. What there is, though, confirms the existence of a rather similar pattern. This pattern is intertwined with differential patterns of institutional growth. Sometimes as a clear result of policy direction, and sometimes as an incremental consequence of policy drift, much of the growth in participation has been associated with the growth of higher education in non-university institutions. The Fachhochschulen, which first opened in 1969, now account for some 461,000 of the 1.9 million students in Germany (Mohr 2002: 150). In the Republic of Ireland, the Regional Technology College (RTC) sector steadily expanded its higher education capacity throughout the 1980s and 1990s; in 1997–98, 11 RTCs were redesignated Institutes of Technology, joining three existing Institutes of Technology with their own degree-awarding powers.

Britain has experienced a rather more complicated pattern, but it is broadly consistent with these wider trends. Much of the growth of the 1980s and 1990s was concentrated in the former polytechnics (which were redesignated as universities in 1992). The UK also witnessed a growth of higher education in further education colleges, although to a much lesser extent than in Ireland, and seemingly with very little in the way of clear policy guidance (Parry and Thompson 2001). In Scotland, for example, the greatest growth within HE has come in the form of entry into programmes taught in

further education colleges. Figure 2.4 shows with respect to full-time education that aggregate enrolments in FECs kept pace with those into HEIs, so
that FECs' collective market share went up dramatically. Figure 2.5 demonstrates that FECs have leapt ahead of HEIs in enrolment of part-time HE
students. Indeed, the extent of FEC domination in this field is even greater
than figure 2.5 suggests, as the doubling of part-time enrolments in HEIs in
the mid-1990s is largely due to changes in the treatment of liberal adult
education. In England, only 6 per cent of the undergraduate population is
currently studying in FECs; of these, the vast majority are part-time students,
and an overwhelming majority of both full and part-time students is studying
for sub-degree qualifications (Field 2002). The distinctive place of FECs
within the Scottish higher education system allows us to consider whether
the pattern of participation found by Lorenzo Morris (1979) for black
Americans is paralleled by the pattern for new types of student in Scotland.

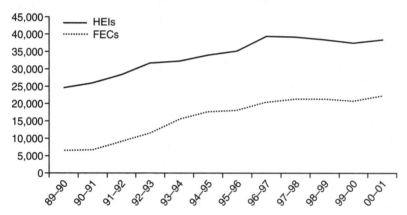

Figure 2.4   Full-time HE enrolments in Scotland, 1989/90–2000/01

Source: Scottish Executive 2002

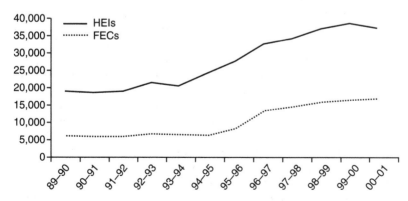

Figure 2.5   Part-time HE enrolments in Scotland, 1989/90–2000

Source: Scottish Executive 2002

A number of studies confirms that non-traditional students in Scotland are tending to cluster disproportionately within the FEC sector of higher education. Postcode analysis has confirmed that students from low-participation neighbourhoods are more likely to enter HE in an FEC than in an HEI (Raab and Davidson 1999), and Gallacher (2002) has demonstrated that mature students and students in full-time employment are also far better represented in FEC than HEI programmes. FECs also have almost twice the capacity of HEIs in respect of part-time higher education (Gallacher 2002). An in-depth study of pupils in their final year of schools where below-average proportions progress to HE found that those coming from middle-class families (mostly with intermediate service professional occupations) were more likely to enter university. Pupils in remote and island communities often made choices on grounds of proximity rather than subject or level. Pupils from the most disadvantaged backgrounds were likely to enrol on a non-degree qualification in an FEC (Forsyth and Furlong 2000). Broadly, then, the evidence suggests that non-traditional students in Scotland are clustering in non-degree levels of study, provided in institutions whose history is that of craft and technical skills training. This is consistent with the pattern discovered by Morris for black Americans in higher education.

For policy makers, the non-university sector has provided an important means of widening access. This sector is far more open to non-traditional students, and more willing to restructure the curriculum to suit the needs of lifelong learners. Policy makers have found this an attractive combination. In 1997, for example, the Garrick Committee welcomed 'good access and articulation arrangements between programmes of higher education at further education colleges and higher education institutions' for reasons of 'both equity and cost-effectiveness' (NCIHE 1997: para. 4.62). Garrick particularly emphasized the equity gains of expanding higher education within further education. Indeed, the Committee attributed the Scottish system's success in attracting students from disadvantaged backgrounds in large part to 'the strong role played by the further education sector in Scotland in providing access to a higher proportion of the total higher education student population than in the rest of the UK' (NCIHE 1997: para. 2.8). Such claims have been echoed elsewhere in the UK, where there is growing policy interest in using the FEC sector as a vehicle for widening as well as increasing participation (House of Commons 2001). Yet if expansion in non-university HE is accompanied by clustering of non-traditional students in lower-status institutions, levels and programmes of study, the goal of equity remains elusive. Non-traditional students are at risk of entering an academic ghetto, which at its best produces outcomes that carry less value after graduation than those enjoyed by students from more conventional backgrounds. I find it surprising, then, that relatively little is currently known about the relationship between patterns of participation and the outcomes of higher education.

So far, scholars and policy makers alike have mainly viewed access and participation in terms of entry. Yet recruitment is not a sufficient basis for judging the extent to which participation contributes to equity. Recruitment itself needs to be opened up: how are choices being shaped and constrained at the point of enrolment?; what opportunities are being taken and what are being missed? We know that young people's decisions are strongly influenced by their cultural capital – that is, their grasp of the often tacit codes and norms by which the education system functions; and by their social capital – that is, their networks and connections. These may be particularly significant in the absence of any formalized system for pre-entry guidance and advice. Those who come with little understanding of the tacit codes and norms that shape higher education's assumptions and procedures, and with little in the way of accurate information about how to make things happen, are most likely to make decisions and choices based on inaccurate or even misleading information. And these factors continue to shape destinies within the higher education system. Inequality may then persist at the stage of graduation, and beyond, when newly qualified graduates enter the labour market.

Evidence on retention is patchy, but in general researchers suggest that disadvantaged students appear to be more likely to discontinue their studies. This confirms findings from the USA, where it was shown in the 1980s that retention rates for specific minority populations are significantly below the institutional mean, even though surprisingly little is known at aggregate and national levels about retention for most minority populations and for other non-traditional groups (Nettles 1988). Overall retention rates in UK higher education are relatively high by world standards; in Scotland, for example, 75 per cent of full-time first degree students achieve the qualification for which they enrolled, with 2 per cent achieving a sub-degree qualification at the same institution, and 6 per cent achieving a qualification after transferring institutions (figure 2.6). Achievement rates for the four UK nations are over 80 per cent, as compared with 72 per cent in Germany and 64 per cent in the USA (NAO 2002). Quantitative analyses of withdrawal point to significant associations with the level of prior qualifications, the quality of pre-entry information, and the degree of existing familiarity with the institution chosen; associations with socio-economic status appear weak or non-existent (NAO 2002). There were also few significant differences between institutions, though a quantitative analysis by the National Audit Office found a marked 'London effect', in that five of the seven HEIs whose non-completion rates were above the mean for their benchmark grouping are located in the English capital (NAO 2002). At first sight, then, retention appears to have relatively little impact upon equality.

A more detailed study, though, reveals a rather different picture. The National Audit Office study measured institutions by comparison with their sector benchmarks, as identified by the Funding Council. Yet different groups of students tend to cluster within these benchmark groups, so that new types of learner are distributed within benchmark groups, and not distributed evenly between them. Of the 15 English institutions where the proportion expected to gain a degree was significantly below the benchmark figures, only five were in London: one was a provincial technological

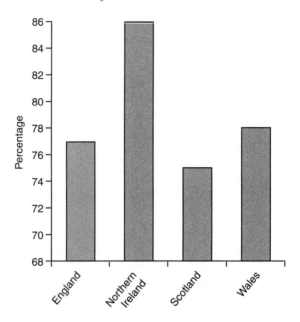

Figure 2.6   Projected results for full-time first degree students starting courses in 1998–99

Source: HEFCE 2001

university and the remaining nine were ex-polytechnics in the provinces. In each case, there was a strong association between non-achievement and the proportions of non-traditional students (HEFCE 2001; NAO 2002). Finally, survey data compiled for the 2003 *Student Living Report* confirm that drop-out is associated with social class: 78 per cent of students from AB backgrounds said they had never considered dropping out, compared with 68 per cent of C1s and 64 per cent of C2DEs (UNITE 2003: S. 2.4).

A similar institutional ghettoizing appears to take place in respect of transitions among higher education students from FECs to HEIs. In both England and Scotland, the vast majority of arrangements for articulation between sub-degree qualifications and entry into degree studies involve the ex-polytechnic sector. Arrangements for progression are also far more numerous in the least popular subjects (as measured by the difficulties faced by HEIs in recruitment); they are particularly numerous in science subjects. Jim Gallacher's research shows that almost two-thirds of those who progress in Scotland from HE in an FEC enter a post-92 university, and a further quarter remain within the FEC sector, with under a tenth moving on to one of the pre-92 universities. As Gallacher has concluded, while 'FECs have had considerable success in widening access, the progression routes available to students after study in FECs are still limited' (2002: 11). This structured inequality is all the more important in the light of Gallacher's finding that many of those who move into degree study make the decision only after experiencing HE within their FEC.

Finally, it should be said that there is little information on retention and achievement in HE within the FEC sector. Although the National Audit Office initially proposed to include this sector, the final study involved only qualitative data on student experiences within FECs. An analysis of Scottish students in the final year of an HNC (Higher National Certificate) or HND (Higher National Diploma) course, covering the period 1989–1999, indicates that that only three of every five students actually achieved their qualification, with most of the rest either withdrawing or failing altogether.* Thus much remains to be known in respect of progression from HN to degree-level study, and subsequent achievement. On the basis of the Scottish evidence, though, it could reasonably be concluded that Scottish HE in FE shows levels of attrition and failure that are relatively high, while those who succeed often find their way into post-92 universities. Scotland's policy of promoting HE within FECs therefore appears to contribute relatively little to wider access.

Labour market outcomes constitute the final stage of my analysis. To date, research attention has focused mainly on the equity aspects of the economic benefits of graduate status. There has been far less attention to the non-economic benefits, even though it is widely recognized that these are considerable, albeit hard to measure. In summary, findings from studies of the returns to graduate status confirm the broad outline of my argument, showing that inequality persists beyond the degree ceremony and the graduation ball.

The returns on higher education vary considerably by the level of qualification. Although there are clear returns to sub-degree qualifications, these lag significantly behind the returns to degrees (Conlon 2002). It has already been shown that such qualifications are typically held by non-traditional learners. Similarly, a follow-up study of people three years after graduation showed that those from new universities were less likely to be in jobs which required their degrees, but more likely to be in non-graduate jobs where they believed that their graduate skills and knowledge were used (Elias et al. 1999).

Even allowing for variations in the qualifications held, non-traditional learners face continued labour market disadvantages following graduation. Kate Purcell and Terence Hogarth (1999) have shown that graduates from lower social groups are disadvantaged in entering and succeeding in higher education and employment. Similarly, it has been shown that the prospects of experiencing unemployment during the years after graduation are significantly higher for some minority ethnic communities than for whites (Elias et el. 1999). Figure 2.7 presents the position of people from different ethnic backgrounds over the three-year period after graduation. Average earnings

* These figures are the result of work by Brian Ramsden, and were drawn to my attention by David Watson.

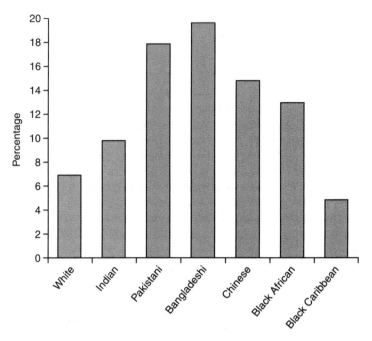

Figure 2.7   Percentage of 1995 graduates from different ethnic backgrounds experiencing six months or more unemployment in the three-year period following graduation

Source: Elias et al. (1999)

three years after graduation are lower for people with non-standard entry qualifications, and for people from manual working-class backgrounds; they are lowest of all, at 10 per cent below the mean, for people from professional families, for those graduates who come from families where neither parent is working (Elias et al. 1999).

Socio-economic inequality is, then, startlingly persistent at every stage of the higher education system. Although the flows into the system from all classes have increased, they have increased unequally for different groups of people. These inequalities, moreover, are sharpened by further stratification within the system. There certainly are new students within the higher education system. Women now constitute a majority and can no longer be considered a non-standard group of entrants, but their entrance into higher education on a mass basis is certainly new, and its impact should not be underestimated. Among those who are truly non-standard entrants, there is a strong risk that higher education is less a passport to the knowledge society than a bus ticket for the second-class citizen. Rather than widening participation, then, the growth of the last two decades has tended to increase it. The new students have come from the transformation of higher education into a mass experience of the middle class.

Changing institutions?

From the analysis above, it might be thought that massification poses relatively little challenge to the higher education institutions. After all, if more students simply means more of the same, then massification simply implies that the system as a whole gets larger. The University of Cologne, with its 64,000 students, is then no more than an extreme form of this development, which is working its way through the entire system. Massification, though, does have consequences, even if it has proceeded on the basis of systematic, large-scale social selection.

Massification, after all, means that something is happening in the world of higher education, and it is happening largely because of external pressures rather than internal decisions. These pressures have become increasingly powerful in recent years. We even hear talk in many circles about a crisis, a term that has been persistently used about the system since the turbulence of the 1960s. This sense of crisis is widespread and multi-faceted, and it has deep roots. The forces that are driving change forward have been widely discussed, and I will not detain you with yet another discussion of globalization, the knowledge society and the information revolution. For the purposes of this discussion, we can take it as given that these wider changes are helping to reshape the context of higher education systems in all countries. If for no other reason, they are doing so because policy makers are agreed on their significance, and are using these changes as evidence of the need for new policies to promote wider participation in education and training of all kinds, as part of a strategy for promoting continuous lifelong learning. These developments are widely held to justify further educational reform, including, of course, reform of the structures, procedures and possibly even the values of higher education. Thus the European Commission has suggested that these developments raise 'fundamental questions about how well equipped traditional education and training systems are to keep pace' (European Commission 2001: 7). The Commission goes on to argue that 'There should be a dual approach to access to learning: making what is already on offer more visible, flexible, integrated and effective, while also developing new learning processes, products and environments' (European Commission 2001: 13).

Reform, then, is a double-sided process. From the perspective of the policy makers it requires not merely greater accessibility to the existing offer, but a transformation of the offer and its institutional settings.

To what extent is this happening in practice? While this question can only be answered sketchily, it seems reasonably clear that the popular picture of higher education study is now substantially out of date. Of course, massification has not been an even process. Student numbers in some subjects have undergone a relative and even, in some cases an absolute, decline in recent years, while in others – notably computing/IT, management and the creative arts – growth has been much faster than the average. I will argue that there have been important changes in the nature of higher education as a result of its growth, but will confine myself here to a relatively concise list of particularly significant implications.

First, massification involves a dual process of redistributing and extending teaching capacity. In so far as this is acknowledged externally, it is largely through journalistic headlines reporting overcrowded lecture halls and empty timetables. But behind the headlines is a germ of truth. Higher education systems are increasingly likely to seek economies of scale by spreading their teaching capacity more thinly over greater numbers. They are also seeking to reorganize their teaching capacity, placing greater emphasis upon the effective application of a general grasp of learning processes and seeking to switch attention to outcomes rather than content. This is having a marked impact on academic identities, not least through attempts to regulate socialization of newcomers into the occupational culture, but also (and significantly so given its generational and age profiles) through the evolution of strategies of accommodation and resistance by more established academic workers. We know relatively little about the evolution of these strategies, other than by anecdotal means, and this is clearly a potentially fruitful area for research, along with other areas of a changing academic labour process. Speculatively, one might predict that students from non-traditional backgrounds might become both subjects and agents of these strategies, finding themselves the target of repositioning strategies by academics facing workplace change, but also spotting opportunities for challenging authority figures whose status is vulnerable and insecure. By creating pressures for autonomous student learning, and eroding established principles of hierarchy, then, massification is ensuring that the higher education experience is less and less like school.

Second, in mass higher education university life is no longer quite so special. The Finnish researcher Tapio Aittola has explored in some depth the implications of mass higher education as a routine phase in what we might call the normal middle-class biography. His conclusions deserve attention. First, he found that the student years no longer constitute a 'classically' academic life stage; instead, the modern student's life is divided between study and part-time employment. Second, the economic and social 'immaturity' of students hampers their identity formation. Third, student culture has lost its independence and vitality. Fourth, the basic structures of the life-world of students have fragmented, and it no longer revolves around the university. Fifth, the curricularization of the university has instrumentalized the study process and the relation of students to the institution itself. Finally, various discipline-based subcultures divide students increasingly sharply. In general, the student generation of the late 1980s and early 1990s differed so greatly from its predecessors that Aittola regarded it as a new student type (Aittola 1995). If anything, these tendencies have intensified since Aittola conducted his fieldwork, particularly perhaps in the so-called Anglo-Saxon countries. Yet there is as yet little acknowledgement of this pattern outside, where expectations appear to be based on ideas of university life in the 1960s and 1970s.

Third, massification is changing the value and the use of academic qualifications. In a comprehensive study of earning data from the Labour Force Survey and social mobility data from the British Household Panel Study, Malcolm Brynin (2002) has provided persuasive evidence that the relative returns to higher education in this country are showing a tendency to decline over time. This is not to say that the relative advantages conveyed by graduate status are about to vanish; these remain clear and substantial, and on Brynin's evidence they seem to be particularly strong for graduate women. He believes that only part of this general decline is accounted for by the growth in the number of graduates in the labour force, attributing at least equal significance to employers' strategies of recruiting graduates for intermediate level positions as part of a drive for greater labour flexibility. Interestingly, the decline in returns has done nothing to affect demand for higher education places in Britain, a fact which Brynin attributes less to the influence of highly skilled employment than to the strength of the social demand for higher education. While the social demand for higher education qualifications may be partly linked to popular perceptions of economic change, as Brynin indicates, it seems plausible to suggest that it may also reflect a desire for relative advantage and security as compared with the risky situation of non-graduates; and it may also be associated with the non-economic benefits of higher education. Given that we do not yet have a clear picture of these non-economic benefits, this again strikes me as a candidate for future investigation.

Fourth, new institutional forms are appearing which challenge the university's authority (Scott 2002). In general, the new institutions can be seen as expressing a different view of knowledge and its application from that embodied in higher education, and particularly in the Humboldtian model of the university. Corporate universities represent one extreme version of this trend. Much of the initial excitement over the appearance of corporate universities can now be seen as somewhat exaggerated, and with the collapse of the dot.com bubble much of the fuss has died away. It is also possible that the existing higher education system will be able, at least partially, to form strategic alliances with corporate universities, though Peter Jarvis in my view is right to conclude that they are more likely to become competitors by seeking to develop their own distinctive theoretical bases, and seeking the capacity to award degrees (Jarvis 2000).

Competition is also represented by the development of private sector higher education within Europe. This is something that has not as yet made much impact in Britain, where there is one significant private sector HEI whose students mainly come from overseas, and where US-owned HEIs have made a very limited impact. In Germany, private sector institutions have grown rapidly, and are now particularly significant providers in the MBA market (Jung 2002: 141). American institutions have made significant inroads in the Netherlands, and any deregulation of higher education markets under GATS is likely to increase this pattern. More generally, as I have argued above, non-university HEIs have tended to grow much more rapidly than the university sector, largely because they have proven more suitable vehicles for reform-minded policy makers. Meanwhile, new forms of public management have tended to bring an element of market differentiation into the state-funded sectors, at least in some countries, including this one. Rather oddly, the British debate has often tended to retreat into a somewhat parochial obsession with a possible reappearance of the pre-92 binary divide. What these developments suggest is rather that we may be witnessing the emergence of a much more complex and multi-faceted pattern of higher education provision, lacking in simplicity and transparency. As Peter Scott argues in an important paper on higher education and lifelong learning, 'traditional taxonomies of post-secondary education are breaking down', but the new forms are at present accompanied by and additional to the old ones (Scott 2002: 39–41). The impact on equity and access is therefore likely to be a complicated one, and is in great need of further research.

Lastly, there is the remarkable persistence of socio-economic and other inequalities within mass higher education. As access to higher education spreads, so it is logical that those who seek relative advantage through higher education will search out the most effective routes within the new and complex landscape, for example by identifying the best institutions and best courses, and avoiding weaker alternatives. It is also likely that social and cultural capital will play an even more important role than in the past in enabling individuals to navigate the new landscape. Access to contacts who are well connected and well informed is an important means of overcoming complexity and managing risk. A capacity for understanding of the tacit rules – of 'how we do things around here' – is an equally significant asset, provided of course that it does not lose its currency for some unforeseen reason. This has significant curricular implications, particularly if we wish to promote equity and inclusion. Further, this new landscape of higher education is likely to present considerable problems of steering for the state, and the probability is very high that new policy measures will have undesirable and even perverse side effects. So, once more, I would see the remarkable endurance of inequality as a promising area for research, including of course research designed to inform policy.

Much more might be said about these developing tendencies, as well as others that I have been forced to neglect. In particular, there has been very little systematic enquiry into the consequences for learning, teaching and organizational culture of the uneven, partial feminization of higher education. This is, then, far from being an attempt to present a finished agenda. What is clear, though, is that the massification of higher education has been accompanied by significant change. It is less clear whether this change represents a radical restructuring of higher education, or whether it has been more akin to the adaptive strategy of Lampedusa's Prince Fabrizio. I am inclined at present more towards the second interpretation than the first. But two concluding points are made.

First, my arguments here have tried to engage with the evidence base on access and participation. This is an area where we have generally been rather well served by our researchers. Broadly, it seems to me that the evidence confirms that some forms of inequality within higher education are remarkably persistent and deep-rooted, if we accept my premise about the shift of attention from participation as recruitment to participation as achievement. It may even be appropriate to speak of institutionalized inequality. Now, this seems to me a good point at which to consider just how good we are in universities at developing an evidence-based approach to our own practice. In his challenging analyses of universities as learning organizations, Chris Duke has rightly pointed to a sequence of managerial failures arising from a reluctance to tap tacit know-how and mobilize commitment through those shared forms of participatory management that alone can promote continuous organizational learning. All too often, Duke rightly claims, neurotic managers actively promote a loss of institutional memory and low-trust methods of working as mechanisms of control, with the result that staff dedication and creativity are driven into opposition and resistance (Duke 2002). I find this analysis persuasive, and would only add that in looking at management in higher education, we are looking at pluralist institutions where power and decision-taking must be viewed as polycentric. When people speak of a 'canteen culture' as a key element of institutionalized racism in the police, they are referring to precisely the same combinations of decisions, non-decisions and inherited procedures that make our universities the socially and racially selective places that they are today. If internal change is persistently blocked by managerial timidity and a staff room culture of obstruction, perhaps we need a Macpherson Report on higher education.

Second, if access and participation are the priorities that policy makers say they are, then there has to be a much clearer policy steer than we have at present. We are all aware that there is a significant debate in a neighbouring country (England) over the future funding of its higher education system. All sides in this debate have sent out either directly or indirectly the message to people from non-traditional backgrounds that they will be financially slammed by the introduction of higher student contributions. Even more striking is the fact that the entire debate has been conducted around the assumption that the gold standard of higher education remains the full-time honours degree.

3

Disabled students in higher education: legislation, teaching, learning and assessment

Sheila Riddell, Teresa Tinklin and Alastair Wilson

Introduction

Widening access to higher education is now firmly on the political agenda, but concerns have focused on the under-representation of individuals from working-class backgrounds rather than disabled people. Positive recruitment measures have also focused on increasing the participation of working-class students rather than disabled students, although the Disabled Students Allowance (DSA) was intended to help defray some of the additional costs incurred by disabled students in higher education. In addition, special needs services have been established to promote access to the curriculum and assessment, although these services have tended to be located within the student welfare rather than the teaching and learning service. Such services tend to emphasize the need for disabled students to accommodate to traditional teaching and assessment practices within higher education, rather than enhancing the accessibility of the curriculum and assessment.

This chapter focuses on moves to redress inequalities experienced by disabled students in higher education through anti-discrimination legislation. Part 4 of the Disability Discrimination Act 1995 (as amended) (DDA), which came into force in September 2002, made it unlawful to discriminate against disabled students or prospective students in the provision of educational services, including pedagogy, the curriculum and assessment. Like other equality legislation, the Act is based on the liberal idea that education may reduce inequality experienced by disabled people if discriminatory practices can be eliminated. Such views would, of course, be challenged by Marxian writers such as Bourdieu (1989), who portray the dynamic of class struggle as determining access to various forms of capital, which may be economic, cultural, social or symbolic. Here, we compare the response of four different higher education institutions (HEIs) in Scotland to the legislation, contrasting their social profiles and academic missions, support for disabled students and approaches to the implementation of the DDA in terms of their interpretation of the concept of reasonable adjustments. Subsequently, we present short case studies of two students in each institution, exploring their experiences of 'reasonable adjustments' and the extent to which they actively challenge the university's approach to teaching and learning. The following questions are addressed in the chapter:

- How is the concept of 'reasonable adjustment' for disabled students understood and implemented in different institutions?
- To what extent are these adjustments made in practice and what types of adjustment are seen as problematic by academic staff?
- How do the experiences of disabled students in different institutions vary in relation to the barriers encountered and adjustments made?
- What are the implications in terms of the ability of anti-discrimination legislation to have a positive impact in terms of tackling inequality in higher education?

The social model and the reproduction of disability

The emergent sociology of disability in the UK grappled with notions of structure and agency. Oliver (1990) and Barnes (1991), the 'founding fathers' of UK disability studies, developed the social model of disability, described as the 'big idea' of the disability movement (Shakespeare and Watson 1997). Within this theory, disability is seen as a product of economic, social and cultural oppression rather than an inevitable consequence of impairment. Abberley (1987) and Oliver (1990) emphasized the Marxist underpinning of the social model. Disability should be seen as the product of material oppression and commentators such as Barnes have been critical of those approaching disability studies from a cultural studies perspective, describing them as 'a particular breed of academic luvvie who write mainly for themselves and other academics rather than for a wider audience' (1999: 580).

Recently, there have been a number of calls, not for an abandonment, but for a more nuanced reading of the social model of disability (Crow 1996; Shakespeare and Watson 1997). Thomas (1999: 120) depicts the social model of disability as a counter-narrative. One defines oneself as disabled, she suggests, because 'one set of strands in one's web of identity – or one chapter in one's ontological narrative – has been subjectively acted upon, rewoven and retold in the light of counter-narratives'. However, she continues, disability is unlikely to be the sole defining element in an individual's identity and should be seen as one of a number of counter-narratives challenging public narratives of gender, 'race', sexuality and age. These do not exist in separate compartments and therefore cannot be seen in isolation from disability politics.

Just as classical social science theories identify education as a major site for the reproduction of social inequality, so too disability commentators have argued that the exclusion of disabled children from mainstream schools and the under-representation of disabled students in higher education is a cause, not simply an effect, of disabled people's social marginalization (Barnes 1991; Riddell and Banks 2001). In the following section, we consider the response of higher education institutions to anti-discrimination legislation. The chapter draws on data from an ESRC-funded study entitled *Disabled Students and Multiple Policy Innovations in Higher Education* (Grant number R000239069). The project ran from 2001 to 2003 and was conducted by researchers at the universities of Glasgow and Edinburgh. The study had the following three main components:

- an analysis of Higher Education Statistics Agency (HESA) statistics on rates of participation by disabled students in different types of higher education institution;
- a questionnaire survey administered to all higher education institutions in England and Scotland;
- case studies of 56 disabled students in eight higher education institutions, four in England and four in Scotland.

Disabled students and the construction of 'under-represented groups' in higher education

Performance indicators produced by the Higher Education Funding Council for England (HEFCE 2001) illustrate the construction of 'under-representation' in higher education. A range of measures of social background are used, including social class measured by the Registrar General's occupational classification system. Students under 21 whose fathers work in occupations designated IIIM (skilled manual), IV (partly skilled) and V (unskilled), or, if over 21, whose previous employment was in one of these categories, are considered to be working class. Those whose home address is in a low participation neighbourhood are also considered to be from socially disadvantaged backgrounds. In addition, attending a state school or college is used as a measure of less advantaged social background. As noted by Archer (2003), all these measures are loose approximations of social class. For example, state schools and colleges vary from selective grammar schools to institutions in very poor neighbourhoods, and some middle-class people live in low participation neighbourhoods. In addition, within a particular family, the occupation of the mother and father may vary, so a student whose father works in a factory may have a mother who is a teacher. Only a third of students provide information about their father's occupation on their university application form, so much of the data are missing. The Higher Education Funding Council also gathers information on ethnicity, age and gender.

Disabled students have more recently come to be recognized as an under-represented group, and performance indicators on rates of participation in different institutions were published for the first time in December 2002. Currently, about 4 per cent of students in UK higher education institutions have disclosed a disability, whereas 15 per cent of the working-age population have a long-term disability substantially affecting their day-to-day activities, the DDA definition of disability (Riddell and Banks 2001). However, a much lower proportion of younger people are disabled and some disabled people, including those with significant learning difficulties, would be unlikely to qualify for higher education. It should also be borne in mind that the majority of disabled students have dyslexia or unseen disabilities such as diabetes, asthma and myalgic encephalomyelitis (ME), and less than 10 per cent have significant physical or sensory impairments. It is likely that many disabled people are currently unable to access higher education due to a range of financial, physical and cultural barriers, but the extent of under-representation is difficult to quantify.

Tackling inequality through anti-discrimination legislation

There continue to be debates about the extent to which legislation is capable of tackling social inequalities. Gooding (2000) summarized some of the major difficulties with the DDA as it now stands. She pointed out that, in contrast with sex and race equality legislation, a disabled person must first prove that he or she is disabled under the terms of the DDA. A person has a disability for the purposes of the DDA if s/he has a physical or mental impairment, which has a substantial and long-term adverse effect on his or her ability to carry out normal day-to-day activities. Many cases have fallen because it was deemed by the court that the person did not comply with the definition set out in Part 1 of the DDA (Meager et al. 1999; Gooding 2000).

There have also been disputes over what is meant by reasonable adjustments and less favourable treatment. Freedman (1999) argued that, for equality legislation to produce a fairer society, the goal of equal representation must be acknowledged, rather than the limited and restricted target of equal opportunities. This requires positive social policy measures including education, training and family-friendly measures alongside anti-discrimination legislation. Despite the limitations of the legislation, Gooding (2000: 548) nonetheless argues that the legislation marks a 'broader change to the cultural value attached to disabled people – a paradigm shift in the way in which disability is understood'.

Part 4 of the DDA, which came into force on 1 September 2002, made it unlawful to discriminate against disabled students or prospective students by treating them less favourably than others or by failing to make reasonable adjustments. In addition, universities were required to make certain types of reasonable adjustments where disabled students or prospective students might otherwise be substantially disadvantaged. Although the legislation has potentially far-reaching implications (DRC 2002), there is a number of 'get-out' clauses which potentially weaken its impact. For example, in deciding what adjustments are reasonable, responsible bodies may take a number of factors into consideration, including the need to maintain academic standards and the cost of taking a particular step. In this chapter we consider the ways in which the reasonableness of adjustments is defined in practice.

The curriculum and pedagogy in higher education: the wider institutional context

As other chapters in this volume demonstrate, there have been major changes in the nature and mode of operation of higher education in the UK. The number of students more than doubled in the ten-year period between the mid-1980s and mid-1990s, whilst the unit of resource fell by more than a third. Despite this rapid expansion, the proportion of students from working-class backgrounds remained stable, with participation rates of higher social groups expanding substantially (Archer 2003). Devices such as the RAE and quality assurance regimes encouraged universities to compete with each other for the staff and students in the highest demand and staff and institutional performance was managed through the publication by the Higher Education Funding Councils of performance indicators and benchmark statistics. The New Labour government established widening access to higher education as one of its policy priorities, and premium funding was instituted in relation to the number of students from under-represented groups in particular institutions. At one level, these changes produced a higher education system which, according to the OECD, was the most efficient in the developed world. On the other hand, academics perceived a decline in their conditions of employment and academic freedom (Halsey 1995).

Bennett et al. (1999) noted that attempts to introduce the teaching of core skills into pre-92 universities were met with considerable resistance, since these were seen as alien to the traditional knowledge-based culture (Dunne et al. 1997). There were also major differences between traditional and new universities with regard to the provision of learning support. Wolfendale and Corbett (1997) noted that new universities and further education colleges had much better learning support services in place than pre-92 universities. A key aim of this research was to investigate the impact of these contextual differences on the ability of a range of institutions to respond to the new duties imposed by the DDA.

Four Scottish institutional case studies

In the research project, higher education institutions were divided into three categories: pre-1992 institutions, post-1992 institutions and non-university higher education institutions. The decision to divide up universities in this way was based on the notion that new and old universities have different histories in terms of governance and degree-awarding powers, although within each sector there is great variation. Table 3.1 shows the number of institutions in each category in the dataset used in this paper.

Table 3.1   Distribution of universities and HEIs by sector and country

	Pre-1992 institutions	*Post-1992 institutions*	*Non-university HEIs*
England	51	36	45
Scotland	8	5	5

Source: Riddell et al. 2002

As noted earlier, in-depth case study work was conducted in eight institutions selected to exemplify particular approaches to higher education. Below, we discuss important aspects of the four Scottish case study institutions.

University 1 was a relatively small (about 6000 undergraduates) pre-92 university in a small town, with most students living in halls of residence. The majority of university buildings were old and many were listed; this was identified by staff at all levels as presenting a major barrier to the recruitment of disabled students. University 1 had a relatively small number of mature students and a high intake from the independent school sector and from England (see table 3.2 for comparison of key indicators). A number of linking arrangements with local colleges and schools had been established, but staff were wary of lowering academic requirements for students from non-traditional backgrounds, fearing a dilution of standards.

Table 3.2   Key characteristics of three universities

	University 1	*University 2*	*University 3*
Number of undergraduates	6,000	14,000	16,000
Number of disability support staff (FTE)	2	4 (5 support for learning staff)	3 (5 support for learning staff)
% disabled students	6	2	4
% from state school/college	59	96	85
% social class IIIM, IV, V	13	36	21
% low participation neighbourhood	8	27	16
% continue or qualify	95	82	86

Of the three universities discussed in this paper, University 1 benefited most from the introduction of premium funding. The university had the highest proportion of dyslexic students and was successful in encouraging them to disclose a disability. Overall, 6 per cent of students disclosed a disability, considerably above the national average. The special needs support service was relatively well resourced and student volunteers compensated for any shortfall in the university's service.

University 2 was a medium-sized post-92 institution with approximately 14,000 undergraduate students. University 2 described itself as a friendly local institution, geared to helping students find work in a range of vocational areas such as business and management, professions allied to medicine, nursing, social work, engineering and journalism. University 2's buildings were all new or relatively new and, compared with other universities in the city, the estate was relatively accessible. The university had little student accommodation and most students lived at home or commuted from the surrounding area. University 2 had the largest enrolment of part-time undergraduates in Scotland and a significant proportion of students were admitted from Further Education Colleges with Advanced Standing. Research funding represented a relatively small proportion of the recurrent grant from SHEFC.

Despite having a relatively accessible modern campus, University 2 had a very low proportion of disabled students (2 per cent), and a particularly low proportion of dyslexic students. Many courses were accredited by professional bodies whose requirements might exclude disabled students. In relation to its student population, University 2 did not have a generously funded disability support service, although its learning support service, which had been in operation for some time, was well resourced.

University 3 was a traditional pre-92 university with a strong research base. The university was proud of its record on widening access, and recruited many of its students from its hinterland, with around half of undergraduate students living at home during their studies. The university had about 16,000 undergraduates and 4000 postgraduates. In terms of its ability to attract students from less socially advantaged backgrounds, University 3 was located mid-way between the other two institutions (see table 3.2).

The proportion of disabled students (4 per cent) was close to the national average. The special needs support service was not as well resourced as that of University 1, and staff were under considerable pressure to meet student demand.

College 1 had pioneered higher education in an FE setting, with 50 per cent of its provision in higher education. Twenty thousand students, including 5000 full-time students, enrolled each year. Of these, 3800 were studying at HE level. The college had a number of campuses and new buildings had been funded through the Private Finance Initiative. Twenty full-time lecturing staff with particular specialisms were in post, and a pool of part-time lecturers also contributed. The college was located in an area of multiple deprivation and 36 per cent of students, including HE students, were from deprivation category 5 based on the Scottish Deprivation Index. For 20 years, the college had been given additional funding by the Scottish Executive to provide higher education to deaf students, who continued to be attracted to the college because of the existence of a well-established deaf community.

Table 3.3 Key characteristics of College 1

	College 1
Number of students	10,000 (2500 undertaking HE course)
Number of learning support lecturers	20 (plus pool of part-time lecturers)
% disabled students (HE)	4
% most deprived neighbourhood	36

Note: Data were gathered according to different criteria for College 1 and have therefore been presented separately.

To summarize, it is evident that the four institutions had very different social profiles, academic missions and approaches to the provision of support for disabled students. The following analysis draws on two student case studies undertaken in each institution. The characteristics of the students are summarized in table 3.4.

Key themes

The limits of reasonable adjustments in the context of the DDA

Table 3.4 summarizes the nature of the adjustments required by disabled students and those which were made by institutions. Additional aids and services funded by the DSA were generally available. However, whilst relatively generous provision was made for students with less significant difficulties, those with higher support needs, such as Lynne, often found that the funds were inadequate. In addition, equipment was often not available until after the course had commenced. Far more problematic was the provision of personal assistants, note-takers and sign language interpreters. Difficulties arose with regard to employment, training and supply of suitable qualified individuals. Students with more significant impairments often relied on informal help from friends, family or volunteers.

Adjustments to institutional policy and practice appeared to be more difficult. Students often had to fight for even simple adjustments to physical features, such as accessible toilet facilities and parking spaces. Adjustments to the curriculum and teaching methods were even trickier to negotiate.

Table 3.4 Characteristics of students within the case study

Name	Institution	Age	Course	Previous education	Nature of impairment	Adjustments made	Adjustments required but not made	Comments
Verity	University 1	20	German/ Social History	Scottish rural comprehensive school	Visual	Specialist computing equipment, extra time in exams	Extended library loans, additional tuition, notes in electronic format, shorter book list	Varying department attitudes. Additional tuition self-funded, disagreements over funding enlargement of texts. Strong parental support/ intervention. Year abroad unsupported
Louise	University 1	20	Art History/ Social Anthropology	English private school	ME, diabetes	Flexible attendance requirements and assignment deadlines, laptop, extra time in exams	Sometimes penalized for late assignments, notes in electronic format	Instrumental approach to university, strong support from disabled students adviser
Phil	University 2	mature	Social Work	Scottish comprehensive, college access course	Visual impairment	Voice-activated software	Notes in electronic format	Highly politicized student, loose connection to university
Shelley	University 2	mature	Psychology	Scottish rural comprehensive school	Cerebral palsy, mobility and speech difficulties	Personal assistance, tape-recorded lectures, extra time in exams	Inaccessible venues, notes in electronic format, lack of cooperation with tape recording	Strong connection with disability movement

Name	Institution	Year	Age	Course	Secondary education	Disability	Support required	Issues	Support network
Kirsty	University	3	20	Genetics	Scottish comprehensive school	Rare chromosomal disorder, visual impairment, deafness, weak muscle tone	Note-takers, personal demonstrator, specialized computing equipment	Notes in electronic format, note-takers with subject knowledge, clear view of lecturer to lip-read	Assistance from parent, commuting meant lack of engagement in university life
Lynne	University	3	19	Law and Spanish	Scottish comprehensive school (peripatetic teacher)	Blind	Specialist brailling equipment, selected reading list, access to all course material electronically, accessible venues	Accessible venues (students' own choice)	Strong support from family, friends and Faculty admissions officer
Robert	College	1	20	Multi-media technology (HND)	Special unit attached to Scottish mainstream comprehensive	Deaf	Sign language interpretation, specialist computing equipment	Shortage of sign language interpreters	Support from lecturers and deaf community in college. Little contact with hearing students
Donny	College	1	mature	Web design (HNC)	Scottish comprehensive school	Spinal injury as a result of traffic accident	Wheelchair access	Access problems: lift, parking space, toilets, slow automatic door, slippery ramps	Director of spinal injury voluntary organization, strong social connections within and outside college

Some lecturers, for example in College 1, were very keen to make their classes interactive and accessible to deaf students:

> I don't want him (Robert) to feel he has got to sit back and because he can't hear doesn't mean he can't ask a question in the normal way as everybody else does. Even if his interpreter is not here, he can always write it on a bit of paper and give me it ... I try and get them into the way of interacting with everybody else, I feel that's important.
>
> (Lecturer, College 1)

In contrast with this was the account given by Verity of her attempt to get lecturers in a particular department to enlarge handouts:

> I've had several talks with them through the couple of years. They are distressed at the time when they realize that things are not going right and they say, 'Oh yes, we will put that right' but it's just words, it's not actions, and it's not sincere and you just need to keep badgering them.
>
> (Student, University 1)

Adaptations to assessment were almost always formulaic, consisting of additional time in examinations, but there were very few examples of modifications to the mode or content of assessment.

One of the most common adjustments required by disabled students was access to notes in electronic format before classes, but lecturers were very unlikely to comply with this request, particularly in pre-92 universities. Circulating lecture notes was seen as deterring students from attending lectures, commodifying knowledge and infringing lecturers' intellectual property rights. A number of lecturers said that they did not have written notes but preferred to teach spontaneously, pulling together information from a wide range of sources just before their lecture. To have a formal written lecture would remove creativity, making the delivery of the lecture a mechanical exercise. However, it was also evident that many lecturers were using old photocopied handouts which had been reproduced so often that they were scarcely legible. A number of students commented that younger lecturers were more likely to use new technology, such as Powerpoint, in a helpful way and were less 'precious' about sharing their lecture notes.

Lecturers in pre-92 universities feared a 'dumbing down' of academic work, and were suspicious of the number of students claiming the status of disability to secure assessment concessions. A lecturer in University 1 distinguished between deserving and non-deserving disabled students:

> I think the issues with academic standards ... will come to the fore when we have a lot more students who fall into the disabled group and what we will get is the student who is disabled and a bad student. A student who is disabled and is a bit lazy, and I think people are not quite sure what to do because of the PC nature of it. These are the cases that will be difficult because the question arises, is the student using their disability as an excuse for being lazy?
>
> (Lecturer, University 1)

A particularly difficult area concerned the adjustments required by dyslexic students who said they were have problems with structuring their work as a result of their dyslexia:

> Yes, I had a student who was making this case to me today when he was talking about advising him to honours. He was saying, 'I have problems with the exams because I can't structure'. I always have questions about structure because there are students who are not dyslexic that we say that to as well.
>
> (Lecturer, University 1)

Generally, adjustments made for disabled students were reactive rather than anticipatory, although College 1 provided an example of a more anticipatory approach, having a permanent contract with a sign language interpretation unit to provide services throughout the year.

Implicit understandings of equality

Particularly in the pre-92 universities, there were concerns that making adjustments for disabled students might involve disadvantaging others. For example, a German lecturer in University 1 explained that, quite apart from the cost, extra tuition could not be made available to Verity because:

> . . . when it comes to tuition, all students would want tuition, there are lots of needy cases that would require extra tuition and it would be hard to argue for Verity to take priority over other students' needs for special tuition.
>
> (Lecturer, University 1)

Other adjustments which were refused in some institutions on ground of fairness to other students included extended access to course materials or library books and additional contact hours with lecturing staff. Some lecturers in pre-92 universities were resistant to the idea that students from under-represented groups should be admitted with lower grades, since this would reflect unacceptable social engineering. The aim, rather, should be to improve state education to erode differential levels of attainment.

The significance of institutional ethos

The ethos of particular institutions, and the degree of 'fit' between institutional and individual student habitus (Bourdieu 1990), appeared to be highly significant in determining the approach to disabled students. Although difficulties existed for all disabled students in all institutions, it was noticeable that some were more willing to make adaptations than others.

University 1 and College 1 were smaller and more socially homogeneous than the other two institutions. Whilst University 1 was traditional and highly socially selective, its paternalistic ethos enabled it to accommodate the needs of the disabled students it recruited, whose social backgrounds mirrored those of other students. The ethos of College 1, attracting a high proportion of socially disadvantaged students, was inclusive across many dimensions. For 20 years the college had received preferential funding from the Scottish Executive to cater for the needs of deaf students. The existence of a deaf community and the college's ability to organize sign language interpretation services meant that the number of deaf students was growing. Higher education students were taught in small classes and lecturers regarded disabled students as part of their core clientele, rather than a small group making additional demands. They were also able to draw on the expertise of lecturers in the Faculty of Learning Support. Raab (1998) and Gallacher (2002) have noted that Scotland's colleges have attracted a much higher percentage of students from disadvantaged backgrounds to their HE courses compared with universities. However, it should be noted that whilst the culture and ethos of colleges may favour disabled students, they may encounter difficulties with modes of assessment, teaching methods and access to staff when they transfer to larger and more impersonal universities (Gallacher et al. 1997).

By way of contrast, disabled students in Universities 2 and 3 received more patchy support. An individual might have a positive experience in a small faculty or department where they received sponsorship from an individual member of staff. However, neither university had a strong system of support for disabled students at departmental level and the disabled students advisory service often had to act as a mediator between student and staff member. Levels of resourcing were low in both universities, with one member of staff having responsibility for at least 200 students, and it was often left up to the student to negotiate their own support. Compared with University 1, where students lived in university accommodation, students at Universities 2 and 3 often commuted in from the large hinterland, thus weakening social ties. The more diverse characteristics of students in these two universities meant that social capital tended to be weaker, and drop-out rates were higher.

Academic cultures and the impact of performativity in higher education

As noted earlier, a major change in higher education has been the gradual erosion of academic freedom and the intensification of academic work, with a new emphasis on performativity. Many academics in pre-'92 universities explained that their efforts had been directed into fulfilling Research Assessment Exercise commitments, distracting attention from teaching:

> Well, the TQA and the RAE have had a disastrous effect on universities and the reason is really very simple. Since the Government in the 1990s

made our funding dependent on student numbers, that automatically meant that, when doing our job, we have to have at least one eye on the finances. We no longer have both eyes on the ball, education and academic matters, scientific work, we have to have one eye on financial matters.

(Lecturer, University 1)

Both the Research Assessment Exercise (RAE) and Teaching Quality Assessment (TQA) were associated with managerialist control of universities. It was pointed out that some practices in universities, which had been introduced on grounds of standardization of practice, such as anonymous marking, were likely to militate against disabled students because such practices ruled out the option to make informal allowances. The RAE was also blamed for prioritizing research over teaching, which meant that lecturers had little time to devote to the type of curriculum change activities promoted in the Teachability project:

> As I was saying, everything is being run by the RAE and with your ESRC grant to do this piece of research you're in that game as much as everyone else . . . So that's your number 1, 2, and 3 priority and everything else is done on some relic of professionalism and goodwill and all the rest of it. So I think, I'm sure the RAE will continue but the sad thing about all this is, I'm sure there are people out there that would love to say, 'Right, okay, well what am I going to achieve this semester as well as all my teaching? I'm really going to try and make these courses accessible', but the difficulty is finding the time to do that . . .

(Lecturer, University 1)

In University 2 and College 1, there was less evidence that the inclusion of disabled students was affected by performativity pressures. Widening access was a central part of the mission of these institutions, and was not seen as conflicting with other goals.

Conclusion

Disabled students may provide a lens through which universities' capacity to respond and adapt to the needs of 'under-represented' groups may be viewed. Returning to the questions posed in the introduction, it was evident that, whilst the DDA requires reasonable adjustments to be made, the nature, scale and scope of such adjustments were very limited. Payments to individual students through the DSA meant that some additional support was available, but this was usually inadequate to meet the needs of students with more significant impairments. Adjustments to teaching methods were rare. Particularly in pre-92 universities, lecturers used very traditional lecturing methods in many subjects and were often unable or unwilling to make their notes available electronically. College lecturers working with small groups were more likely to be flexible in their approaches to teaching and to have less fixed views about a body of knowledge to be conveyed.

In pre-92 universities, the widening access agenda was perceived as being at odds with some fundamental institutional values. There were concerns that making adjustments for some students, particularly those with dyslexia, might lead to a reduction of standards generally. There was resentment of a wide range of managerialist measures, including the Research Assessment Exercise and Teaching Quality Assessment, which were seen to erode academic freedom. The widening access agenda was seen as another example of the Government interfering with university autonomy and was met with similar suspicion. In addition, the demand for accessible curricula was considered to be at odds with the demands of the Research Assessment Exercise, which required a focus on research rather than teaching.

The ethos of individual institutions, which was linked to their sectoral position, appeared to have a marked effect on the willingness of lecturers to make adjustments to teaching, learning and assessment. Both University 1 and College 1, small institutions with relatively homogeneous social profiles, appeared to find it easier to meet disabled students' needs. By way of contrast, University 2 and University 3 were larger and more amorphous, and found it harder to muster the energy or resources to respond to requests for support. In all institutions, disabled students were themselves expected to act as change agents, cajoling staff to make adjustments in addition to coping with the pressures of coursework and assessment.

As we noted earlier, the DDA is based on the idea that discrimination occurs if adjustments are not made to 'level the playing field' for those who experience substantial and adverse effects of long-term impairment. There seems to be considerable evidence, however, to suggest that many staff, particularly in traditional universities, operate with the idea that equality means treating everyone the same. This is perhaps not surprising, since universities are highly exclusive institutions which draw on meritocratic ideologies to justify the role they play in perpetuating social inequalities. Bourdieu and Passeron (1977) argued that the politics of formal equality, applied in this way, are a robust mechanism for guaranteeing inequality since they assume that all learners come equally equipped for the process of learning. This assumption accentuates the social and cultural advantages already possessed by some learners which educators assume to be normal. In the same way, by expecting disabled students to perform in exactly the same way as everyone else, institutions may accentuate their existing disadvantages.

Current debates on social justice in access to higher education, occurring in the light of the recent English Government White Paper (DfES 2003), are just as relevant to disabled students as to those from working-class backgrounds. Opposition to positive action reveals the lengths to which socially advantaged groups will go to protect their existing privilege. Clearly, continuous pressure will be needed to ensure that the prohibition to discrimination against disabled students is not interpreted as merely providing formal access, but is taken further to ensure fairness of representation and treatment within higher education. This will require radical changes to established methods of teaching and assessment, whose legitimacy has often been taken for granted.

4

Rurality and higher education: a conceptual analysis

Neil Moreland, Joyce Chamberlain and Kepa Artaraz

Introduction

This chapter is based upon our experiences as a manager and researchers in a Rural Opportunities Project in the West Midlands region of England. The project covered the three rural counties of Herefordshire, Shropshire and Worcestershire, and involved collaborating with 17 further and higher educational institutions. The main aim of the Rural Opportunities Project was concerned with increasing the supply of people into higher education, either directly or via pathways established within the three counties and the 'new town' of Telford in Shropshire, established in 1963.

The project was one of many such widening opportunities projects funded in the years 2000 to 2003 by the Higher Education Funding Council for England (HEFCE). The national context of the Rural Opportunities Project is briefly considered before the regional context and the project activities are described. The rest of the chapter considers the implications for widening opportunities based upon our experiences in the project.

The national context of the Rural Opportunities Project

There is a number of factors that collectively constitute the national context of the Rural Opportunities Project. The first of these factors arise from changing concepts and discourses about the nature and constitution of rural life. A Government White Paper, published in 2000, *Our Countryside: The Future – A Fair Deal for Rural England*, articulates a vision of rural England as:

- A living countryside, with thriving rural communities and access to high-quality services;

- A working countryside, with a diverse economy giving high and stable levels of employment;
- A protected countryside, in which the environment is sustained and enhanced, and which all can enjoy; and
- A vibrant countryside, which can shape its own future, with its voice heard at all levels.

(DEFRA 2000: 6)

Whilst this vision may be laudable, Gray points out that, '[t]he White Paper pays scant regard to lifelong learning and misses many opportunities to point out both the success stories and the potential of lifelong education and learning in rural areas' (Gray 2002: 6). Though there is little space given to education in the White Paper, it significantly does go on to say that, '[w]e intend to make sure that people of all ages living in rural areas have full access to the range of opportunities available and that obstacles to access will be addressed' (DEFRA 2000: 36). This is a bold statement, and justifies the activities of projects such as the Rural Opportunities Project (of which more below). At the same time, the statement perhaps displays a naïvety, given national concerns and preoccupations with the quality and standards of educational provision, including higher education (see, for example, the Quality Assurance Agency (QAA) website on subject benchmarks). Gray (2002: 7) sceptically suggests that the statement that 'obstacles to access will be addressed' is not the same as saying that the obstacles will be removed, whilst ensuring full access to the range of opportunities available can mean nothing if there is no provision to access.

Perhaps the solution lies in government proposals elsewhere, such as that of rural proofing. Rural proofing is 'a commitment by the Government to ensure that all its domestic policies take account of rural circumstances and needs' (see www.countryside.gov.uk/ruralproofing/default.htm). Rural proofing accordingly 'applies to all policies, programmes and initiatives and it applies to both the design and delivery stages'. What is not clear from such statements, however, is the extent to which such regulatory requirements apply equally to Quasi-Autonomous Non-Governmental Organisations (QUANGOs) such as the Higher Education Funding Council for England (HEFCE) and the Learning and Skills Councils (LSC), established in 2001 to address the training and development needs arising from and within local and regional as well as national economies in England and Wales. The jury is still out on the issue of rural proofing and higher education, though the recent White Paper *The Future of Higher Education* (DfES 2003) does contain a proposal to establish an Access Regulator, a proposal not universally welcomed by the higher education community. There is a diversity in rural areas; the dispersal of rural exclusion and poverty is often found amidst affluence (Rowntree Foundation 2000). As the Rowntree Foundation Report says:

The main axes of inequality in rural Britain are social class, gender and age. The principal groups affected by exclusion are older people, young people, low-paid people in work, self-employed people, people detached from labour markets, and women . . . Other factors which are more important in rural than urban areas include low pay, inadequate pensions, poverty in self-employment, lower levels of benefit uptake, and fear of stigma in small communities.

(Rowntree Foundation 2000: 4)

Such factors are not likely to be addressed by free markets in educational provision at higher education. If higher education does the same as it always has done, then the outcomes will be the same as they always have been.

Developments in rural areas, and especially the decline in public services and rural amenities such as public houses and shops, allied to poor or non-existent public transport, make the lives of potential rural students difficult if not impossible (Davidson 2002). To this we can add the reality that, 'rural England is growing but ageing. It is mainly the result of in-migration of older people and out-migration of the young' (Ryley 2002: 41). Ryley subsequently goes on to write that a major effect of such migration patterns is that the

Displacement (of locals) and loss of esteem lead to low educational attainment and patterns of local employment that sees locals working in the lowest paid sectors. Professional, well-paid work is often the province of the incomer. In this way, social exclusion is created through a process of social change, but it has different effects on different sections of the community.

(ibid.: 42)

Another aspect of the national context of the Rural Opportunities Project is the current government's policy target of achieving a 50 per cent participation rate among all 18 to 30-year-olds in higher education by 2010 (Woodward 2001). Irrespective of whether we question the need for such a policy, its wisdom or the likelihood that it might be achieved, a Widening Opportunities (WO) policy has taken place in the context of changing notions or discourses of education towards 'education for work'. According to Hyland 'the vocationalisation of education and training at all levels has been the *leitmotif* of developments from school to university over the last two decades or so' (Hyland 2001: 677). That is to say, education has been refocused to a considerable extent towards meeting the needs of industry and commerce. Furthermore, as Woodward (2001) suggests, in order to reach the current government's 50 per cent participation targets, higher education has to improve on the 25 per cent of entrants who come from the 50 per cent of the population in skilled manual, semi-skilled or unskilled families – social classes IIIM, IV and V (ONS 2000).

The problem is that the majority of people in those social class categories do not have the entry qualifications appropriate to enter higher education, despite there being continuous and clear evidence of a 'pool of ability'

(Robbins 1963) untapped. This failure to attract larger numbers of these lifelong learners, or so-called non-traditional students, into higher education is a particular feature of the three rural counties covered by our project. Consequently, this means that widening opportunities projects have to innovate in ways that current providers do not in order to attract such students.

Besides, according to Burke (2002), the access to higher education movement that so successfully led to the opening of educational opportunities to traditionally excluded groups in the late 1970s and 1980s has undergone enormous changes in the recent past. These changes include formalization, standardization, marketization and centralization of processes and procedures. The end result is that the access to higher education project may be in danger of stalling, in particular by having moved away from a commitment to social equality and justice and becoming tied ever more closely to a politics of vocationalism, competition and individualism (Burke 2002: 8). As we shall see, such trends are not attractive to a large number of rural learners, though obviously such a vocational focus has an appeal to them.

The regional context of the Rural Opportunities Project

Although the project has a central physical base in Telford, individual county project workers who also have a local base within their areas carry out the development activities in each county. The key characteristics of the counties include the following:

- They constitute the three rural counties of England bordering Wales;
- They are situated in the main rural 'fringe' of the West Midlands conurbation with low population densities, with the exception of the 'new town' of Telford;
- Employment is typically in micro- and small enterprises, and with low-skilled personnel (with the exception of Telford);
- There is limited higher education access or provision in the area;
- There is a tradition of migration out of the area to participate in higher education.

This latter migration tends to be the norm in rural areas, with those who participate in higher education often not returning to their places of origin. Besides the obvious 'brain drain' out of the rural areas, this internal migration can seriously erode the skill base of the local economies. This then brings two additional challenges. Firstly, to 'bring higher education to the people in rural areas'; secondly, to make their studies relevant to the local economic needs.

The organizational context of the Rural Opportunities Project

Supported by 17 institutions of higher and further education, the Rural Opportunities Project is led by the University of Wolverhampton and the Open University. Under the aegis of Project and County Management Boards, the strategies adopted by the Rural Opportunities Project for widening access can be classified under the following headings:

- Stimulating new opportunities (for example, promoting curriculum development in order to provide locally mediated distance learning);
- Providing information about existing opportunities (for example, websites, targeted advertising, careers conventions, taster courses);
- Assisting access by associated colleges and universities to opportunities/ information (for example, undertaking needs research and analysis, providing transport costs to centres);
- Providing practical support (for example, study centres for students); and
- Providing assistance to help overcome obstacles (for example, assisting institutions to recognize the variety of routes into HE and the disparate but valid experiences of potential students).

The project has been successful to some extent, involving well over one thousand potential higher education students in the final year alone, as well as supporting numerous innovations that would not have occurred, or have occurred much more slowly, without Rural Opportunities stimulation and support. That being so, the rest of this chapter will focus upon the lessons learned by the project based upon our experiences and theorization of rurality, rural living and educational need. To do this, we begin with the concepts and realities of rurality and social capital.

The nature and realities of rurality and social capital

Rurality and ruralism are problematic concepts, both empirically and ontologically. Empirically, rurality has been defined in relation to urbanity, and the absence of compressed populations and their associated urban areas and space usage (for example, Richardson 2000; Phillips et al. 2001; Ward 2002). Ontologically, rurality is both a category and a set of experiences. By category, we mean an understanding of a particular phenomenon as having a set of related characteristics. For urban dwellers, for instance, rurality is usually defined in terms of green fields, agricultural and forestry land use, and possible beliefs of the arcadian existence where people are in communion with, and closely related to, the land. In the UK, however, there is a developing conflict over countryside, and role and nature of rural space and economic activities (Marsden 1999), though there appears to be a movement towards what might be called a leisure or culture economy of ruralism (Ray 1998) in which farming is very much a reduced activity in favour of the stewardship of land and diversification of land use (Curry 2002).

Ontologically, however, the understanding of rurality and rural living by individuals and groups has to be initially constructed, and continually reconstructed. That is, rural life and living is not always or only a chocolate box cover of rural life, but an existence and set of identities that have to be established and continually refurbished or altered as the circumstances of the lives of individuals and groups alter. Images of settled rural communities abide in arcadian perspectives, despite the existence of inequality and poverty on a par with, if not in excess of, that in towns and cities (Farmer et al. 2001). Accepting inequalities, and their articulation in a variety of social processes and contexts, has allowed sociologists of rural areas to present and analyse more intricate and accurate pictures of rural lives and existence. As Panelli et al. note:

> Recent social theorists' interests in discourse, heterogeneity, identity, space and change provides researchers with the opportunity to re-fashion studies of community as 'inquisitions of power' where a politics of contrasting voices, spaces and actions can be considered. Such an approach to 'community' would acknowledge that different people could share a notion of 'community' yet simultaneously relate to one another in unequal ways creating both experiences of privilege and marginalisation.
>
> (Panelli et al. 2002: 111)

Marginalization too is a collective ontological as well as a spatial concept. For instance, at a conference in 2002 on 'Community Education in the Margins' in Herefordshire (Herefordshire Strategic Lifelong Learning Partnership: entitled Herefordshire: Towards a Learning County, 6 March 2002), it became clear that the 'margins' referred to the county of Herefordshire being physically on the edge of the West Midlands, but also outside the mainstream activities of the West Midlands region. At the same time, whilst there was an awareness of separateness from the people in the West Midlands conurbation centred upon the City of Birmingham, the ontology of marginality, involved perceptions of being isolated, and of not being 'incorporated into' or 'included' in the main arenas of public life. In a sense, the empirical reality is irrelevant (though not completely in this case as significant parts of the three rural counties of Herefordshire, Worcestershire and Shropshire have been designated a Rural Regeneration Area by Advantage West Midlands). Ontologically, if people believe that they are excluded, then that is a significant reality that informs their perceptions and activities. Figure 4.1 encapsulates this process of negotiating reality, with dimensions such as space and place, work, rural living regimes and activities as well as participation leading to lived but negotiated concepts of rural knowledge, including what it means to be rural.

What figure 4.1 emphasizes is the necessity for social realities to be nego-

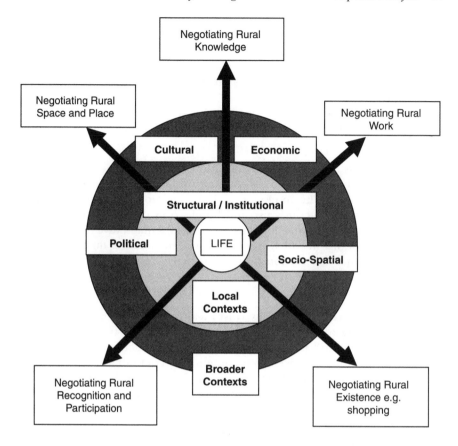

Figure 4.1 The individual learner in the broader context: 'people make their own histories, but not in circumstances of their own choosing'.

Source: Panelli 2002: 115

tiated and/or reaffirmed (or altered) if they are to continue to be a significant framework for living. Access to resources and power to define such realities, however, is not evenly distributed, but structured and unequal, sufficiently for Shucksmith to comment, in relation to rural social class, that:

> Class divisions and inequality can be partly defined in terms of differential access to forms of self-actualization and empowerment. It follows that attempts to address inequality and social exclusion must seek both to alter the structures which constrain individuals' actions and also to build the capacity to act of those actors with the least power and opportunities.
>
> (Shucksmith 2000: 209)

Numerous studies are available of such inequalities, including generational ones (for example, Mulraney and Turner 2001; Panelli 2002; Panelli et al. 2002). There is thus a necessity for the rural dweller to 'make out' in the ongoing attempt to live a tolerable or acceptable life. For rural communities (as in all societies), a key part of such attempts concerns the nature of local social capital.

Though there is neither the space nor the time here to go into any analysis of social capital, we share the interpretations with Falk and Kilpatrick that,

> Social capital is the product of social interactions with the potential to contribute to the social, civic or economic well-being of a community-of-common-purpose. The interactions draw on knowledge and identity sources and simultaneously use and build stores of social capital. The nature of the social capital depends upon various qualitative dimensions of the interactions in which it is produced, such as the quality of the internal-external interactions, the historicity, futuricity, reciprocity, trusts and shared values and norms.
>
> (Falk and Kilpatrick 2000: 103–4)

The use of terms like historicity (historical contexts), futuricity (possible trajectories of life and communities in the foreseeable future), and reciprocity (mutuality and provision of complementary services or activities), imply that rural people have some common or communal understanding and interaction. As Meert (2000: 321) reminds us, for instance, 'reciprocity implies that each participant has the capacity to produce some resources, and assumes a social network with symmetric links between members'. Key aspects of reciprocity are thus the consolidation and extension of social capital, and the provision of opportunities (such as rural higher education) that does not denude a community of its talent except by agreement and aspiration. In this context, therefore, the provision of local rural higher education, and pathways to that provision, is potentially a key contribution to social capital. There has thus to be a supply-side rationale for widening educational opportunities in rural areas.

A supply rationale for rural opportunities: assisting the well-being of the rural population

The provision of local higher education possibilities is an aspect of what has been called 'well-being'. In Nordic languages, we are told by Konu and Rimpela (2002) that the word 'welfare' means not just welfare in the sense that the British know it, but also well-being. Whilst it is hard to separate the more materialistic aspects from subjective understandings of social structures and processes, the concept of well-being developed here clearly links to Amartya Sen's (1999) concept of development as freedom.

Instead of well-being, Sen writes of the development of a person's capabilities as part of the range of freedoms (for example, political, economic and social freedoms) intimately associated with the quality of life (Sen 1999: 24). Sen persuasively suggests that definitions of freedom incorporate both social processes and 'the actual opportunities that people have, given their personal and social circumstances' (17). Where such freedoms do not exist, people experience 'unfreedoms', in which Sen includes inadequate opportunities for achieving what they would like to achieve. This last aspect is an important supply-side argument for widening rural opportunities, for the individuals concerned ought not to have to leave their homes and local areas to enter higher education, unless they so wish. If one accepts Sen's analysis, then rural higher education should be provided, as it could well 'influence the individual's substantive freedom to live better' (39). Poverty for Sen (and for us) is thus seen as 'the deprivation of basic capabilities rather than merely as lowness of incomes', including the capacity to study for higher education if that is what a person values and wishes to participate in. For significant numbers of rural people, a valued 'functioning' ('the things a person may value doing or being' – Sen 1999: 75) is the capacity to enter and study education (including higher education where appropriate) without leaving their own rural locations.

In the UK, the Open University is of course a significant provider of higher education opportunities in rural areas. Increasingly, the World Wide Web and IT-mediated higher education learning opportunities also are becoming available. However, what such provision lacks, for many rural people, particularly those who are relatively immobile or do not wish to travel for learning, is the social element of learning. By social element of learning, we mean two related experiences or situations. The first is the purely physical and interactional aspects of meeting other similar people in a common social situation. Historically, this first aspect of the social element of learning is most people's prior experiences of learning at schools, at least in the UK. A second aspect, however, is the aspect of socializing and social interaction that occurs during learning, often defined as social constructivist learning environments and experiences (Hung 2001).

Constructivism is based upon the proposition that all learning has to be actively created by a person within the neurological pathways of the brain. This is so, even when the 'knowledge' learned is 'taught' or memorized in a rote fashion. By extension, social constructivism emphasizes that all knowledge that is learned has a social basis to it, even if it is at the level of deciding what is to be learned. In an analysis useful for us, Kasl et al. (1997) distinguish between: fragmented learning (individuals learning separately, even in a group); pooled learning (sharing information learned individually); synergistic learning (mutual study and learning); and continuous learning, in which synergistic learning becomes habitual. The Open University, despite individual and group tutorials, can be constructed as essentially fragmented learning using study materials, whilst local rural study centres (a focal development of the Rural Opportunities Project) have the capacity to be synergistic and even continuous if a group of people decides to continue to meet to learn once any initial instrumental needs have been met. In our view, synergistic learning has to start from the perceived (felt and expressed) concerns of rural individuals and groups as a major development point for rural education, including rural higher education.

At the same time, it cannot be assumed that there are thousands of people in rural areas just waiting to have a higher education experience, as that palpably is not true. Nonetheless, our project points to significant numbers of rural people who may, or could, benefit from educational experiences including getting onto local ladders of opportunities that may lead to higher education. To create such opportunities locally is a supply-side issue, though creative approaches have to be grasped if such people are to be attracted to educational opportunities. Many and varied, the approaches require some prior preparation by educational providers, such as clear procedures for the assessment of prior experiential learning (learning arising from life experiences), the provision of study skills support, and user-friendly informational gateways to opportunities such as websites.

Principles of rural opportunities: the six Es

The outcomes of the experience of the Rural Opportunities Project to date can be summarized under six principles – the six Es:

- Endogeneity: An emphasis upon working and collaborating with local communities and providers to enhance education and training provision.
- Engagement: Generating commitment to lifelong learning by engaging the potential and actual learners on their terms, for example needs identification processes.
- Enablement: Providing appropriate support systems, such as ICT and Study Skill Support.
- Empowerment: Supporting and mentoring people in the development of confidence and authority to participate in lifelong (higher) education.
- Entitlement: Ensuring access to local learning opportunities as a right.
- Environment: Providing local study opportunities and formats conducive to lifelong education.

It is worth considering these aspects a little further.

Principle One: Endogeneity. The principle of endogenous development has been subject to analysis, such as that by Shucksmith (2000). Shucksmith, whilst clearly in favour of endogenous development, is aware of tensions, particularly those arising from the existence of social class structural differences and local elites.

A central question has been how to build capacity at a collective, territorial level (perhaps through the symbolic construction of a 'community' or territorial identity), while at the same time positively redistributing power and building the capacity to act of the least advantaged individuals.

(Shucksmith 2000: 215)

Shucksmith goes on to say that

There is a tendency for endogenous development initiatives to favour those who are already powerful and articulate, and who already enjoy a greater capacity to act and to engage with the initiative. This may even lead to a capturing of the initiative by elites or sectional interests, in extreme cases. More marginalized groups are less able to participate or engage with the programme, and are less likely to be empowered unless explicit attention is given to their inclusion.

(Shucksmith 2000: 215)

These are real concerns, for the provision of local facilities such as study centres ought not to be the preserve of a select few who have already won the battle for educational attainment and privilege. At the same time, we have no magic wand to wave in response to this, but it is clear that continuous efforts have to be made to work with both involved and dispossessed people. This requires a long involvement with individuals, collectivities, groups and communities that are not always best served by short (three years is short in these terms) projects that 'parachute in and out' as the funding ceases. There thus remain real tensions in government policies and funding of projects designed to promote and facilitate inclusion (Alexiadou 2002).

Principle Two: Engagement is the process of winning individuals, groups or organizations over to something, which in this case is a commitment to involve them in an educational endeavour of some sort. The important point here is that engagement does not necessarily imply selling to people a pre-existing commodity such as a module or course unless it fits their needs. Rather, engagement is predicated upon the explicit attempt to start from their needs and wants, whether it be youth (for example, Panelli 2002), micro-businesses or small businesses (Pengelly 2002a and 2002b), or other categories such as low achievers or the educationally disenchanted (Golden et al. 2002). According to Golden et al. (2002: ii), critical success factors in re-engaging with hard-to-reach young people are, 'building relationships, gaining their trust, and giving clients a sense of ownership and choice. Projects combined structure with flexibility to meet individual need, provided clients with targets to aim for, and offered practical activities with minimal written work.' Whilst such young people are a particular category, engaging them, as with all rural learners, means starting from where they are, and addressing their needs. Engagement must thus be a key aspect of widening opportunities work.

Principle Three: Enablement is a service concept that focuses upon the provision of services such as study support that increase the chances of someone succeeding in education. As the DfEE report suggests, '[s]tudy support is, accordingly, an inclusive term, embracing many activities – with many names and many guises. Its purpose is to improve [young] people's motivation, build their self-esteem and help them become more effective learners. Above all, it aims to raise standards' (DfEE 1999: 1). The importance of such support should not be underestimated, even at degree level study, as we have found out in our study centres. In many cases, the issue is not just one of a lack of study skills, but also a lack of confidence. Consequently, study centre tutors can be engaged in confidence-building as often as study skill support.

Principle Four: Empowerment, by which is meant the gaining of confidence to apply knowledge to the solving of educational issues such as retention or underachievement. This may involve arguing against and overcoming scepticism, such as the scepticism that small employers have about the supposed benefits of training to them and their company (Johnson 2002: 293). Similarly, Pannelli (2002) argues that engaging young people requires wide-ranging efforts, whilst Devins et al. (2002) note that the attractions of ICT as a medium for learning centres remains unclear, and requires a great deal more research, despite intuitive perceptions that ICT is one of the possible ways of addressing exclusion. Empowerment is concerned too with providing a variety of support mechanisms, including crèches and assistance with transport costs, so that the student does not have to worry about such factors, or feel guilt whilst studying.

Principle Five: Entitlement is a supply-side approach to the provision of learning opportunities. As higher education is essentially an urban phenomenon, people in rural areas who wish to study at higher education level have to leave their homes in order to do so. Whilst leaving home should still be allowable for those students who want to, it should not be a requirement to do so. Whilst the development of collaborative arrangements such as franchises and jointly developed degree courses are to be found in rural areas, the range of such offerings tends to be small, and moreover tend to be based upon assumptions about what people want to study, such as rural tourism. For the principle of Entitlement to work, therefore, there needs to be a sustained attempt to work with communities to provide what is wanted and needed, rather than what it is thought such communities need.

Principle Six: Environment of learning. Whilst ICT may obviate the necessity for study centres to have masses of resources such as books, the requirement for some such resources has to be addressed, as does ensuring that local students have access to ICT facilities (Grimes 2000), and particularly broadband (Devins et al. 2002) to enable speedy access at a distance. Additionally, local study centres should be pleasant places to be in, and be sufficiently large and open to accommodate a range of needs and numbers of participants. Failure to do so will result in such centres gaining reputations of niche access and bias in provision, an unwanted situation.

Conclusion

This chapter has sought to make sense of the many developments with which the Rural Opportunities Project has been engaged. In doing so, the chapter has drawn upon a range of perspectives generated from philosophical principles as well as theoretical studies and sociological analysis. Our experiences suggest that only by systematically incorporating all six Es will any educational provision be attractive to rural learners, both existing and potential. The analysis suggests that a variety of approaches – as well as staying power to overcome initial scepticisms and inertias – are necessary for the successful engagement of learners in rural areas. Finally, approaches to tackle these needs must be:

• multi-layered
• engaging
• integrated into overall strategies at regional and institutional levels; and
• coordinated.

The difficulties of generating cooperation and collaboration between educational institutions should not be underestimated (Griffiths 2000; Das and Tang 2002; Moreland et al. forthcoming). Underlying all of this, of course, is a general belief in the value of education, and specifically the need to widen access to new groups of lifelong learners to higher education opportunities.

Section II

Higher education and lifewide learning

5

Student feedback, learning and development

Dai Hounsell

> Ultimately, the intention of most educational systems is to help students not only grow in knowledge and expertise, but also to become progressively independent of the teacher for lifelong learning. Hence if teacher-supplied feedback is to give way to self-assessment and self-monitoring, some of what the teacher brings to the assessment act must itself become part of the curriculum for the student, not an accidental or inconsequential adjunct to it. In other words, the processes and resources that are accepted as natural and normal for the professional teacher need to be replicated for the students and built into their learning environment.
>
> (Sadler 1998: 82)

It has long been recognized, by researchers and practitioners alike, that feedback plays a decisive role in learning and development, within and beyond formal educational settings. We learn faster, and much more effectively, when we have a clear sense of how well we are doing, and what we might need to do in order to improve. And while we can of course monitor, and reflect on, our own performance, there are many situations in which self-appraisal is of only limited value; we also need feedback from someone more expert (more knowledgeable, better informed, more highly skilled) than ourselves.

In universities and colleges, as in other educational settings, students can get feedback intrinsically or extrinsically (Laurillard 2002: 55–6, 126–7). Intrinsic feedback is an inherent consequence of an action and arises from a student's engagement in a task or activity. Extrinsic feedback, by contrast, takes the form of external comment on an action, and has traditionally been provided by the teacher or tutor. While extrinsic feedback may be found in, for instance, a tutorial discussion (Anderson 1997) or a laboratory practical, where it is more or less simultaneous, it is most commonly associated with a specific assignment (for example, a report or an essay) which has been undertaken in the student's own time and formally submitted by a given deadline. A tutor's feedback on the assignment follows later, in the form not just of a mark or grade – which may not be very informative in itself – but also of comments of a general and specific kind on the quality of the work the student has produced.

There are, however, growing concerns that the provision of feedback on assignments may be in decline, for a number of reasons. One stems from the shift towards modularization and semesterization, and with it the advent of course units which tend to be 'short and fat', that is compressed into a few weeks rather than extending over a full academic year – with the result that opportunities for assignment work may shrink as assessment becomes more 'end-loaded', or that feedback can come too late to be of real benefit to students (Yorke 2001a; Higgins et al. 2002). A module may have actually finished, or be close to finishing, before there is any significant feedback, leaving students with little or no opportunity to capitalize on what they have learned from that feedback in a subsequent assignment or assessment (Gibbs 1999). A second is anxieties about divulging any information to students about coursework assignments until marks or grades have been formally reviewed by an examination board, paralleled by scepticism on the part of some tutors about whether students (seen as increasingly instrumental in their attitudes to their academic studies) take feedback seriously, or 'are only really interested in what mark they get'. Third, and most importantly, the backwash effects of much larger class sizes and a lower unit of resource have also been fewer and less frequent assignments, together with greatly increased marking loads on tutors or lecturers, and less time to write helpful comments or discuss work with students face-to-face. Nor has there been any compensatory rise in opportunities for intrinsic feedback – quite the opposite, in fact, as tutorials and practicals too have in many subject areas been subject to 'downsizing'.

At the same time, ironically, evidence has recently emerged of the potentially very powerful impact of constructive feedback on the achievement of learners at all levels. The evidence comes from a very substantial and searching review by Paul Black and Dylan Wiliam of the research findings on formative assessment (that is, assessment that is developmental in its aims, enabling students to raise the quality of their learning through feedback which pinpoints the strengths and weaknesses of the work they have produced). The implications of the findings for universities and colleges call for some caution: the largest gains in achievement were for below-average learners in primary and secondary schools, where the majority of the studies reviewed had been undertaken. The overall conclusions, nonetheless, are striking:

> The research reported here shows conclusively that formative assessment does improve learning. The gains in achievement appear to be quite considerable, among the largest ever reported for educational interventions. As an illustration of how big these gains are, an effect size of 0.7, if it could be achieved on a nationwide scale, would be equivalent

to raising the mathematics attainment score of an 'average' country like England, New Zealand or the United States into the 'top five' after the Pacific Rim countries of Singapore, Korea, Japan and Hong Kong.

(Black and Wiliam 1998: 61)

Against this uncertain background of declining opportunities, on the one hand, and evidence of potency on the other, it seems timely to take stock of what is known and understood about the provision of feedback to students on coursework assignments. Focusing in the main on higher education, this chapter will review studies of feedback as conventionally provided, survey recent developments in feedback practices, and consider changing conceptual perspectives on feedback.

Studies of conventional feedback comments

In the world of empirical research on higher education, feedback has for the most part languished in a Cinderella role. The available studies of feedback, in its well-established guise of written and/or oral comments on essays and other kinds of written assignments, are neither large in number nor, typically, more than relatively modest in scope. They are for the most part subject-specific (and predominantly clustered in the humanities and social sciences); often confined to a single setting such as a particular course or department in one institution; and often lack a well-defined conceptual anchorage. But despite the limitations of these studies, and a consequent need to proceed with care, collectively they do yield up a relatively broad-based and thought-provoking portrait of contemporary provision.

The studies of feedback in higher education fall into three broad clusters: studies of students' understanding of assessment criteria and tutors' expectations; investigations of students' experiences and perceptions of feedback; and scrutiny of tutors' comments on assignments. Each of these will be reviewed in turn.

Students' understanding of criteria and expectations

The first small cluster is of studies that have investigated students' understanding of tutors' expectations for essay writing and of the relative weighting and interpretation of assessment criteria. Studies of this kind are germane to feedback because it is these expectations and prioritizing of criteria by tutors which provide the basis for their judgements of the quality of the work being assessed and thus of the comments they relay back to students.

In a study of essay writing in psychology, Norton (1990) found evidence of a mismatch between staff and first-year students in their perceptions of criteria for assessing essays. A significant area of divergence was in the relative importance of argument and content. Argument was much more highly ranked by tutors than students, while the latter placed a premium on content. Similar findings emerged from an Australian investigation of essay-writing by first- and third-year education students (Campbell et al. 1998; Smith et al. 1999). Interviews were combined with analyses of a sample of essays using the SOLO taxonomy (Biggs and Collis 1982). The interviews included questions on students' understanding of three key assessment criteria, which had been set out in guidelines circulated at the beginning of the semester. The criteria were concerned with the organization and synthesis of information and critical evaluation of the literature. Campbell and her colleagues found that substantial numbers of the students were unable to give definitions which approximated to the conventional academic ones, although third-year students generally fared much better than the first-years, suggesting a developmental progression in understanding over the degree programme. Differences in students' grasp of the criteria were also associated with differences in conceptions of essay-writing: students who had written essays with *relational* conceptual structures (that is, in which a theme or argument was used to integrate the essay into a coherent whole) were much more likely to be able to offer appropriate definitions of the criteria than those whose essays displayed *unistructural* or *multistructural* conceptual structures (that is, were characterized by sequential description and 'knowledge-telling').

Both the Norton and the Campbell findings offer clear echoes of other studies (for example, Branthwaite et al. 1980; Prosser and Webb 1994) as well as of my own earlier research on differences in second-year history and psychology students' conceptions of essay-writing (Hounsell 1984/97, 1987). Some of the students in my investigation had conceived of an essay in ways which were congruent with those of their tutors: as an ordered argument well supported by evidence (in history), or (in psychology) as a well-integrated and firmly grounded discussion of a topic or problem. But other students' conceptions lacked this interpretive character: an essay was seen as an arrangement of facts and ideas (in history) or as an ordered discussion of relevant material. Not surprisingly, these non-interpretive conceptions were associated with uncertainty about tutors' expectations together with difficulty in making sense of feedback comments.

In trying to account for these findings, I had found it fruitful to draw on the ideas of the Norwegian psycholinguist Rommetveit (1974, 1979), for whom intersubjective communication, if it is to be effective, depends on both participants in a dialogue having a common set of underlying premises or assumptions. Thus some students misconstrue a tutor's guidance or comments, or fail to grasp the significance of these, because they do not share the tutor's assumptions about what an academic essay entails, or more fundamentally, what constitutes academic discourse in the discipline concerned. Likewise, tutors fail to acknowledge 'the subtle interplay between what is said and what is taken for granted' (Rommetveit 1979: 96) and so do not seek to narrow the gap between their own and the students' understanding of expectations.

Students' experiences and perceptions of feedback

The second cluster of studies brings together research which has sought to investigate feedback as it is experienced and perceived by students. The most substantial of these is a questionnaire-based survey by Hyland (2000) of nearly 700 second- and final-year students in 17 UK history departments. The survey focused exclusively on students' experiences of the feedback they had received on their assessments.

Hyland found that feedback largely took the form of written comments on coursework: the practice of returning assignments via tutorials had become quite rare, and 70 per cent of the students (95 per cent in all but two institutions) had received no feedback on their examination work beyond notification of the grade awarded. Feedback on coursework was highly valued by the students, over 90 per cent of whom believed that feedback could help them to identify academic strengths and weaknesses, feel a sense of achievement in their studies, and raise their marks for future work. Three-quarters felt that feedback helped them to deepen their understanding of what they had learnt and appreciate its importance. And, interestingly, most (70 per cent) shared their feedback with one another.

However, the students' experiences of feedback had been mixed, and often disappointing. In general, tutors' comments had tended to dwell on the students' shortcomings and weaknesses. As Hyland observes:

> The fact that so much written feedback appears to students to be primarily judgmental rather than developmental, and to reflect a 'deficit' model for measuring their learning and achievements, may help to explain why only a minority speak of it as encouraging, stimulating or confidence building, and why one in six admit to having left some coursework uncollected.
>
> (Hyland 2000: 243)

Students' difficulties with feedback were compounded by variations from tutor to tutor in requirements and personal preferences, and uncertainties about how to interpret or act on comments. A study by James (2000) followed a very different research design: not a large-scale questionnaire survey but an intensive, interview-based study of 21 mature social science students' experiences of being assessed. Many of the students' comments were concerned with the utility of tutors' feedback on their written work, which in the majority of cases had not met their expectations. They expressed disappointment with the considerable variability in tutors' comments with respect to matters such as length, scope, timing and usefulness to them, whether their wish was to gain higher marks for their essays or to continue to get high grades.

In several cases, students had approached tutors to get more information about why they had been given a particular mark, but these encounters had left them in ignorance of the criteria underlying marks, or with little or no idea of how they might improve their written work. Marks and feedback could also have powerful effects on students' self-confidence, buoying up some, while leaving others 'devastated'. James discusses the students' experiences from a sociological standpoint, drawing particularly on Bourdieu's concept of habitus to consider how much scope students had to make strategic choices about the content and process of their written work:

> The burden of many of their complaints was that tutors did not give sufficient information for them to make these choices more intelligently, or in other words to modify their strategies. At the same time, the systematic arrangements for assessing written work (in large numbers, alongside staff's other priorities and so on) made such information hard to come by. Arguably, the students were in a situation organized to provide an initiation into an academic discipline rather than one designed to nurture them as learners. This in turn led them to overestimate the scope for the development of their capacities as learners.
>
> (James 2000: 163)

The final example in this cluster is also an interview-based study, but of honours-level students' experiences of a less traditional, non-written assignment, the oral presentation: a short, prepared talk followed by questions, comments and discussion, before an audience of one's tutor and fellow students. The 39 students who took part in the group interviews were drawn from three contrasting subject areas, in the humanities, social sciences and physical sciences (Hounsell and McCune, forthcoming). Two aspects of the findings are especially germane to an understanding of feedback practices. First, in only one of the three courses was there formal, written feedback; in the other two, it was at the tutor's discretion, and, if provided, informal. Students' earlier experiences of feedback on oral presentations had been equally unpredictable.

Second, even where feedback had been provided, its impact was not necessarily pivotal; rather, it represented one of a number of potentially telling influences on the development of the students' expertise in presenting their work orally. The students had also been influenced by their past experiences of presenting; by the pre-presentation guidance given by their tutors; by the experience, often anxiety laden, of giving the prepared talk and handling the subsequent discussion; and – perhaps most interestingly of all – by what they were able to learn from observing the presentations of their peers.

Studies of tutors' comments

Reviews of tutors' comments, and of students' efforts to make sense of these, make up the third, and probably slenderest, cluster of feedback studies. The approaches followed differ markedly. Chanock (2000) used a questionnaire to survey the reactions of 101 politics, history and cinema and media students at La Trobe University to a commonplace form of essay comment by tutors: 'Too much description (/narration/retelling); not enough analysis.' She found that half of those who had received a comment of this kind had either not understood it or felt that it needed more explanation.

Two other studies adopted an 'academic literacies' perspective which blends linguistic analysis with a more sociologically inspired dissection of identities, discourses and institutional relationships of authority (Lea and Stierer 2000). In one, Ivanic, Clark and Rimmershaw (2000) analysed and discussed with students essay comments by five social science and four EAP (English for academic purposes) tutors at Lancaster University. They found very large variations in the tutors' comments, ranging from none – and an occasional tick – to almost 30 numbered comments together with equally extensive general comments in the case of one social science tutor. Comments served various functions, including explaining the grade awarded, evaluating the match between the student's essay and an ideal or high-quality answer, and giving advice on how to improve that or a subsequent essay. However, comments which attempted to engage in dialogue with a student about what he or she had written were 'surprisingly rare'.

In the other study using an academic literacies approach, Lea and Street (2000) undertook linguistic analysis of students' writing and tutors' feedback, as part of a wider interview-based study involving 23 staff and 47 students in two UK universities. They observe that the language of tutors' comments was often cryptic ('Explain', 'Meaning?'), displaying a tendency to use imperatives and assertions with little by way of qualification or mitigation. In the interviews, the students would often describe how they had completed a piece of work that they believed was well constructed and appropriate to the subject, only to receive a very low grade and fairly negative feedback, which had left them feeling confused and unsure about what they had done wrong. As Chanock had also found, what seemed to be an appropriate piece of writing in one discipline or module, or for one tutor, was judged to be quite inappropriate for another. Lea and Street locate these difficulties in what Lillis and Turner (2001) have since called a 'discourse of transparency', the assumption on tutors' part that the meaning of their comments is self-evident.

There are also strong parallels here with my own findings [see above] on the intersubjective gap in communicating and making sense of feedback.

Innovative approaches to feedback

The great variety of innovative approaches to generating feedback which have been experimented with in higher education in recent years can also be seen as falling into three broad groups. These are: much greater clarity about the criteria used by tutors in marking and feedback; steps towards involving students themselves in generating feedback; and the rise of collaborative authorship and 'on-display' assignments.

More explicit criteria and proforma feedback

Probably the most widely practised of these has been the shift towards the finer-grained articulation of the evaluative criteria which underpin an assignment grade and any accompanying comments, and with this greater explicitness, the adoption of proformas or 'assignment attachments' to provide each student with criterion-specific ratings or feedback comments in a more consistent and relatively economical format. The impulses underlying this shift are complex but probably have more than one mainspring: most obviously, a burgeoning concern with greater transparency of academic expectations, on grounds of equity in assessing students and in the interests of fuller public accountability, together with attempts to achieve greater consistency across markers, course units and programmes of study (Hounsell 2000: 187). But the shift has been given much greater impetus by two related developments: quality assurance guidelines pressing for fuller and more formal articulation of assessment criteria and outcomes-led curricula (QAA 2000); and the widespread advocacy of assignment proformas in guidance to new and established tutors on assessment and feedback strategies (see, for example, Hounsell and Murray 1992; Gibbs 1995; Brown et al. 1997). However, and despite the fact that this shift can be seen as addressing the gulf identified in research on feedback between tutors' and students' grasp of assessment criteria, significant empirical evidence substantiating its benefits for student learning has yet to appear.

Greater student involvement

A less widespread but no less vigorous innovative push has been towards greater student involvement in assessment and feedback. This has been accompanied and supported by a fast-growing literature which now includes not only thoroughgoing discussions of principles and practicalities (Boud 1995; Brew 1999; Falchikov 2001) but also surveys of changing practices across subjects and institutions (Hounsell et al. 1996; Nightingale et al. 1996) and meta-analyses of research findings on both self and peer assessment by students (Falchikov and Boud 1989; Falchikov and Goldfinch 2001). The rationale for student involvement is essentially that it encourages greater learner autonomy and self-direction, principally by nourishing a more profound understanding of the criteria relevant to work of high quality, and by furthering the capacity to apply these criteria to arrive at informed judgements.

Needless to say, there is great potential here for improving the quality of feedback, not only indirectly, through student engagement with criteria, but also more directly, since peer involvement can help to develop expertise in giving and receiving feedback – a worthwhile skill in itself (Jaques 2000).

Indeed, as Cohen et al. (2001) have observed, where there is 'rich peer feedback', that is where students do not simply allocate marks or grades:

> The giver of feedback has to identify what constitutes good work in a given subject area and express these ideas in a coherent form, while also communicating effectively with the prospective receivers about their feedback needs. The recipient of feedback benefits from identifying and articulating these needs, from receiving detailed comments from a peer who has faced a similar challenge and from responding appropriately to the feedback.
>
> (Cohen et al. 2001: 249)

Self-generated feedback is of a somewhat different character, to the extent that it seeks to stimulate focused, systematic *reflection* on what has been achieved (Brew 1999) rather than introducing a measure of externality through the comments of fellow students. It is therefore feedback not in its conventional trappings, but considered much less restrictively as 'any information that is provided to the performer of any action about that performance' (Black and Wiliam 1998: 53). However, both self and peer student involvement are also seen as engendering a greater sense of interest in, and ownership of, the process of feedback, and thereby, greater responsibility for interpreting and acting on it (Sadler 1998; McDowell and Sambell 1999).

Frustratingly, however, and with a few notable exceptions (see, for example, Falchikov 2001) there has been little research to date which seeks to validate the positive effects of self- and peer-generated feedback on the quality of learning. Most studies of student involvement have been pre-occupied with the role of self and peer assessment in marking and grading, seeking to address (and for the most part allay) the understandable fears of teachers and administrators that students might prove to be unreliable or over-generous markers.

Collaborative and on-display assignments

A third development in feedback practices is what can be called, borrowing from the language of architecture, a 'spandrel' – a design feature which was developed for one purpose but, fortuitously and in a way that was not originally intended or foreseen, can be co-opted to serve another and different one (Gould 1997). In this instance, the spandrel is the emergence of the 'on-display' assignment. To grasp its significance, it is first necessary to appreciate the extent to which assessment practices, in the UK at least, have traditionally been a private and solitary activity. Though there may be a degree of informal interchange between some students, formally speaking, essays are produced by, and returned to, individuals (Hounsell 1998). In most disciplines, it has not been commonplace for students to be encouraged to share their work with one another – with the consequence that many, perhaps most, students have limited experience of what their peers have achieved in their assignments and assessments.

Two developments have brought about a sea-change. One is the advent of assignments which call for collaborative 'authorship': for example, group or team reports on a project, panel debates, collaborative book reviews, group problem-solving, or paired essays (Hounsell 1998). The other is the growing adoption of oral presentations and poster presentations, in which the work of an individual student, or of a group of students, is not privately submitted to the tutor but is openly displayed to peers. Cooperative learning in both these forms opens up rich opportunities for students to acquaint themselves with one another's work and thereby develop a common understanding of what has been – and can be – achieved. As was noted in the study of oral presentations which was reviewed earlier, for example, being able to observe other students' presentations at first hand could have a number of positive effects.

In collaborative and on-display learning the role of *observation* is akin to that of *reflection* in self-assessment. Both processes can have feedback-like effects, as 'information to the performer of an action', or, put more meta-phorically, as accelerants or affordances (Laurillard 1997) to learning, enabling students to attain particular standards of achievement more rapidly or more effectively than would be feasible by their own efforts alone.

New conceptual perspectives

A concern with conceptualizing feedback can be traced back to the begin-nings of psychology as a subject of academic study and Edward L. Thorn-dike's 'law of effect' (Hounsell 1987). Thorndike demonstrated that repeated practice or 'exercise' alone was insufficient for learning to occur; knowledge of the results of a given action was also necessary. 'Knowledge of results' subsequently played a central part in the behaviourist learning theor-ies of Skinner (1954), who stressed the need for prompt reinforcement of right answers and correction of wrong ones. But it seems that the term 'feed-back' itself became the favoured currency much later, and was probably imported from electronics (Black and Wiliam 1998: 47) or systems engineer-ing, where it was defined by Norbert Wiener in the following way:

> When we desire a motion to follow a given pattern, the difference between this pattern and the actually performed motion is used as a new input to cause the part regulated to move in such a way as to bring its motion closer to that given by the pattern.
>
> (Wiener 1961: 6)

What was common to each of these conceptualizations was a view of feed-back as a process which entails both diagnosis and remediation, with the latter, in Skinner's and Wiener's formulations, considered as integral. Subsequent perspectives, however, have tended to problematize the relationship between these twin facets of feedback. As we saw earlier in reviewing studies of feedback in higher education, even where there is accurate diagnosis of the gap between actual and desired performance, it may prove difficult to communicate the nature of the gap to students or learners, or for them to know how to act on this diagnosis to attain the desired end. There is also an affective dimension, as Ramaprasad (1983) has pointed out. If a student is content to receive marks close to the class average, feedback is unlikely to spur them to raising the quality of their assignment work to a higher plane of achievement.

In the most recent perspectives on feedback, Sadler (1989, 1998) has argued, higher achievement is viewed as dependent on nourishing in students an appreciation of what counts as high-quality work in a given subject and at a given level, together with a grasp of the strategies needed to attain those high standards:

> The indispensable conditions of improvement are that the *student* comes to hold a concept of quality roughly similar to that held by the teacher, is able to monitor continuously the quality of what is being produced *during the act of production itself*, and has a repertoire of alternative moves or strategies from which to draw at any given point. In other words, students have to be able to judge the quality of what they are producing and be able to regulate what they are doing during the doing of it.
>
> (Sadler 1989: 121)

In this conceptualization of feedback, then, student engagement is at the heart of the process. Self-assessment is not one among various options for generating feedback, but integral. This in turn places a responsibility on the tutor or teacher to go beyond simply providing feedback, by developing students' capacity to make the best use of it.

Concluding thoughts and implications

The backcloth with which this chapter opened was two-edged: robust evidence of the impact of formative feedback on learning across the full span of sectors and levels of education, side-by-side with widely voiced concerns that opportunities for students to get prompt and constructive extrinsic feedback on their assignments and assessments have been shrinking. What emerged from the subsequent review of studies of feedback in higher education added further weight to those concerns. There was evidence that while feedback was widely valued by students as a crucial aid to their learning, their experiences of getting feedback from their tutors had been uneven, often unrewarding, and on occasions confidence-sapping. The quantity of feedback provided by tutors seemed to range widely: rich and extensive in some instances, perfunctory or absent in others. Its quality was equally erratic. Sometimes feedback was perceived as helpful, sometimes opaque, obscure or a source of uncertainty and confusion, particularly since requirements for assigned work seemed to fluctuate, in ways that could appear unconsidered if not arbitrary, from subject to subject, course unit to course unit, and from one tutor to another. And there seemed to be a pervasive lack of awareness on some tutors' part of the difficulties students experienced in making sense of comments or taking appropriate action in response to feedback. Many tutors appeared to take it for granted that their expectations of academic work, and the criteria they applied in evaluating it, were relatively self-evident and readily communicable, or that students would know how to remedy any shortcomings identified.

Set against this often dispiriting picture of current practices was more heartening news of imaginative attempts to remould the provision of feedback. The most widespread of these, fuller explication of marking and feedback criteria, can be seen as an attempt to bridge, in part at least, the intersubjective gulf between tutors' and students' expectations of academic work, and to communicate these more systematically through feedback comments. How successful these efforts have actually been, however, has yet to be empirically substantiated. Moreover, seen in terms of feedback as traditionally conceptualized, these efforts may help bring about more consistent diagnoses but strengthen only that part of remediation which is to do with a surer grasp by the recipient of feedback of what he or she has, or has not, achieved. They do not necessarily help a student to resolve what appropriate action to take in order to attain higher standards.

In that and other respects, the remaining two innovative directions identified – student involvement in the generation of feedback, and a more open and collaborative approach to assignments – may have a greater likelihood of success. For in drawing students into the closer and more interactive engagement with academic requirements advocated by Sadler, they capitalize more effectively on students' lifewide experiences and capabilities as well as holding out the prospect of a fuller mastery of academic processes and outcomes.

Equally fundamentally, they represent not simply the enhancement of feedback as conventionally practised, but the beginnings of its transformation, on two mutually reinforcing axes, into a new and perhaps more potent guise. Sighted along one axis, feedback is becoming less exclusively magisterial. It has started to shed its skin of dependence on the tutor or teacher and to re-emerge in a form in which the tutor's role as provider of feedback can be complemented or augmented (if not necessarily replaced) by peer- or self-generated feedback. Along the other axis, feedback's hitherto distinctive function, the acceleration of learning, achieved through the provision of informed, third-party comment, no longer appears quite so unique. For it seems that both focused, systematic reflection (through the medium of self-generated feedback) and reflective observation (where there is collaborative or on-display learning) can also serve as potentially powerful affordances or accelerants to learning. If these conclusions are indeed valid ones, it follows that the pedagogical challenge in any given learning-teaching situation is not simply to provide high quality feedback, but to seek to optimize the activation both of feedback as conventionally conceived and of other feedback-like affordances to learning.

6

Reconstructing students as consumers: power and assimilation?

Louise Morley

Introduction

The previous chapter investigated the possibilities for enhancing learning by drawing on students' lifewide learning experiences through innovative assessment and feedback procedures. In this chapter the focus switches from the academic assessment of students to the evaluation by learners – increasingly constructed as consumers – of their academic experience.

Based on interviews with 36 academics and managers on quality and power in higher education, this chapter focuses on how students are constructed in quality discourses, the interplay between consumer values and contractualism, risk reduction, and shifting pedagogical relations. Questions are posed about the extent to which, in a market economy, care appears to have become commodified and pedagogical relationships possibly reduced to service-level agreements. Conversely, attention is given to claims for the potential gains and benefits to students from a commitment to transparency, entitlements and student satisfaction.

Delighting the customer

The customer care revolution and an outcomes-based approach, with the emphasis on product specification, entitlements and consumer rights has changed social and pedagogical relations in the academy. In a market economy, students arguably are less likely to be constructed as recipients of welfare, than as purchasers of an expensive product. In market approaches to higher education choice and services, is there a danger that elitism and poor equity practices of the traditional academy are being repackaged into seemingly user-friendly and 'transparent' procedures? Transparency does imply a challenge to the discriminatory practices of the hidden curriculum (Margolis 2001). It also assumes that there is a truth or property that can be revealed and measured. However, as Apple remarks:

Rather than democracy being a *political* concept, it is transformed into a wholly *economic* concept. The message of such policies is that of what might best be called 'arithmetical particularism', in which the unattached individual – as consumer – is deraced, declassed, and degendered.

(Apple 2000: 60)

In spite of the many studies (for example, Lynch and O'Riordan 1998; Ball et al. 2002; Shiner and Modood 2002) demonstrating the role that social class, gender and ethnicity play in higher education choice, participation and experience, quality discourses tend to treat students as a social bloc. The term 'student experience' combines the universal with the particular. It suggests that students were previously excluded from academic citizenship and that some advocacy and remedial action are required.

To a considerable extent, modern consumption involves the manipulation of signs (Baudrillard 1998), and signs of quality have been introduced to reassure consumers that their interests are being met. In the arena of higher education there has been the introduction of an array of mechanisms, including learning contracts, guidelines, assessment criteria, learning outcomes, core skills, all of which in various ways attempt to systematize and codify student/teacher interactions. Care is being commodified, with higher education becoming more like the hospitality industry (Atkins 1999). Quality assurance, while appropriating and re-articulating concepts such as student empowerment and entitlement, is viewed by some as a profoundly conservative construct; conservative, because it is about disembodied standardization. For example, Bensimon (1995: 608) believes that quality, or total quality management (TQM) in particular, is a 'natural ally of those who believe it is more important to defend traditional values than to reconstruct the academy to make it more responsive to diversity'. Howie (2002) also argues that students are now educated within a system that promotes a form of thought antithetical to the recognition of 'otherness', and indeed to issues of social justice. Quality audits from this perspective are essentially relationships of power between observers and observed. An important part of the power relations is the way in which norms are created and maintained. Norms can constitute an invisible web of power because the norms become internalized and more difficult to recognize and contest (Shore and Wright 1999). Customer care hence can be perceived as simply a regulatory device, with considerable moral potency.

On the other hand, new norms and relations of power are being forged. In Britain, the Quality Assurance Agency (QAA) claims to take the perceived interests or desires of customers as the starting point of delivery. The National Union of Students in Britain (NUS) supports quality assessment as it provides the possibility for, in Spivak's (1988) phrase, the subaltern being allowed to speak. Quality assurance is seen as a form of student empowerment as it encodes rights and entitlements, gives students a 'voice', privileges the student experience and is assumed to inform consumer choice. Hence, the NUS vigorously opposed political moves to lighten the touch of higher education quality audits in 2001. The then president Owain James said that the 'NUS is in favour of universities undergoing Teaching Quality Assessments because they give students clear and consistent external information on which to base their decisions when researching courses and colleges or universities' (cited in Major 2001: 9).

Choice and decision-making

A common belief in my study was that student decision-making was influenced by codified information. Scores gained in the different audits are seen as important information by a curriculum leader in a new university:

> And of course it's also good for students, getting back to this issue of students becoming more like customers. I think it's good that they can refer to a QAA score as a point of reference. I know, I mean I'm slightly biased because we got a better-than-we-expected score.

The university is perceived as a knowledge outlet, with students/customers browsing and selecting from marketing documentation. Yet Segal Quince Wicksteed's survey (1999) discovered that only 12 per cent of respondents considered QAA reports to be the single most important source of information about quality. However, a professor in a new university believes that enhanced consumer information and the introduction of tuition fees have led to more discriminating and informed decision-making and higher aspirations of the service and product for all students and their parents:

> Students are increasingly sophisticated and their parents are, in looking at league tables, QAA scores and so forth so I think that's one issue. I think students are more aware now of their position as quote customers unquote, than they were heretofore ... Part of it is external quality procedures and so forth. But also part of it has been the changing nature of funding. So if you're paying for something overtly out of your own pocket, it changes your disposition a bit.

In this analysis, information is seen as part of the democratization process. Blackmore (2000: 144) identifies how human capital theory is premised upon 'the self-maximising, autonomous, individual chooser and upon national productivity measures'. However, the market economy tends to overlook the influence of habitus, and how choice is frequently structured by gender, social class and ethnicity (Ball et al. 2000). Findings in Britain and the USA suggest that students from middle-class backgrounds, with university-educated parents, are more likely to find rankings important and to devote time to strategic decision-making (McDonough et al. 1997; Ball et al. 2002). Pugsley (1998: 85) observes that 'there are class inequalities involved in making decisions about higher education which have persisted for the 40 years since Jackson and Marsden's 1962 study'. Reay et al. (2001) discovered that conceptions of the 'good university' are both racialized and classed.

In their study, working-class students were more concerned with feeling comfortable, safe and 'happy' than with league tables. Just how happiness is defined is, of course, another issue.

New modes of description

A principle of Total Quality Management (TQM) is customer delight and planned satisfaction – happiness has to be measurable. There are fears that this process is eclipsing traditional identifications with academic disciplines and that presentation and contract are gaining hegemonic power over content. This is part of a significant realignment of the university away from epistemological foundations of the knowledge base and towards a more technocratic, instrumental view of knowledge (Brooks 2001).

The culture of continuous improvement in public services has resulted in the need for professionals to evaluate and represent their practice and organizations within new modes of description. The debate on standards, accountability, customer care and transparency of decision-making in the professions is demanding enhanced skills relating to representation, measurement, resource management and evaluation. Image and efficiency underpin the representation of quality services. A professor in a new university notes:

> I think presentational matters have been quite dramatically changed . . . QAA seems to have focused attention a great deal on procedures related to teaching rather than the actual quality of the teaching.

Shore and Selwyn's (1998: 161) analysis of a Scottish university document prepared to help students evaluate courses revealed nearly twice as many columns devoted to the lecturer's 'style' and 'communication skills' than to the content of the course (Shore and Selwyn 1998: 161). The form of teaching, in their view, has assumed dominance over the content. Meadmore (1998) argues that what is being taught or researched has become less important than that it should be done 'excellently'. Excellence is represented as value-free and the student is a disembodied sign. However, the focus on peripheral details paradoxically means that the pursuit of 'excellence' can potentially result in its opposite: mediocrity.

In a mass system, there is a danger that students are not constructed as scholars to be handcrafted, but rather as entities in an industrial or manufacturing battery process. Johnson and Deem (2003) suggest that some senior manager-academics tend to see students as rather abstract entities, or units of resource. The introduction of tuition fees in Britain has nominally raised the influence of students and their families as stakeholders. A registrar in an old university relates it to new market relations:

> . . . students will simply not accept poor quality teaching in the way that perhaps they have in the past . . . And since students are now, some of

them, and their parents, paying for the higher education they get, they're entitled to get a quality service I think.

Quality assurance is perceived by many as an essential component in the modernization of public services. A polarization that emerged in my study was the 'now and then' binary. Now, the bureaucracy is onerous and burdensome, but the past was a cauldron of secrecy and inefficiency. Quality assurance is strengthened by the repudiations it implies.

Access: democratization or income generation?

Quality has achieved policy prominence at a time of massification in higher education. Widening participation in higher education has both economic and democratic intentions. Over recent years, student numbers in the UK have increased dramatically. However, elitism is never far from the surface and access policies have been accompanied by a moral panic over standards and 'dumbing down'. There are contamination fears expressed in the idea that massification and the entry of 'non-traditional' learners presents a threat to academic standards. This sentiment was expressed, for example, by the Conservative Secretary of State for Education, John Patten (1993).

Expansion is represented as chaos, with working-class students, or 'all and sundry', perceived in terms of cultural disadvantage and as potential pollutants. This raises questions about the lack of intertextuality between different government policies. Even with a change of government, espousing an access agenda involves taking risks that can be penalized in quality assessments. There is an assumption, underpinned by some research findings, that 'non-traditional' students have a higher rate of non-completion (Yorke 2001b). Shiner and Modood (2002) found that non-elite new universities were more likely to widen the social and ethnic basis of participation. Ambivalence towards students permeates higher education policy. They are perceived as contributors to wealth creation, consumers of national wealth, high-risk investments and agents of innovation and change. The construction of students has shifted over the decades. Whereas in the 1960s students were seen as change agents, radicals and transgressives, their identity at the beginning of the twenty-first century is described in the language of the market. The Dearing Committee made reference to the development of a consumer consciousness:

> There is now greater emphasis on recognition of the individual as customer or consumer. People's expectations of publicly funded services have risen and they no longer accept unquestioningly what is offered.
> (NCIHE 1997: 64)

It is debatable whether students have ever unquestioningly accepted what they were offered. The history of university students internationally is riven with protests, uprisings and challenges to the establishment (see Marcuse 1969; Thompson 1970; Habermas 1971; Touraine 1971; Riesman 1998; Delanty 2001). Today, however, empowerment seems to have been reduced to service-level agreements (Barnes 2001).

Words, words, words: writing risk reduction

Service-level agreements are part of the low-trust/high-risk society (Beck 1992), and the quality movement demands that every academic activity is broken down into simpler and more manageable parts. Hence a fragmenting or fracturing process results, with complex processes translated into empirically identifiable indicators, measures, competencies and outputs. Whereas this was once seen as Taylorization (Dominelli and Hoogvelt 1996), a term that is sometimes used today is 'granularization'. An entity is decomposed and reduced to a myriad of parts and reconstituted to represent a 'pure' whole, containing certain knowledge about processes and practices (Guile 2001). The search is for some specific feature or logic that permeates the reconstituted whole. External conditions of audit are rearticulated in terms of internal procedures and priorities.

There is a morality of visibility, with transparency a keyword in quality assurance (Strathern 2000). Documentation is proliferating in the academy as transactions are required to be specified and formalized. A new 'contractualism' has emerged (Yeatman 1995), and the rights of one group become the duties and responsibilities of another. Transparency of operation, according to Strathern (2000: 2), is 'endorsed as the outward sign of integrity'. If we are asked to trust the measures, rather than the professionals delivering the service, then education comes to be delivered defensively. A registrar describes how procedures are documented and formalized now in anticipation of student complaints:

> Students – well perhaps in some ways it's the formalization of procedures and in particular putting in place grievance procedures which we've had for quite a time, and a complaint's procedure has chimed in with the increasing litigiousness of students anyway.

If professional judgements are subjected to managerial prerogatives, they too can become granularized. A reader outlines how student questioning is now more related to grades, entitlements and credentialism than to intellectual debates. Students are more demanding.

> I mean like . . . 'Tell me what's a 2i and what's a 2ii. Why haven't you given me a 2i?' Also questioning marks, asking for double marking and so on. I don't know whether that's just a general part of the whole atmosphere in academia, more pressure on students to achieve.

The mass system also means that, for many, there are fewer opportunities to engage face-to-face with students. It is suggested that a decrease of trust means that the spoken word is replaced by documentation as both communication and contract. A senior lecturer describes the cultural shift:

> There are too many students for us to carry on with that sort of closed personal sort of environment. So we had to start documenting things . . . We're having to really, really move very dramatically from a culture where there was very little paper, everything was word of mouth, to everything being documented . . . and I think it's to the good.

A noticeable feature of my research is that no informant actually cited improved teaching or enhanced disciplinary knowledge as outcomes of quality assessment. They all tended to focus on procedures, structures and documentation. In response to my direct question about whether quality assurance has impacted upon his actual teaching, a director of quality in a new university responds:

> Well, I mean only in as far as it's made me more aware I suppose, of quality mechanisms, and how important it is to get student feedback for example, and to do something about that feedback. But I think I always realised that, you know, even before I moved in to this post . . .

Is this a case of making tacit professional knowledge explicit, or performativity? As Howie (2002) notes, academics have to pretend that they do not know what they know. Confession and disclosure of the redemptive power of quality assurance is required. A professor in an old university argues that enhanced documentation might have resulted in more reflexivity about process, but he has doubts as to whether it has enhanced professional practice:

> There have been advantages in the sense that it's made all of us think more carefully about how we proceed, and the amount of documentation that students, rightfully, can expect. I think that's the advantage, and I don't think it's actually made us any better teachers.

A reader comments on enhanced reflexivity:

> I suppose it does make you think about the structure of lectures, perhaps, you know the educational achievements you're trying to achieve.

There are questions about whether enhanced reflexivity automatically leads to improved practice. There are also issues about whether this constitutes 'counterfeit reflexivity' (Clegg 1999) as it is within prescribed taxonomies of effectiveness. Some informants report how they have learned to discipline themselves in relation to performance indicators. This is evocative of Butler's argument that there is a psychic life of power (1997). A principal lecturer in a new university describes how external requirements have impacted on her self-management:

> In relation to my teaching I suppose it's tightened up. I mean I think we did have good practice in place, but it's certainly made us tighten up more on the quality of feedback that goes to students, ensuring that we

were clear in our module handbooks, so it actually subtly led to improvements in quality to a certain extent.

A theme emerging from the interviews was the irony that while quality assessment of teaching and learning is supposed to focus on 'student experience', it is widely perceived as impoverishing or retarding it as the labour intensity reduced time available for students. The QAA is thought by some to damage what it claims to improve. A director of learning and teaching notes:

> What I have noticed is that . . . I've got less and less time to see the students as often as I'd like to . . . I certainly don't see them as often as I used to.

For some, service-level agreements appear to damage the service itself. For others, there are implications that improving the quality of documentation leads to improved quality of the service.

Students as sites of danger: as time bandits, plaintiffs and greedy institutions

Whereas fears of litigation are well established in higher education in the USA, they have now entered the UK academy. This has resulted in a performed solicitousness, with numerous tests of the new forced 'unconditional love'. Sennett (1998) observes that the focus on instrumental relationships is a characteristic of work in late modernity with an imperative to demonstrate capacious, flexible responses. There is a strong notion of relational responsibility, with an intensity of interdependency (Hey 2001). Several of my informants noted that it was becoming increasingly dangerous, in the academy, to set aside time for writing and research. This creates considerable anxiety in the context of the pressures of the Research Assessment Exercise. They believed that they are expected to be permanently accessible to students for fear of grievance procedures and negative student evaluations. Presenteeism is facilitated by new technologies, and multiple modes of communication are now possible between students and academics (Blackmore and Sachs 2001). A philosophy lecturer in an old university observes how there has been some cultural reversal as providers and 'customers' enter new forms of relationship. Academics now have to be acquiescent and accountable to students. Her observation raises questions about the discourse of demands, the parameters of professionalism and the climate of anxiety:

> . . . you are in a position where you can't refuse the students anything, you know you really can't, if they knock at the door at any time of day you have to say 'Please come in, you know what would you like me to do for you?' Just in case one of the SPR [Subject Provision Review] team stops them and says 'What's your experience?' And they could be the one that says 'Well, they're never in', or even 'They don't help very much'.

The issue of boundaries is evocative of Shaw's (1995) theory that teaching is often elided with mothering. Part of the traditional construct of mothering is to have no boundaries, needs or limits. Allowing oneself to be used up is a prerequisite of maternal care. In this context, consumption is about devouring. Some social groups are more easily able to 'sign off' from duties of care than others. Bernstein (1996) observed that power both creates and legitimizes boundaries. The material and symbolic resources of some members of the academy allow them to evade the pastoral and emotional labour requirements demanded by the changing economy of higher education. Autonomy can be understood as lack of vulnerability to others, a kind of solipsism or lack of sociality or imperviousness that ignores community and proximity. Autonomy is also associated with the elite who can protect their boundaries. The boundary has gendered implications. Many women academics appear to negotiate a hybrid position between academic autonomy and the demands of compliance to traditional femininity. However, all academics have to mediate between their own depletion and increasing student demands as total expenditure per student over the 20-year period between 1976 and 1996 has suffered significant decline (Watson and Taylor 1998; Becher and Trowler 2001; Yorke 2002).

'Edutainment' and student evaluation

Within the context of the learning organization, students, as customers and consumers, are also perceived to be a source of knowledge production. Critique is a democratic value, with student evaluation seen as the yielding or redistribution of academic power in order to apprehend the demands and views of others. Ramsden (1998) argues that feedback from the client, the customer, the consumer, the student, the lifelong learner is the one measure of performance that should count in any organization. This tends to assume that the 'voice' of the consumer is stable, pure, concrete and is the authentic indicator of democracy (see Moore and Muller 1999). This view suggests that there is a culturally untainted place from which students speak and theorize. It homogenizes student voices and overlooks power relations within the student body. Furthermore, it suggests an algorithmic relationship between input (student evaluation) and output (organizational change). Marginson (1997: 5) critiques the idea of an 'imagined line of causation from competition to consumer sovereignty to better efficiency and quality'.

Student feedback can also be methodologically unreliable because it tends to be driven by provider assumptions and concerns (Clouder 1998). The given represents the extent of the possible. There are concerns that student committees can be little more than reception mechanisms – mere opportunities to seek the student 'voice' on a never-ending array of documentation for quality assurance (Morley 2003). There are issues of power and interest representation. Power relations can compel people to consent to what constrains them. Student evaluations and feedback can propel students into identities and definitions bound up with the terms by which they are regulated.

There are also questions about what constitutes an authentic and stable 'student voice' when briefings and selection are endemic in the methodology, and the terms of engagement and identification are so heavily prescribed. Externality is a central constituent of quality assurance procedures. In a therapeutic sense, good attention with someone carefully listening can provide the preconditions for a range of feelings to surface. Quality managers have to ensure that students do not mistake quality audits for appeals hearings or therapy sessions. It is representation and promotion rather than disclosure that it is required. The briefing/coaching of students was noted by a pro vice-chancellor:

> I'd challenge anybody to find me a department that hasn't coached its students. If they say they don't coach and they get high scores then great. I mean they're running an extremely wonderful university . . . So what students will do will be to go to the reviewers and complain. Because they think that they've then got strength in the arm of the department . . . And one of the first things we have to do of course, is to disabuse them of that. It changes the relationships with our students . . .

A senior lecturer observes how, in her institution, some students saw the subject reviewers as ombudspersons to whom they could complain about quotidian irritations:

> We had a mock review here, and the mock review didn't go terribly well, because the students, some of our overseas MA students, basically thought that the process was about telling some nice people about the difficulties they were having so that these difficulties would be sorted.

When students and teachers are interpolated in quality discourses that are scrutinized by third parties, distortions can occur. Student evaluation can be seen as a form of perpetual referendum, providing the opportunity for a quasi-therapeutic catharsis. Furthermore, they can reproduce gender inequalities. Luke (2001: 59) reminds us that 'teaching performance indicators, such as those commonly culled from student evaluations, do not always account for students' (sceptical and often negative) perceptions of women in positions of intellectual authority'. While there is an increasing emphasis on accountability and transparency in the public services, student criticism is often an unaccountable and anonymized one-way gaze. This poses questions about the reliability of the evidence, as a lecturer in a new university observes:

> I don't think that the really good systems of student feedback that are part of quality assurance always help. They encourage students to be critical; rather than encourage students to develop a healthy critique . . . I don't see that as much kind of evidence.

Another view is that students' voices and time are colonized for the purposes of continuous improvement. The endless production of documentation for students, evaluation procedures and student consultations could also be perceived as a form of domination. Students are asked to evaluate courses, to take time off work to sit on committees, meet auditors, and mentor new students. The emphasis on outcomes-based education is reducing their academic experiences to trades-based notions of competences. Performativity involves students too. In the tradition of managerialism, every organizational member is responsibilized or co-opted into achieving corporate goals. It is questionable whether incorporation into quality procedures represents greater democratization or an assimilationist politics.

Student satisfaction: new settlements of power

Quality assurance can operate rhetorically in the interests of power and the emphasis on student satisfaction can have potent moral authority. There are proposals to introduce performance-related pay in relation to how academics score in student satisfaction surveys. McWilliam et al. (1999) note how criteria for best practice are no longer being driven by the dictates of the intellectual field, but by the degree of client satisfaction. In Britain, the media has recognized the news potential of student satisfaction. *The Independent* (Abbott 2001) conducted a survey of 40 students and found that a little more than half (57 per cent) of students claimed that the teaching that they received was good on the whole. However, Bensimon (1995: 595) suggests that categories such as 'customer', 'quality' and 'satisfaction' have no fixed and intrinsic meaning, but rather their meaning is produced locally by 'the culture, history, mission and power relations that mark the institution'. Policy priorities and corporate cultures are impacting on student identities. A lecturer in a new university identifies how students describe themselves now in new managerialist terms of purchaser and provider:

> I think that also in the culture of, you know, legacies of Thatcherism, that education increasingly becomes seen as a product by very many of our students. And I actually had a student say to me a fortnight ago, 'We are the purchasers you know, you do have to listen to us' . . .

The passivity and blame culture that this informant describes is reminiscent of Henkel's observation: that the closure enforced by subject review was disempowering students:

> Concepts of quality that elevated clarity of exposition, comprehensive handout material, contained and predictable learning formats above other values were encouraging passivity and dependence in students.
>
> (Henkel 2000: 100)

A head of department in a new university explores how the consumer ethos ultimately disempowers students:

> . . . the extent to which students have begun to define the whole experience as a consumer, as a consumer choice. They have become much

more litigious . . . At one level it's an empowering of students who previously were, I think, quite oppressed. They were de-powered in the
situation. But I think that there are some fundamental contradictions in
the relationship where students are engaging with learning, and almost
regard the fact that if they don't learn that somehow it's a fault of the
staff, or the course, or the institution, as some kind of deficit model . . .

In this analysis, students are engaging with a product, not a process. This
informant feels that it has perverted rather than improved teacher/learner
relations and that higher education is now about the reproduction, rather
than the production, of knowledge:

> . . . students use the quality assurance process, the complaints frame-
> work, all of the codes of practice, and all of their rights as stake-
> holders . . . What it does is to create the notion of, as a commodity to be
> transmitted in the most efficient manner possible, rather than a shared
> journey in to the exploration of the frontiers of knowledge . . .

This informant's observations on the changing political economy of higher
education reflect Lyotard's view that the transmission of knowledge is to
supply the system with players capable of acceptably fulfilling their roles in
the pragmatic posts required of institutions (Lyotard 1984: 48). The construction of students as passive recipients of wealth-creating skills and
knowledge also contradicts the OECD (1996) view and that of the British
government (DTI 1998) that innovation is the driver for economic growth
(Marceau 2000). It is relevant to ask what values and dispositions are
being produced in the consumer culture. Student protest no longer occurs
through mass mobilization in favour of a cause, or in opposition to oligarchic
regimes. Instead, it is articulated in everyday social relations, or the micropolitics of academic life, raising questions about whether there has been a
domestication of 'the student voice'.

Who knows?

Struggles for power and knowledge can configure around who is the authority on students' learning. A question relating to user-based definitions of
quality is whether the client or consumer is the ultimate authority. Like
surgery and legal advice, it is difficult for purchasers to evaluate at the point
of delivery. Entertainment, rather than education, is sometimes the key to
positive student evaluations, as a senior lecturer reports:

> there is, therefore, a lot of pressure, when students dislike any aspects of
> courses immediately. For the sake of the Subject Review any element of
> students disliking modules is bad.

There are questions about whether the 'feel good factor' is conducive to
intellectual growth. The emphasis on keeping students happy and in the

comfort zone contradicts Said's view on the role of the intellectual, whom he believed should fulfil an abrasive function, challenging certainties and rigidities of thought. Least of all should an intellectual be there to make his/her audiences feel good: 'the whole point is to be embarrassing, contrary, even unpleasant' (Said 1994: 9). If intellectual challenge becomes constructed as a risk, it is questionable if the quality movement has added value to the student experience.

However, there are views that suggest that quality discourses mean that students need no longer be the subordinated other. Academics have had positional advantage over students and have been traditionally located in a different class position. An academic development officer in an old university argues that quality assurance has raised the significance of students in the hierarchy of interest in universities:

> It's been a positive benefit in persuading, you know winning hearts and minds between departments, that students need to be moved up the pecking order a bit.

In this sense, the democracy of the consumer and knowledge capitalism appear to have been more successful than earlier notions of student empowerment. An academic development officer in an old university felt that academics were complaining inappropriately about the effects of quality assessment – particularly as academic professional judgements had long played a role in the naming and shaming of students:

> I think there's been a lot of whingeing about the quality assurance. If you turned it, you know, about negative effects upon institutions, a poor review, you know marked for life, all that sort of thing, the subjectivity of these judgements and so on. All I would say is just turn that spotlight round, and say what about all the judgements that are made upon students, you know, and happily classified in to, you know, firsts, 2i's, 2ii's, thirds, passes and so on. I don't think most staff think that much about it, or they're absolutely damn sure they're right.

Student evaluation for this informant is an opportunity to reverse the roles of critical authority. For him, judgements of worth involve identification and labelling. However, the quality score is seen as temporary, whereas the classification of students by academics is a permanent piece of capital, posing questions about who has the last word.

Conclusion

Based on a review of the literature and the findings from interviews with 36 academics and managers, it appears that students are increasingly perceived as carriers of power in the changing economy of higher education. On the one hand, it seems as if quality audits do take into account students' wider views of their academic experiences. However, it also appears that their 'voices' may be appropriated, rejected and selectively included for organizational and other purposes. Ostensibly, in the context of contractualism, students appear to have gained some recognition. It is still questionable, however, as to whether this has been accompanied by an authentic redistribution of rights and entitlements, or whether these remain at the level of text. In some cases, students have been successful at strategically capitalizing on transparency and accountability to open up practices and procedures. But the rights discourse can evoke 'possessive individualism', and ignore systemic disadvantage (Blackmore 1999: 50). The granularization of teaching and learning into skills that can be assessed has significantly altered the education process. The emphasis on fragments, rather than a whole, can encourage a particular cognitive orientation that is not compatible with social justice and change agency (Howie 2002). Improvements in the 'student experience' could imply an acceptance of the changing purpose of higher education and its transmutation into a speedy, utilitarian, corporate university (Kenway and Langmead 1998). Are students being co-opted into 'battery higher education' (Russell 1993: 100)? Are they being reduced to their position in the market? While students might gain more consumer leverage in terms of turnaround time for essays etc., are they in danger of losing more complex identities as scholars and social agents? Is the democratization of users with solicitousness employed to pacify? Quality assurance could operate to make students more docile; by transforming them into consumers, they become more governable.

Methodological note

Semi-structured interviews were used to elicit the views of people with a range of engagements in quality assurance. My sample of 36 comprised 18 women and 18 men in 35 higher education institutions in England, Scotland and Wales. Twenty-two informants were from old universities and 15 were from new/post-1992 universities. Nineteen informants were academic members of staff and 17 were administrative. Academic staff comprised 4 professors, 1 reader, 3 principal lecturers, 5 senior lecturers and 6 lecturers. Administrative staff comprised 1 pro-vice chancellor, 2 registrars, 4 assistant registrars, 3 heads of department and 12 Quality Assurance managers. The disciplines included Philosophy, French, Spanish, English, Economics, Education, International Studies, Technology, Applied Science, Social Policy, Sociology and Veterinary Medicine.

7

Self-directed learning on-line

Philip Candy

Introduction

Today, it is almost impossible to imagine life without the internet, so integral has it become to many aspects of our lives. Yet it is only as recently as the 1980s that Gooler (1986) wrote speculatively of a time when information would be provided across the community in the same way as other services such as electricity, gas, water and the telephone. To describe this imagined confluence of information and communication technologies, he coined the term 'The Education Utility', whose potential 'as the cornerstone of a lifelong learning society' was, he wrote, nothing short of 'awesome'. He went on:

> The Utility could prove to be the focal point around which a new coalition might form to enhance the quality of education available to all citizens. That is, the Utility might bring together in common purpose a host of associations, agencies and individuals whose combined talents, carefully orchestrated, could change the countenance of education. Suppose this new coalition began by bringing corporations, teachers, associations, administrative associations, state boards of education, local boards of education and colleges of education personnel together to discuss how best to implement the concept of the Utility. And, further, suppose you added other groups to the coalition, such as educational researchers, continuing and adult educators, vocational/technical educators, philosophers and liberal arts professors. Suppose creative people and groups *outside* the education system, but with ideas for education, joined the coalition. And suppose each of these groups and individuals focused on how to make high quality individualized education a reality? Why couldn't this coalition bring about a renaissance in learning?
>
> (Gooler 1986: 179–80)

Gooler envisaged dramatic new possibilities for teaching and learning in universities, schools and colleges; he also foresaw its application in workplaces and communities, in continuing professional education and in international education and exchanges. Unconsciously echoing the enthusiasm of those who, 140 years earlier, had predicted that through the telegraph 'all the inhabitants of the earth would be brought into one intellectual neighbourhood' (Jackman 1846), he suggested that:

> the Education Utility, used correctly in international settings, could very well play a critical role in promoting international peace and understanding. To the extent that individual citizens have a better understanding of their fellow world citizens, world peace is made more possible.
>
> (ibid.: 176)

Today, we know the Education Utility as the World Wide Web, and it is clear that global peace is no closer – indeed it may be further away – than it was in 1846. What about other aspects of Gooler's vision? Are we closer to realizing the vision of the Education Utility as 'the cornerstone of a lifelong learning society'?

This chapter draws on a major new Australian study to explore the interconnections of learning with other significant life activities which should not be ignored by higher education (see Methodological Note). In particular, it investigates the inter-relationship between self-directed learning and the use of Information and Communication Technologies (ICT) and on-line learning in higher education and elsewhere. How are self-directed learners – within and outside higher education – to be supported? What is the potential role (and responsibility) of higher education in supporting on-line independent learners, including 'conventional' students as well as those who are not part of the formally enrolled student body? What support is required by different types of learners? The conclusion points to new forms of partnership required to meet learners' needs, including, amongst others, higher education, professional bodies, employers and community groups.

Interconnection of learning with other significant life activities

For many people, learning is synonymous with schooling, and whenever they are asked about their learning activities and outcomes, they refer only to their (often unsatisfactory) experiences with and memories of the formal education system. In his pioneering research into self-directed adult learning back in the late 1960s and early 1970s, this was a recurrent finding reported by Tough (1966, 1971). However, one of the defining characteristics of the learning society must be that learning is inextricably interwoven – intellectually and socially – with other aspects of life. It is not simply that it is widely or even universally available, although this is also vital, but rather that it occurs naturally and unselfconsciously in the context of many everyday activities.

In recent decades, there has been increased (or rather renewed) attention to the diverse kinds of learning that occur in settings such as workplaces, homes and communities. It has become recognized that learning is an everyday occurrence, and indeed that there is much to be gained through the study of learning in its 'natural habitat', as opposed to that which occurs in the more rarefied and contrived environment of classrooms or for accreditation by formal education providers (see, for instance, Resnick 1987; Lave and Wenger 1991). Indeed, this blurring of boundaries has led Edwards to posit that learning is akin to a 'moorland' – an open and unfenced expanse of territory – rather than a series of 'fields' (1997: 95).

While this development has been occurring at a theoretical level, the widespread uptake of digital technologies has amplified and accelerated the convergence of learning with other life activities at a practical level. This has occurred in two different ways. On the one hand, since so many aspects of life are now dependent on digital technologies, it has become necessary for people to learn about them in order to participate fully and actively in a range of day-to-day tasks. On the other hand, technologies provide a common platform for the conduct of many everyday tasks, of which learning is one. In fact it is not only the common platform, but rather the endless universe of interconnected hypertext documents that makes it so easy for one activity to seamlessly shade off into another.

As technologies become more ubiquitous and applications more user-friendly and intuitive, it is to be expected that there will be even greater convergence between learning and a range of other activities including entertainment, work, e-commerce and social communication (Candy 2003). An extension of this general principle is the convergence between self-directed and other-directed learning. While for some people there has always been a link between their own self-directed learning activities and participation in formal study towards a qualification, for many others – perhaps a majority – this link is more potential than real; the differences between the two worlds have represented an unbridgeable gap. The advent and rapid diffusion of digital technologies has gone some way towards abolishing the distinction between self-directed learning and that which occurs in other, more formal instructional settings.

One obvious and widespread example is that, for many people – even those enrolled in formal courses of study – the acquisition of ICT literacy represents a significant self-directed learning effort in itself. Research into ICT literacy of students in vocational colleges and universities likewise bears out the assertion that, to a significant extent, they are self-taught (Oliver and Towers 2000). Again, for adults, whether their use of ICT is predominantly work-based or not, their skill as users is commonly acquired through reading manuals, through trial and error, or through the well-established practice of seeking out a more experienced person and asking for help and advice.

All this independent learning is occurring against a backdrop of increasing availability of courses and programmes for learners of all ages. Whether in schools, colleges or universities, in workplaces or continuing professional development courses, or in community-based settings, learners from the very young to the very old are clamouring to participate in courses and programmes in order to learn ICT skills. Indeed, in a survey of learning needs and interests among Australian adults, virtually the only field that held near-universal appeal – even for those who were otherwise resistant to learning – was the ability to use computers for a variety of purposes, including to access a range of learning opportunities and possibilities.

The interpenetration of self-directed on-line learning and formal instruction using technology is not, of course, limited to the domain of technology. For instance, those enrolled in formal programmes of study are liable to be drawn away from the strict limits of their curriculum into specific areas of interest that appeal to them and which are accessible via the internet. Conversely, learners of all ages using technologies to pursue their own interests may well happen upon readings, illustrations, bibliographies and other resources that have been developed and are provided by educational institutions for the benefit of their enrolled students.

Whether or not such resources are, or should be, made available to the general public is a matter for institutions to consider. Certainly some deliberately seek to attract self-directed learners, either because of an ideological conviction about the value of learning, or because they see it as an opportunity to showcase the quality of their materials.

It has been an enduring aim of educators throughout the ages to engender in their students a love of learning and a level of enthusiasm that will carry over from the classroom to the 'real world' (Candy et al. 1994). Perhaps for the first time, therefore, there is a potentially seamless connection between self-directed and other-directed learning, mediated by information and communication technologies. Certainly, as this study showed, much can be learned from the experiences, interests and priorities of self-directed learners that can be applied to supporting the learning efforts of those engaged in more formal studies.

There are, however, a number of downside risks to this development. The first is that learners who experience very high quality resources and materials through their own self-directed inquiries, or who come to relish the freedom of pursuing their own interests on-line, may be less than enchanted with the often amateurish resource materials and the lock-step restrictions to which they are subjected by their lecturers, teachers or trainers. Allied to this, the ease with which learners can 'click' their way out of the classroom means that it is difficult and perhaps impossible to constrain learners to the strictures imposed by a formal curriculum. On the other hand, as young people who are highly accomplished users of technologies pass from school to college or university, and on to the workplace and the wider community, they are likely to expect high standards of connectivity and sophistication in the design of sites they encounter in the outside world. Thus, in both cases, the longed-for articulation between learning in formal settings and beyond them may prove to be a double-edged sword, if not for the learners, then at least for those offering courses and programmes of instruction.

Distinguishing self-direction from learner-control

There is a huge body of literature pertaining to the phenomenon of on-line learning, of which the greater proportion focuses on learning in the context of being taught. Although much of it refers to concepts such as independent, self-paced, self-directed, autonomous or learner-managed learning, on closer examination, the majority of it actually turns out to refer to a severely circumscribed kind of independence, in which the learner is 'permitted' to take control over a relatively narrow range of choices. It is certainly a far cry from the kind of entirely self-directed learning with which I have been dealing, and is instead more akin to the concept of 'learner-control'.

In earlier work (Candy 1991), I distinguished between true unconstrained self-direction, or autodidaxy, on the one hand, and what I labelled learner-control of instruction on the other. In conventional off-line education, there is a long tradition of teachers, lecturers, instructors or others giving learners some control over certain instructional functions (such as the pacing or sequencing of various topics within a course), often on the dual bases that this increases the sense of ownership and hence motivation to learn, and that it may lead to an enhanced capacity for undertaking the other sort of self-directed learning. While there is considerable support for the claim that increased learner control can increase ownership and hence motivation, the link between learner control of instruction and self-directed learning in other contexts is more tenuous. In fact, it can prove to be little more than an article of faith, especially if no explicit attempt is made to develop learners' capacity to manage their own learning beyond the institutional setting.

From the point of view of an outside observer, it can be difficult to detect whether a given learning project is more properly defined and viewed as an example of learner-control or of self-direction, since the external manifestations may be the same in both cases. However the distinction is an important one, because it goes to the heart of where true control of a learning event actually lies. In the case of learning on-line, the same distinction can usefully be made, and throughout this study I have consistently sought to concentrate on self-directed learning rather than learner-control.

However, there is an important caveat to be noted here with respect to learning on-line. In the pre-digital world, there was obviously potential for confusion between these two phenomena. A purely self-directed project could conceivably make use of materials developed for formal courses; perhaps even more likely, participation in a formal programme of study could give rise to the independent pursuit of learning beyond the classroom. However, the learner would be reasonably sure when that invisible line had been crossed, as he or she had moved from one context to another. In the on-line environment, however, the possibility of such connections is dramatically enhanced. Because there is a unified platform for the storage and delivery of materials, learning projects that start out as independent and self-directed can subtly merge across into courses and programmes offered on-line – with or without the formality of enrolment. Conversely, participation in an on-line course can give rise to the pursuit of more self-directed activities and interests. Indeed, the hypertext environment is such that a learner can seamlessly and sometimes even unintentionally move backwards and forwards between different learning resources and environments in a way that was not possible in the pre-digital era. Thus, there is a greater transparency in the on-line environment, a fluidity between formal education and training, and the independent pursuit of learning, which needs to be recognized by information and education providers alike.

Supporting self-directed and on-line learning

The focus now shifts from the perspective of the learner to that of the people and organizations that might be able to help with the learning process – of which higher education is just one, albeit important, player. Central to the argument here are two propositions: first, that a great deal of valued learning occurs outside the boundaries of formal education and training; and second, that whether learning takes place inside or outwith the context of formal courses and programmes, there is still a need for learners to obtain some help and assistance with their learning.

Despite the fact that, as previously discussed, there is an increasing convergence between the worlds of formal, non-formal and informal learning in the digital domain, there are nevertheless several features that distinguish most, if not all, providers of education and training including, in particular, higher education, from those organizations and individuals outside the formal education systems that might also seek to support self-directed learners. The first such difference is the concept of *curriculum*; a cumulative developmental programme of learning that is mapped out in advance by a subject-matter expert. When a person embarks on a formal course of study, he or she may reasonably expect that someone will have developed a programme that, if appropriately followed, is likely to lead to certain learning outcomes. The truly self-directed learner, on the other hand, is basically blazing his or her own unique trail – at least insofar as the pace, sequence and direction of learning is concerned – and is unlikely to be following a route mapped out through the learning territory. This is one of the trade-offs that the self-directed learner makes; that of freedom over convenience.

Linked to the notion of curriculum is the idea of deliberate *scaffolding*; some conceptual apparatus that is erected at the beginning of a learning endeavour, and progressively dismantled as the learner proceeds. For this to happen, someone needs to have a concept of what the learner already knows at the outset, the desired or likely finishing point, and a proposed route from one point to the other. In the case of the self-directed learner, not only is the concept of a 'finishing point' less relevant, but the actual trajectory is far from clear, especially to the learner himself or herself, and it is therefore difficult to know how and by whom such scaffolding could be erected in advance.

Discussions about scaffolding inevitably lead to consideration of another difference between the formal educational process and that of autodidactic learning; namely, the concept of *assessment;* a process that makes judgements about the learner's progress. Such assessments are of two principal types: formative – discussed extensively in chapter five of this volume – which may result in some direct instructional intervention or other corrective action; and summative, which commonly leads to some form of certification. The self-directed learner generally has to judge for himself or herself how a learning project is proceeding, or at least to seek external advice with respect to the criteria he or she has adopted, and as far as summative assessment is concerned, is usually more interested in the learning itself than having it attested to by some external authority.

A final major difference revolves around the degree of integrated *support* available to the learner. For the 'student' it is reasonable to expect that higher education will offer an integrated range of support; not only in relation to the substantive area of learning, but in such matters as getting and staying on-line, locating and using relevant websites portals and search engines, setting up email accounts or personal homepages, developing a level of both technological and information literacy consistent with the demands of their studies, and coping with the likely uncertainties and set-backs involved in learning. The self-directed learner, on the other hand, may have to draw together such support from a diverse range of sources. For example, difficulties relating to communications may be the province of the telecommunications company or the Internet Service Provider; problems pertaining to hardware or software may have to be resolved by the dealer who supplied them; questions relating to the domain being studied might be dealt with by a librarian, a website owner or by other users with a shared interest in the field; and when it comes to the human side of the learning effort there may be fewer obvious sources of support or guidance to which he or she might turn.

A useful model on which support might be based is that provided by Lonsdale (2002), who identifies four different categories of learners:

- the task-specific searcher;
- the general searcher;
- the participator;
- the self-improver.

Each type of learner requires different levels and amounts of support. The **task-specific searcher**, for example, is aiming to locate a specific item of information and will require those forms of assistance that enable him or her to locate rapidly and accurately the needed information. Increasingly this is achieved through the technology itself, which utilizes more intuitive software and greater amounts of artificial intelligence to resolve the inquiry.

The **general searcher** may wish to gain an overview of a field of knowledge or practice. Sometimes this is facilitated by a portal or subject gateway, sometimes by a directory, sometimes by a browsing facility, and sometimes by a human agent who helps to identify the major parameters of a field and assist the learner to conceptualize how the field is constructed, its major tenets and its principal elements.

Participators in the on-line context are those who enjoy the social contact afforded by technology. Their support is likely to derive from the group itself, although depending on the size and nature of the group, and the technology used, it can be difficult for other members to detect whether they are experiencing difficulties. In the case of formal educational settings, when there is a nominated tutor or group facilitator, this can be a problem; certainly it is an issue that has confronted distance education providers since long before the advent of on-line learning. It might be possible to build in a protocol whereby learners have to 'check in' periodically, but most general interest groups are very loosely organized and, in any case, participants might find such a requirement onerous. Indeed, one reason why some learners choose not to participate in formally structured courses is precisely because they find such restrictions unacceptable or inconvenient.

Lastly, there is the **self-improver** who, as defined by Lonsdale, is a classic self-directed learner; someone with an interest in (and frequently a wide knowledge about) his or her subject area. Novice learners are likely to require considerable direction and support, whereas those with more experience may be more independent, although both can suffer from the difficulties of navigating in cyberspace and from the loss of motivation and direction that commonly afflicts the independent learner. At such times, membership of a group, whether formally structured or not, can be decisive in determining ongoing commitment.

Not only is it possible for an individual to be more than one of these kinds of learners simultaneously, depending on the particular learning effort or topic, but perhaps more importantly, a learner might shift his or her orientation in relation to a particular learning effort. When these four categories of learners are combined with different aspects or domains of on-line learning, it is apparent that the provision of support – whether built-in to the technology or provided by human agents (the 'mortal in the portal') – is far from a simple matter. This leads us to a consideration of exactly what skills are demanded of the person doing the supporting.

Skills required to assist self-directed learners

Because learners have very diverse learning needs and interests and varying levels both of subject-matter expertise and of technological fluency, their individual requirements for help can differ quite markedly. As a basis, however, it may be assumed that at different times and in varying measure learners may require help with:

- the substantive basis of their inquiry;
- handling technology;
- participating in on-line groups and forums; or
- some combination of the above.

When stated like this, it appears that the needs of the 'learner' are not too different from those of the 'student,' and accordingly that the skills involved in offering assistance to such people look remarkably like those required of professional on-line educators or 'e-moderators'. In 1998, the Australian National Training Authority and the Victorian Office of Training and Further Education jointly published a study which contained a detailed checklist of 'Competency Units', each with subsidiary Skill Elements, found to be required for those operating in the on-line environment (OFTE 1998). The eight main Competency Units were how to:

1. use the internet;
2. use the internet for research;
3. use the internet to communicate;
4. plan a course of delivery on-line;
5. design an on-line course;
6. create an on-line course;
7. teach on-line; and
8. assess on-line.

(OFTE 1998: 31–7)

Goodyear and his colleagues have put forward an eight-part model according to which the on-line teacher has to be:

- a process facilitator;
- an adviser-counsellor;
- an assessor;
- a researcher;
- a content facilitator;
- a technologist;
- a designer; and
- a manager administrator.

(Goodyear et al. 2001)

Each of these domains subdivides into a number of more detailed competencies; for instance the 'process facilitator' role has 23 competencies nested within it. There is no suggestion that any one person would have to evince all of these competencies, or that they would be equally good at all eight of the roles; indeed, as Goodyear et al. acknowledge, 'These roles are unlikely to have equal importance in any specific instance of on-line

teaching. In some circumstances, some roles may be of negligible importance' (Goodyear et al. 2001: 68).

The person seeking to help an independent self-directed learner would of
course be unlikely to perform those roles that are specific to the formal
education and training context, such as the assessor role or that of the man-
ager-facilitator, and the extent to which he or she might be involved as a
designer or a technologist may well depend on the range of resources or the
complexity of the applications involved. Nevertheless, both lists noted above
are salutary for the simple reason that all these functions, certainly those that
relate specifically to learning *per se* (facilitating processes, advising and coun-
selling, contributing to the information base through research and helping
the learner to master specific content), are equally applicable at least to
some extent in business, community or other settings where self-directed
learning might occur.

Towards a model of support for on-line self-directed learners

Self-directed learning is often portrayed somewhat unfairly as a dilettante
activity, an adornment to the real business of learning that occurs in universities and other education and training institutions. While this was probably never a fair characterization, it is even less true today, when the sheer
volume of information combined with the rapidity of change has catapulted
us into an era of continuous learning, most of which is self-directed. Far from
being a marginal activity, self-directed learning is now a major way in which
people cope with the turbulent and unpredictable worlds in which they find
themselves both personally and professionally.

If the move of self-directed learning from the periphery to the core is
notable, so too is the move of technology within self-directed learning
from the periphery to the core. Technologies are no longer the province
of the 'geek', but are increasingly a key part of most people's experience.
Today, many people are more likely to log onto the Internet to answer a
question, find a service, consult an expert or check the specifications of a
product than they are to visit the local library or even to pick up the
telephone. On the one hand, new technologies have created a potent incen-
tive for a great deal of learning, since they are so ubiquitous and versatile.
On the other hand, the growing demand for learning, and the increasing
sophistication of learners, have stimulated the development, expansion and
refinement of technologies to satisfy the hunger for information and
knowledge.

It is probably fair to say, then, that technologically assisted self-directed
learning has assumed a priority never before seen, but with this new-found
prominence has come the need for all sorts of help. This help starts with the
six domains I identified in my study: *connectivity*, one of the essential pre-

conditions for on-line engagement; the *capability and confidence* to engage with the digital technologies and the on-line environment; the availability and affordability of appropriate digital *content*; ensuring *credibility* and trust-worthiness both of the information and of the environment; techniques for *capturing* and harvesting needed information; and finally help with realizing the transformative potential of technologies through *collaboration* with others.

Many of these issues lie beyond the reach of any one organization or sector; their realization will entail an unprecedented level of collaboration between a diverse range of players: governments, telecommunication pro-viders, hardware and software manufacturers, educational institutions, business corporations, the media and community groups. And the need for help does not stop with these threshold issues, either, since people's deci-sion to participate in on-line learning – both individually and collectively – invokes another suite of concerns that likewise call for a conspiracy of cooperation.

From the study, it seems established that attempts to learn in this context are a great deal more sophisticated than the direct and unproblematic acquisition or transmission of neatly packaged and pre-digested elements of knowledge; it is equally clear that there is a lot more to providing support than simply placing digital information onto websites. These support strat-egies may be clustered into four major groups as follows:

- those that pertain to the content, organization or accessibility of websites;
- those that pertain to the orientation and assistance provided (either on-line or off-line) to users and potential users;
- those that pertain to discovery, capture, organization and display of information; and
- those that pertain to the sharing of information and insights and to the creation and support of virtual learning communities.

When a student enrols to undertake on-line learning through a formal course of study, whether provided by a university, college, school or training institution, he or she reasonably expects the provider to take care of these various facets. This is one of the value-added services that a learner expects when he or she becomes a student. For the self-directed learner, on the other hand, pursuing his or her interests independently and without institutional affiliation, different kinds of support (when available) may be provided by different stakeholders.

Of particular note is the convergence of many activities, programmes, concepts, technologies, users and outcomes that were previously separate from one another. This raises the question of whether, taken together, these changes presage a new world in which learning occupies a central unifying role. Are we, as so often claimed, about to enter the age of learning or the learning society?

Conclusion: Partnerships and public recognition of learning attainments

One of the features that distinguishes a 'learning society' from a 'society of learners' is the extent of public commitment to and public acknowledgement of the learning that is undertaken. In a strongly individualistic society, learning is a private and highly personal activity, in which people succeed or fail by their own efforts. Much of our formal education system, and a good deal of our work-based learning, depends on this as the basic defining characteristic, which tends to be supported by the individualistic nature of many digital technologies.

Yet intriguingly, it is becoming increasingly fashionable to acknowledge the contextualized and socially embedded nature both of learning and of the workplace. As Bollier puts it, 'the new conversation about the [information] commons is burgeoning for cultural reasons as well. Now that communism is dead, it has become more permissible to talk in respectable company about co-operation and collaboration' (Bollier 2002). With respect to the issue of partnerships in the creation of a learning society, there are two different manifestations: one pertaining to the imperative to get everyone on-line, and the other to the shared nature of much on-line learning.

Throughout the study on which this chapter is based, I have emphasized that, if we are to avoid the worst excesses of the digital divide, and instead to reap the benefits of the digital dividend, there has to be a shared concern amongst governments, businesses, education providers, telecommunications carriers, community groups, libraries and cultural institutions to collaborate in order to get as many people on-line as possible. If the digital world simply replicates, or worse still exacerbates, the traditional inequalities of the off-line world, then there is little hope for a learning society. However, if it is recognized that these technologies provide an unprecedented opportunity to create a new and more egalitarian dispensation, with learning at its heart, then there is a requirement for unprecedented levels of partnership. Manifestly, governments must take the lead, but there are many other stakeholders who need to be enlisted in the programme to provide access for all.

There is a second, and perhaps more localized, sense in which the on-line world is an arena for novel partnerships. This is the potential they offer for genuine networking and for interdependent learning. So long as computers and other devices were freestanding, indeed even when they were simply linked to databases and virtual libraries, all they could offer was an enhanced version of independent learning. But their truly radical and transformative potential arises from the opportunity they offer to network with others – both experts and co-learners – in the creation of collaborative communities of inquiry. However, even here, as Brown and Duguid (2000) point out, the on-line world excels at 'learning about' rather than 'learning to be'. Thus, to the extent that a learning society transcends propositional knowledge to embrace procedural knowledge as well, there must inevitably be learning partnerships both on- and off-line. The implications for the future of higher education in these new partnerships are profound.

Methodological note

The study on which this chapter is based was undertaken during 2002, while the author was a National Research Fellow with the Australian Department of Education Science and Training. The Final Report of the Fellowship is due to be published during 2003 on the Department's website (www.dest.gov.au).

8

Access to what? Opportunities in education and employment

John Brennan and Tarla Shah

Introduction

Some graduates do better than others in the labour market. Whether this is to do with simple good fortune, the superiority of some courses or some institutions over others, the larger ambitions and capabilities of some graduates, or the needs and preferences of employers, there is little doubt that as the numbers of people entering higher education have grown so too have the range of employments they enter. To increasing diversities of students and of higher education courses and institutions must therefore be added an increasing diversity of graduate jobs.

In this chapter, we consider some of the factors associated with success in the labour market and whether there are aspects of the higher education experiences of some students that disadvantage them in their search for suitable employment following graduation.

There has been no shortage of initiatives over the last 20 years attempting to make UK graduates more employable. Students have been provided with opportunities to gain experience of the workplace, to acquire skills and competencies required by employers, to become more aware of the requirements of the job market, more conscious of the need to sell themselves to employers, and more knowledgeable about how to do it. In recent years, greater emphasis has been placed on the need for students to possess generic employment skills rather than to follow explicitly vocational courses. Thus, an economic rationale for investment in higher education has been emphasized, for both individuals and society.

Following the advent in the UK of a Labour Government in 1997, issues of social equity became added to the agenda for higher education reform, alongside economic and employment issues. Policies to extend access and to widen participation were increasingly promoted and these, like the drive for employability, came to embrace most parts of the higher education sector.

With the expansion of higher education, questions were increasingly asked about the appropriateness of some of the jobs that graduates were obtaining. Although there has been little evidence to suggest that graduates in large numbers are failing to obtain suitable employment – at least after an initial few years of transition into the labour market – the belief has nevertheless been voiced that a degree is no longer necessarily a passport to a decent career. Certainly, some graduates do much better than others in the labour market.

In this chapter, we look at issues of equity not primarily at the point of admission to higher education but at the point of exit. We consider why some graduates do better than others in the labour market and whether higher education's efforts to enhance the employability of graduates have benefited some students more than others.

The effects of social background and educational experiences on employment

The UK now has a higher education participation rate of well over 40 per cent. There are more mature, female and ethnic minority students undertaking some form of higher education study, although lower social classes (IV and V) still remain under-represented (NCIHE 1998; Hodge 2003). The current government strategy is to have 50 per cent of young people (those aged between 18 and 30) into university or college by the year 2010, with particular emphasis on raising the participation rates of young people from social classes IV and V.

Earlier studies have shown that these 'non-traditional' students are not evenly distributed among the different types of higher education institutions and different subjects of study (NCIHE 1997; Connor and Dewson 2001). They are more likely to study at the less prestigious institutions (post-1992 universities and colleges of higher education [the latter referred to hereafter as 'colleges']) and are under-represented in the traditionally high prestige subjects of study (for example, medicine and law). In addition, because of the above-average drop-out rates amongst these groups, their proportion is even lower among those graduating (HEFCE 2001).

Nevertheless, there are growing numbers of graduates who do not come from the class and ethnic backgrounds of the traditional majority and who do not possess the social and cultural capital, in Bourdieu's terms (1986), typically associated with the possession of a degree. Lacking some or all of the accompanying social characteristics of a graduate, are educational qualifications by themselves sufficient to guarantee success in employment? In the following section we show that there are variations in employment outcomes of graduates which can be at least partly attributed to socio-biographical differences.

The chapter will draw on a study of the employment prospects for graduates from socially 'disadvantaged' groups. The study investigated the transition from higher education into employment of (i) ethnic minorities,

(ii) lower socio-economic groups, and (iii) mature students. We were able to use data on UK graduates collected as part of a wider international project on graduate employment. The graduates were contacted three and a half years after graduating through a postal questionnaire. Over 4300 questionnaires were returned (a response rate of 34 per cent). For the purposes of the analyses presented here, we used the responses from 2997 full-time students (see the Methodological Note).

We were interested in the relationship between the social and educational characteristics and experiences of graduates and their subsequent employment. In particular, we were interested in the extent to which experiences during higher education might be able to compensate for disadvantages arising from social and educational biographies prior to entering higher education.

In brief, the analysis showed that a relationship existed between the social and educational characteristics and that, together and separately, they both could have consequences for a student's post-graduation life. Socio-economic background, ethnic background and age all have indirect effects upon employment through their association with factors such as institutional type, subject of study, entry qualifications and degree classifications – but they also appear to have direct effects on employment. Even when the educational factors are controlled for, graduates from the disadvantaged groups do rather less well on several employment criteria in the labour market than their counterparts. Many of the differences were not large, but taken together they suggest a situation where employment opportunities at graduation are likely to be affected by a graduate's social class, ethnicity and age. The following sections describe some of the disadvantages graduates from different backgrounds can face.

The measures used

Socio-economic background was measured by parental occupation and by education attainment levels of both parents. The numbers in our sample from *ethnic minority* graduates was quite low and therefore the differences for ethnic minority graduates were more thoroughly analysed using datasets from the Higher Education Statistics Agency (HESA). Three *age* groups were used to differentiate between 'traditional' and older entry age groups and those who postponed their studies by only a couple of years. The age bands used were: under 21, 21–24, 25 plus.

We measured *employment success* using the following information from our data: periods of unemployment; level of income; level and type of job – graduate/non-graduate as defined in the *Moving On* study (Purcell et al. 1999); managerial/professional; level of education required and skills utilization; expectations regarding promotion and salary increases; and job satisfaction.

Having identified the socio-biographical and employment measures using the data available to us, we then used these to identify the effects of different educational experiences (entry qualifications, institution attended, subject studied, degree class) on employment prospects. These are described below.

The effects of educational background on graduate employment

Effects of entry qualifications

We know from earlier studies that the entry qualifications of students have an impact on labour market opportunities (for example, Purcell et al. 1999; Naylor et al. 2002). This was confirmed by our own study. Moreover, students from lower socio-economic backgrounds (though not ethnic minorities) were less likely than others to enter higher education with good entry qualifications. We, along with other studies, found that obtaining a degree in itself does not fully compensate for not having good school-leaving qualifications, and that this was something that works against the employment prospects of students from disadvantaged backgrounds.

Effects of institution attended and subject studied

As well as entry qualifications, the reputation of the institution attended and the characteristics of the subject studied both affect subsequent employability. Most of the employment success measures used in the study show clear differences according to type of institution and field of study.

As reported in other recent studies, graduates from pre-1992 universities ('old' universities) experienced relative advantages compared to new university graduates, and all university graduates had advantages over college graduates (Brown and Scase 1994; Purcell and Hogarth 1999). Old university graduates were more likely to be in managerial or professional positions than new university or college graduates, and they were also more likely to describe their job as one which required a degree. They also found their tasks more challenging and felt they had more opportunities to use their skills and knowledge. In salary terms, old university graduates earned on average more (about £1700) than new university graduates, and new university graduates earned about £2400 more than college graduates. As regards job satisfaction, old university graduates were happier in their jobs than new university graduates, who in turn were more satisfied than college graduates.

Graduates from vocational subjects such as law, engineering and business did better in the labour market than graduates from more academic courses in the humanities or sciences. And students from science-based courses tended to do better – on some measures at least – than students from arts or social science subjects. Subjects with the greatest employment prospects were computing and medicine. Engineering, law, architecture, mathematical sciences and business studies also provided above-average employment opportunities. The least favourable outcomes on average were in areas such as arts, humanities, languages and biology.

Graduates who studied a non-vocational subject were almost twice as likely to be unemployed within the first three and a half years after graduation as those who had studied a vocational subject (12 per cent and 7 per cent, respectively). Three and a half years after graduation, 62 per cent of non-vocational arts graduates were working in a graduate-level position, whereas the respective rate for vocational science graduates was 81 per cent. Vocational subject graduates were more likely than non-vocational graduates to be in jobs which they perceived as graduate level and demanding, and there was a similar (although weaker) divide between science and arts graduates. The income difference between vocational science graduates and non-vocational arts graduates was around £5600 a year. Non-vocational science graduates and non-vocational arts graduates were between the two extremes, but somewhat closer to the lower end of the scale. In terms of job satisfaction, however, the only group that was significantly different from the others – in the negative direction – was that of non-vocational arts graduates.

We have seen how entry qualifications, type of institution and field of study are related to subsequent employment success. We now look at the relationships between social background and those features of higher education.

We found that unequal access to different types of institutions was very likely to contribute significantly to employment inequalities among graduates from different social backgrounds. The proportion of old university graduates is around 4 per cent among graduates from the least qualified families, whereas over 60 per cent of graduates with both parents holding a degree studied in an old university. Subject choices were more socially mixed, though graduates from more affluent backgrounds were over-represented in some traditionally high-prestige subject areas such as law and medicine. As has been found in several earlier studies, the subject choices of students from lower socio-economic groups, mature students and also some ethnic minority groups tended to be more instrumental and were led by more direct employment expectations than those of other students (for example, Connor and Dewson 2001).

Type of institution attended can be a factor contributing to relative labour market disadvantage for students over the traditional entry age since younger students have much better access to pre-1992 universities. For example, more than half of the 'traditional age' female graduates studied in pre-1992 universities, whereas only one-third of the older ones did so. However, older students tend to choose fields with more direct employment relevance, that is better than average labour market prospects. The only high status field in which they were under-represented was medicine.

Unequal access to different parts of the higher education system was discussed in the Dearing Report (NCIHE 1998) and was analysed further in later studies (for example, Forsyth and Furlong 2000; Connor et al. 2001). However, disadvantaged student backgrounds are not simply associated with 'higher education of lower prestige' but through this with 'degrees of lower labour market value'.

Effects of degree class

Once again, as has been found in earlier research, a high level of academic achievement seems to be an important factor associated with employment success (Elias et al. 1999; Smith et al. 2000; Naylor et al. 2002). This was also confirmed by our own study. However, there were no strong relationships between social origins and degree class results, so in this respect at least students from socially disadvantaged groups were not placed at a further disadvantage.

The effects of socio-biographical background on graduate employment

The effects of social class

The above paragraphs indicate that graduates from socially disadvantaged backgrounds might be further disadvantaged by virtue of the characteristics of their educational experiences and qualifications. But even when the effects of educational differences are controlled for, such students are further disadvantaged in some important respects. For example, male graduates whose parents had left higher education at the minimum school leaving age were receiving 10 per cent less income than their peers whose parents had degrees. They were also less satisfied with their jobs. First generation female graduates were only half as likely to feel that their qualifications were necessary for their jobs (compared with graduates who had graduate parents). More generally, graduates from lower socio-economic backgrounds received lower average salaries (£1500 a year in the case of men and £1000 a year in the case of women). They were also less optimistic about expecting salary increases. Male graduates from lower socio-economic groups faced further disadvantages: they were less likely than their peers to be in managerial or professional jobs and were more likely to have experienced a period of unemployment.

The effects of ethnicity

National statistical data indicate that graduates from most ethnic minority groups have a higher likelihood of being unemployed six months after graduation compared to their white counterparts. This disadvantage is even more apparent when ethnic minority graduates with similar educational and socio-demographic characteristics are compared. Bangladeshis, Pakistanis, Indians and black 'other' males experienced the highest rates of unemployment. More moderate, but still considerable, rates were seen amongst black Africans, black Caribbean and females from black 'other', Asian and the Chinese minority. Chinese males were also in a worse position than whites, but the difference here was fairly small. This high unemployment rate might account for why graduates from most non-white ethnic groups are involved in some form of further study or training six months after graduation. The acquisition of additional educational capital might be a strategy to offset the effects of a lack of social and cultural capital.

However, our data show that the advantages of white graduates are apparent in terms of getting a job only. Once they find a job, most ethnic minorities have as good a chance as their white counterparts of being employed in a graduate level job and they are usually not more likely to be in non-graduate jobs.

The effects of student age on employment

The Dearing Report (NCIHE 1998) indicated that those groups that have not traditionally participated in higher education at the age of 18 are increasingly doing so at a later age. Our data also suggest that there is a higher incidence of participation in higher education after the traditional age by people from disadvantaged socio-biographical backgrounds. These differences are not particularly notable in the 21–24 age group. Twenty per cent of students with parents having completed only compulsory education enter higher education in their late 20s or after compared with only 7 per cent of students with graduate parents.

Our data suggest that such a long delay in commencing higher education has serious implications on the employment benefits from having a degree. Men entering higher education after the age of 24 were at greater risk of being unemployed and had a greater likelihood of being in a non-graduate job. For women, age of entry seemed to have more limited effects. In their case too, entering higher education between the ages of 21 and 24 has positive effects (in terms of level of job) but starting their studies later increased the likelihood of being in a non-graduate job and also in being less satisfied with the job.

In conclusion, our analysis of the employment experiences of graduates nearly four years into employment confirmed that there were differences that could be related to social and ethnic background and to age, and that these differences could partly be related to the nature of their educational experiences and qualifications, but not entirely so. Even after educational differences had been controlled for, differences remained in the employment outcomes for graduates from different backgrounds.

Higher education experiences that can make a difference

We now address the extent to which higher education institutions could help these graduates to overcome their apparent disadvantages in the labour market.

Using our data, we identified a number of 'intervening factors' which seemed to influence in a positive way the employment outcomes of graduates. Table 8.1 provides a summary of the association between successful employment outcomes and some 'intervening' factors from the higher education experience, the approach to job search and the characteristics of the employer. In addition to an early start in job search, other job search techniques which were associated with successful employment outcomes were: using contacts established through employment undertaken during the course of study; contacting employers without knowing about a vacancy; seeking assistance from teaching staff; using the institution's careers service; and using personal connections. Some factors which appear to benefit other groups of students are not accessible to mature students or to students from the lower socio-economic backgrounds. Indeed, the advantages appear to be more accessible to those that need them least. However, these data should be interpreted with caution as a statistical association does not necessarily imply causality. Even though our study controlled for some factors, others were beyond its scope. The main ones are, of course, the attitudes and aspirations of the students themselves.

Table 8.1   Factors associated with successful employment outcomes

	All	*Older graduates*	*Lower socio-economic groups*
Work experience in HE	✓	*	✓
Absence of term-time working	✓	✓	✓ *
Extra-curricular activities	✓	*	✓ *
Overseas experiences in HE	✓	*	*
Early job search	✓	*	✓
Techniques of job search	✓	✓ *	*
Private employer	✓/X	✓/X *	*
Medium/large employer	✓	✓ *	✓

(✓ = positive effect; X = negative effect; * = limited access to the positive factor)

The part played by higher education

In the second phase of our project, we took the results of our analysis of the relationships between social, educational and employment experiences to four universities in order to explore whether universities could in fact 'make a difference' to these underlying processes of social inequality. We took both a problem – the way in which social background and educational experiences combine to determine, and in many cases limit, employment prospects – and a solution – opportunities available within higher education that could, to some degree at least, enable a student to overcome disadvantages deriving from class, race or age. Or so we thought. Our interviews and meetings in the universities suggested a different and more complex picture than the one presented by the analysis of our survey data.

The four universities that participated in this phase of the project were from different parts of the UK and had different histories and traditions. But what they shared was an interest in the project and a commitment to the issues it sought to explore. At each institution, the results of the analysis of phase 1 of the project were presented at a seminar of interested staff, generally a mixture of academics, staff from student and career services, and representatives from the management of the institution. The purpose of the seminars was to test out the findings of the project against the experiences of the institution and to identify actions being taken within the institution to deal with the problems that our analysis had exposed. In all cases, the seminars and initial interviews with staff were followed up by repeat visits and further interviews. Around 30 staff were interviewed in each institution, representing a range of academic departments and central services. Only a few students and graduates were interviewed. The student perspective was obtained mainly second-hand from staff, a major limitation which we hope to rectify in future work.

Missing the target

Our earlier analysis had given some support to the effectiveness of various institutional measures to improve employability. In each of the four universities, we learnt of initiatives that were being taken to assist students to prepare for their entry to the labour market. Opportunities for students to have experiences like mentoring or volunteering, practice at job interviews or preparing a CV, awareness raising and skills development through career management courses, either within the main curriculum or as optional add-ons, were present at all of the institutions. These were frequently collaborative ventures between careers services and interested academic departments. Not all departments were interested. There is evidence to suggest that many of these kinds of employment-enhancing activities are quite successful in easing the transition from higher education into employment (for example, Mason and Williams 2002). As indicated by the results from our own survey, it appears that students can improve their employability during higher education if they spend their time wisely and make good use of the opportunities available to them. But our survey data suggested that students from disadvantaged backgrounds tended not to make use of these opportunities and, as a consequence, were further disadvantaged compared with their peers.

Before our visits to the institutions, we had thought that early awareness-raising and a greater targeting of services to those who stood most to benefit from them would be part of the solution to their employment disadvantage. We soon learned better. We encountered a few examples of targeting support services to mature students that appeared to have been reasonably successful. However, the examples we found of targeting to ethnic minorities had not been successful; the ethnic minority students had not apparently wanted this help. And we did not find examples of services being targeted at students from particular social class groups. The reasons were not hard to find. For many staff, there was first an ethical issue. 'This institution treats all students equally.' Although easy to understand, by treating students equally, we are in practice confirming existing patterns of inequality. But there are also practical reasons why targeting disadvantaged groups was not possible. Targeting the 'disadvantaged' could be akin to stigmatizing them, drawing attention to 'deficits', real or imagined. Staff rightly perceived that this was unlikely to be effective and indeed might instead undermine confidence and aspiration by suggesting 'problems' where students had not seen any.

Many people in institutions emphasized the importance of raising awareness at an early stage among all students of career matters and the sorts of things that students could be doing to enhance their job prospects. Turning up at the careers office mid-way through the final year of study was widely seen as being too late, although careers staff also had concerns about whether they were adequately resourced to deal with increased demand from students in their earlier years of study. But it also seemed that students from disadvantaged groups were least likely to turn up early, or indeed in some cases at all. In part, this was of course because they were not aware that they lacked awareness! But it was also because they were simply too busy. These were students who were often working more than 20 hours each week alongside their studies. Some had domestic responsibilities as well. It was enough to fit in the core requirements of attending classes and submitting required assignments. The difficulties and pressures of the immediate prevented consideration of the future. Getting into higher education was an achievement in itself. Finding out what was required and seeing if you could cope with it was more than enough for most students.

Thus, targeting and early awareness raising were more easily said than done. Like involvement in extra-curricular activities and studying abroad, take-up of the various employment-enhancing opportunities present in universities is more likely to be experienced by students already aware of their needs and opportunities and with the time and resources available to pursue them. Such students are less likely to belong to socially disadvantaged groups.

Competence or confidence?

Much of the literature on graduate employability has focused on the kinds of competencies and skills that employers say they want and graduates will need to possess when they enter the labour market. Although some of these skills and competencies are occupationally specific, there has been more emphasis in recent years on the need for more generic skills and competencies reflecting the greater flexibilities required in today's labour force. Some have suggested that such generic skills are in fact class-based and are part of a broader social reproduction function of higher education (Brown and Scase 1994).

However, many of the staff we interviewed in the four universities did not appear to feel that it was a lack of necessary skills and competencies that was the chief reason for the difficulties that some students were encountering in seeking employment. Much more important were feelings of confidence and self-esteem, a sense of personal identity and the aspirations and ambitions to go with it. A staff member at a Scottish institution told us of mature students 'who go through four years at this university desperately hoping not to get "found out" '. For such students, this was participation without assimilation, studying for a degree without being a student in some wider sense, a partially glimpsed experience but one that was out of reach for a host of practical and cultural reasons. In spite of their huge personal achievements in getting into higher education, for some students there remains a strong sense of insecurity, a feeling that they are missing something, perhaps a largely indefinable something, but nevertheless a something that may deny them access to opportunities normally associated with the possession of a degree. A perception that the institution where you studied is not regarded as a 'top university' may add to this sense of insecurity.

This emphasis given to the importance of confidence and self-esteem had implications for both employment success and academic success. The confidence that could be achieved through success in academic work could, it was suggested, be translated into employment success through the rising aspirations of the students, the confidence to be assertive in approaching employers, the image presented to employers in applications and during interviews. By the same token, the lack of confidence and self-esteem that was associated with risk of drop-out was also associated with a lack of success in the job search process. The question of the extent to which confidence is something that the student brings into the university – reflecting life experiences outside the university – or is something that the university experience can provide or undermine may be central to a consideration of the university's responsibilities for the employment prospects of its students.

A feature of the student experience relevant to these questions of confidence and identity lay in the relative anonymity associated with study on large modular programmes. The few hours each week that students spent at the university were passed in large lecture theatres or in classes with different groups of students in each. There were thus few opportunities for making friends, for sharing experiences, for helping each other, in short to experience some of the most powerful socializing aspects of university life. If all around were also feeling insecure, these students were deprived of the reassurance of knowing it.

The street and the office

It used to be the case that going to university meant leaving home and spending three or four years almost solely in the company of one's peers, similar in age and social and educational background, in lecture theatres, libraries and bars. While this kind of life may still be the experience for some students, for many others it has been replaced by something much more complex and varied. 'Study' takes place in parallel to a whole set of other life experiences. Around 50 per cent of students now work during term-time, often doing substantial hours each week. As we have already seen, such work appears to be negatively related to employment success after graduation. In addition, many mature students have significant domestic responsibilities to fit in alongside study. The student body is made up of a much more diverse group of people, large numbers of whom are permanently balancing a whole range of responsibilities outside their studies.

If life during higher education is more varied, so too is life prior to higher education. Differences in class and ethnic culture are associated with varying degrees of 'fit' with the life and expectations of university study.

The sociologist Richard Sennett has used the terms 'street' and 'office' to describe the competing sources of personal identity in modern life (2001). By emphasizing its role in preparing students for employment, higher education is siding with the 'office'. But insofar as students are bringing with them the culture of a street far removed from the traditional norms of university life, there may be a clash of cultures for some students on campus. However, one of the four universities that participated in the project had a student population of whom well over 50 per cent were from ethnic minorities and almost all were from working-class backgrounds. Many were mature students. Whether the culture of this institution was the reason for or the consequence of this distinctive social mix of its student body is not clear, but it was certainly the case that it provided an environment where first-generation students from varied social backgrounds could feel comfortable, could make friends easily, could achieve a sense of familiarity and acceptance. In a sense the culture of the street had engulfed the university and was a crucial factor to its success in widening participation. But at the same time, it was a factor that had negative implications for employment prospects. The culture of the 'office' was weak and employers did not find in the students of this university the attitudes and expectations normally associated with graduates. Success in widening participation was creating problems for achieving success in employment.

Increasingly, universities need to balance the cultures of both street and office if they are to fulfil the aspirations of diverse groups of students. Where academic culture sits in all of this must vary by subject. More vocational subjects clearly relate most easily to the office and offer career goals that are explicit, although not always attainable for students lacking the right sorts of social and cultural capital. In academic subjects, however, neither street nor office may be readily apparent, although there may be much hidden relevance to both. For the essentially part-time student (even if formally full-time), making connections between different 'lifeworlds' being experienced simultaneously poses considerable challenges – and considerable learning opportunities if the challenges can be overcome. The ability to operate successfully in different cultures may be a crucial pre-requisite for employment success for such students, and also an important determinant of personal confidence and self-esteem. Can universities help them to achieve it?

Who is responsible and what can be done?

In addressing broad higher education policy issues such as widening participation and enhancing employability, universities frequently set up special units or projects, sometimes with external funding secured from the funding councils or government departments. Central student services – especially careers – have clear responsibilities for supporting students through and beyond their higher education, both by means of special projects and through the more regular activities of their staff. But what of the responsibilities of academic units? The four institutions in our project differed in the relationships between central student services and academic units and in the expectations placed on the latter. These partly reflected larger organizational and cultural differences between the institutions, the relative autonomy of faculties and the resources available for central support services. However, the dominant view of staff in student services was that their colleagues in academic units shared the responsibility for supporting students, including support for their future employability. The extent to which academic staff accepted such responsibilities differed between subject groups, predictably reflecting the extent to which courses had identifiable vocational goals. Among other academic groups, awareness-raising among staff was regarded as a pre-requisite for awareness-raising among students.

The issue of locus of responsibility is an interesting one. Academic staff are frequently working with high staff-student ratios and are under pressure from the Research Assessment Exercise (RAE). They may possess little knowledge about employment outside academic life. Even if they had the time and inclination to do so, would they really be much help to students? Yet many of the interesting ideas we encountered for assisting students to obtain good jobs required the active support of their teachers. Thus, there is probably a general issue about the role, expectations and workloads of academic staff that institutions will need to address before tackling the specifics of what might be done to achieve greater equity and enhanced employability among their students.

Of the many interesting initiatives being taken in institutions, we shall focus here on just two: making a positive experience of term-time working and the role of career management courses. We consider both of them from the standpoint of tackling social disadvantage at the point of entry to the graduate labour market.

Term-time working

Work experience as part of an organized placement has long been regarded as beneficial to future employment. Analysis of our survey data added further confirmation of this. However, the survey did not support the contention that other forms of work experience during higher education had a similarly positive effect. In fact, the relationship was a negative one. This was the one finding that surprised some of the people we spoke to in institutions, who regarded these other forms of work experience as valuable, if second-best to a supervised placement. Our interpretation of the finding was not that term-time work was necessarily without benefit, but that it took time away from activities that would have been more beneficial to the student. Whether these were extra-curricular activities, more time for study, or just visits to the careers service, the effect was to deprive students of some aspects of the student experience that could have benefited them and which *were* benefiting their peers and competitors in the labour market.

In some institutions, staff are attempting to find ways of turning the experience of term-time work to positive effect. This is frequently linked to the introduction of student profiles or personal development plans which encourage students to reflect on what they have learned – from various sources – and to assess their strengths and their weaknesses in the light of this. In practice, however, there were considerable differences between staff in relation to the kinds of work that could be regarded as potential learning opportunities and still more differences between them in whether such learning could be assessed and accredited. Some staff would limit the relevance of term-time work to semi-professional jobs in areas that could be linked to the content of the course. Others were prepared to see relevance in virtually any form of work experience, providing the student could demonstrate it. One English lecturer had set his students an essay assignment to describe some recent job experience in the style of George Orwell's *Down and Out in Paris and London*. The use of term-time working as a positive learning tool may call for a measure of creativity for both teacher and student.

Students from socially disadvantaged groups are more likely to have to work during term-time than other students. Many work long hours. Unless such experiences can be viewed positively – by the students themselves, by their teachers and by potential employers – they will be a source of further disadvantage for them.

Issues of term-time working were linked in one institution we visited to questions of drop-out. It was suggested that drop-out was an understandable outcome in the circumstances that some students faced. Instead of stigmatizing it, opportunities should be provided for students to 'drop back', perhaps after working full-time for a while in order to finance a further period of study.

Careers within the curriculum

Several institutions were introducing career and employment issues into the curriculum. There were a number of approaches to this. Free-standing modules could be available as part of a large modular programme. Or they could be specially designed as part of a specific course and related to a particular area of study and employment. Careers staff were frequently involved in the design and teaching of these courses.

Most of these initiatives had been too recent to be evaluated. Take-up of free-standing modules could be quite limited and completely absent from students in some subject areas. Integration within a subject-based programme at least had the advantage that it was taken by all students and also implied a measure of support by subject-based staff.

Students taking vocational programmes could expect their teachers to be interested and knowledgeable about employment opportunities, whether or not career issues were directly addressed in the formal curriculum. The survey indicated that many students found the careers advice of their teachers to be extremely valuable. Teachers in the more academic subjects may have little advice to give. The employment outcomes from their courses may be very diffuse. And, as we have already noted, they may be particularly influenced by factors associated with the social background of the student. Thus, on those courses where socially disadvantaged students most need information and advice, it is most likely to be lacking.

The introduction of career management issues into the curriculum would be regarded as inappropriate in some quarters, especially if it were to be assessed and contribute to the final degree award. Not all students will welcome it or see the point of it. Yet it is by ensuring that *all* students become aware of employment issues that the disadvantages faced by some groups of students can be offset and some measure of a level playing field achieved.

Conclusion

Widening participation in higher education is also extending opportunities in employment, but it is not equalizing them. Social background, ethnicity, the gender route taken into higher education, age at graduation and many other factors will directly and indirectly affect employment opportunities after graduation. Getting into a 'top university' and getting a 'top degree' may well be the most effective ways of compensating for social disadvantage, but they are hardly options for the majority. For them, the time spent in higher education needs to be used carefully and effectively to maximize opportunities after graduation. The obstacles to their doing so lie in the demands posed by the other aspects of their lives. Perhaps it is by finding value in knowledge derived from these aspects of life, by sometimes challenging the hegemony of academic knowledge, that characteristics of the person that we have perhaps unkindly called 'socially disadvantaged' in this chapter can one day be viewed in a more positive light.

It is hard to say that universities bear a responsibility for helping these students to overcome the difficulties they face. Yet if they do not, they are instead reinforcing a cycle of social disadvantage. In this project, we found universities that did accept some measure of responsibility for turning educational opportunity into employment opportunity and achieving a measure of social equity at the point of exit from higher education. This is not to deny that a possibly larger measure of responsibility might rest with employers, or with the school system, or with government. But all is connected. Most universities do accept a large measure of social responsibility. It may be difficult to deliver on sometimes but, after all, universities are meant to be about achieving difficult things.

Methodological note

A report of some of the results of this study has been published by HEFCE in Brennan et al. (2001). The detailed report of the analysis used in this chapter is published on the HEFCE website (www.hefce.ac.uk/Pubs/RDreports).

Section III

Perspectives

9

The global challenge

Brenda Gourley

As soon as we start thinking of students as whole people, with not only immediate life goals which have to do with employability in the short term, but as individuals whom we seek to equip with skills, attitudes and knowledge which remain relevant over their whole lifecourse, then the framing of the university experience becomes something different. It forces us to consider what their futures are likely to encompass and what is most likely to equip them best. More than that, however, institutions of higher education have always known (or perhaps they have forgotten) that education is, or should be, a transformatory experience and that its effects are likely to extend over many facets of the student's life. It is, in the terminology of this volume, a 'lifewide' experience.

Taking this task of thus equipping the students of our institutions is indeed a responsibility which requires deep wisdom and foresight.

How one views the future is of course powerfully influenced by one's own worldview, background, culture, religion and other factors. Whatever the future, however, it is difficult to imagine anybody omitting globalization as a powerful driving force likely to affect many dimensions of any student's life. Globalization has been described as 'the widening, deepening, and speeding up of world interconnectedness in all aspects of contemporary social life – a widespread perception that the world is rapidly being moulded into a shared social space by economic and technological forces' (WFS 2001: 3).

I am particularly taken with this definition of globalization because it high-lights the concept of a shared social space. As soon as we conceive of ourselves in a shared social space, it seems to me that a whole range of other issues falls into place. These include a consideration of what collection of people constitutes the institution, what the institution does (in terms of research and teaching) and how it governs itself. Together these define the institution and, at the same time, define the student experience. Together they will determine whether the students' education is indeed a transformatory experience or simply a transfer of a particular set of limited knowledge (or even just content) and a confirmation of previously held prejudices.

The elements that go to constitute the lifewide student experience are many indeed and not all are affected by globalization but the ones that are can be grouped. I will consider just six and try to explore how each is affected by globalization. They are set out below.

Elements pertaining to students' cultural and social life

The concept of globalization as meaning the inhabitation of a shared social space raises deep questions of whether we can properly understand this social space without an understanding of, and dialogue between, elements of our shared cultural heritage. Kofi Annan describes this very well in the foreword to a book entitled *Crossing the Divide* when he says: '[t]oday, globalization, migration, integration, communication and travel are bringing different races, cultures and ethnicities into ever closer contact with each other.' More than ever before, people understand that they are being shaped by many cultures and influences, and that combining the familiar with the foreign can be a source of powerful knowledge and insight.

> There is a set of common values that humanity has shared over centuries. The United Nations itself was founded on the belief that dialogue can triumph over discord, that diversity is a gift to be celebrated and that the world's people are united by their common humanity far more than they are divided by their separate identities.
>
> (Annan, in Picco et al. 2001: 11)

The General Assembly of the United Nations unanimously proclaimed 2001 as the UN Year of Dialogue Among Civilizations. The Secretary-General, Kofi Annan, appointed an international group of eminent persons to bring together the distinct questions elicited by that Dialogue. Their research and discussions have been brought together in *Crossing the Divide*. Kofi Annan's Foreword goes on to say:

> The need for dialogue among civilizations is as old as civilization itself. But today, the need is more acute than ever. Individuals who live in fear and lack of comprehension of other cultures are more likely to resort to acts of hatred, violence and destruction against a perceived 'enemy'. Those who are exposed to the cultures of others and learn about them through communication across cultural divides are more likely to see diversity as a strength and celebrate it as a gift.
>
> (Annan, in Picco et al. 2001: 11)

I use this powerful quotation from one of the world's great human beings because UNESCO has now specifically challenged educational institutions to join in promoting, maintaining, reinforcing, enriching '. . . and in many cases even reintroducing – cultural diversity in society' (2002: 17). We have a responsibility to our students and to our communities, wherever they may be, to join in the great endeavour that Annan and his fellow commissioners seek to promote.

One of the important questions that we obviously have to ask ourselves is whether our curricula are conceived to cover the main issues framed by the globalization debate?

It is a source of perplexity and grief to me that educational institutions do not recognize their explicit social responsibility in this regard. This will have to do as much with staff as it does with students. We cannot expect staff who have only one kind of experience to have the knowledge and skills that are needed for designing a different kind of educational experience.

Education is, of course, concerned with building intellectual and social capital, but not only particular sets of intellectual and social capital. It must do this yet it must also concern itself with building global citizenship. It must aim to build bridges across cultures as we all learn more about each other and come to accept that we occupy the same planet where our destiny is a common one. I would argue very strongly indeed that this is as important to employability as specific knowledge is about a profession or discipline. As the workplace too becomes more multicultural it is those people who mix easily and well across cultures who will be more valuable and more likely to succeed. Would that we had more people in positions of corporate, political or other power who see themselves as global citizens and exercise their power as inhabitants of a shared social space.

The curriculum sends powerful signals as to what is valued and what is not. Recently I was told by a student that in signing up at her local university she was committing 'cultural suicide'. Many universities and the new brand of 'super universities' – many of them distance-teaching institutions – have students all over the world and yet in their teaching materials they often seem culturally myopic (to say the least). Many universities have established 'partnerships' with institutions in other countries and yet fail to appreciate the marvellous opportunities for the joint preparation of material that students in many cultures could appreciate and learn from without feeling themselves distanced from the material. Daisaku Ikeda, in a speech entitled *A New Road to East/West Cultural Exchange*, points out that 'economically developing countries all have cultures as rich and complex as nations who outstrip them in wealth and power. It is desirable to use standards other than economics (alone) in evaluating the achievements of a people'.

In terms of non-economic aspects of human culture, 'developed' nations might appear much less advanced than others that are now regarded as 'developing'. We would possess a more varied and accurate picture of our green planet and its six billion people if it were examined in the light of the 'art, religion, traditions, lifestyles, and psychology of its inhabitants' (Ikeda 1996: 70). Ikeda envisions 'an enchanting, peaceful future when many peoples . . . will be able to travel a new Silk Road of cultural and mutual understanding' and reminds us of the lines written by the poet Yunus Emre: '[t]he world to me is sustenance; its peoples and my own are one' (ibid.: 20, 21).

Many universities encourage students from other countries to study with them and yet fail to appreciate the opportunity such students represent to create spaces for cultural dialogue – both in the classroom and outside. I applaud the effort to create a more international experience for all students but cannot help but wonder if they are not simply seen as 'customers' who help revenue flows rather than other occupants of our shared social space.

I ask for some humility on the part of the educators – and I would hope that this humility would extend to the examination of their curricula even for their indigenous students. Culturally myopic curricula do no service to students who we would hope aspire to being global citizens – conscious of the obligations that being educated brings with it the need to understand more of the world they occupy.

UNESCO has rightly highlighted linguistic diversity as a necessary dimension of cultural diversity. It urges educational institutions to encourage 'linguistic diversity – while respecting mother tongue – at all levels of education, wherever possible, and (foster) the learning of several languages from the youngest age' (UNESCO 2002: 28). I would draw attention to UNESCO's *Universal Declaration on Cultural Diversity* and its website (UNESCO.org/ culture) where it has collected a pool of ideas for the implementation of its cultural diversity agenda.

Elements of globalization pertaining to students' political and civic life

In his *On My Country and the World*, Mikhail Gorbachev remarks that 'the character of political activity even in democratic systems seems to be increasingly less democratic' (WFS 2001: 4). Globalization certainly puts the role of the nation state in a new light. It would seem that the nation state is too small for the big problems of the world and too big for the small problems. In those nations governed by democratic principles there is disenchantment with what democracy can deliver. Voting, for example, attracts fewer people than it should. This is entirely non-trivial in a world where a country like the United States exercises unprecedented global power and where so much power comes to reside in the hands of so few individual people.

The role of non-governmental organizations is growing as people find alternative ways of trying to influence those things that they care about. The role of regional or local government is growing for the same reason.

Jan Aart Scholte has written most thoughtfully about what public policies must be designed to govern responsibly. They include those which are needed to contain global regimes for arms control, suprastate mechanisms for conflict management, global environmental codes, socially sustainable global economic restructuring, suprastate financial regulations, global taxation, greater roles for global civil society (Scholte 2000). These are just some of the issues involved in a global world where we seek to prepare students for their global citizenship.

The Association of Commonwealth Universities (ACU) has published a consultation document on *Engagement as a Core Value for the University*. It quotes a study inviting universities to be 'part of the conscience of a demo-cratic society, founded on respect for the rights of the individual and the responsibilities of the individual and society as a whole' and to 'play a major role in shaping a democratic, civilized, inclusive society'. It goes on to assert that 'university study should enable students to acquire not only such skills as are useful in the working world but also those skills necessary to participate in society' (ACU 2001: 4).

It is instructive to ponder on the World Bank's Task Force Report on *Higher Education in Developing Countries: Peril and Promise* (2000) where it says that:

> higher education promotes values which are more inclusive and more public than other civic venues, such as religious communities, house-holds and families, or ethnic and linguistic groups. Higher education is expected to embody norms of social interaction such as open debate and argumentative reason; to emphasis the autonomy and self-reliance of its individual members; and to reject discrimination based on gender, ethnicity, religious belief or social class. The best higher education insti-tution is a model and a source of pressure for creating a modern civil society.
>
> (World Bank 2000, quoted in ACU 2001: 5)

Civil engagement with local and other communities may well be the best way for students to learn about the issues of social concern. More and more universities are engaged in one form or another of what has come to be called 'service learning' where students are actively engaged in community projects of various kinds and gain academic credit for doing so.

It is important in this context that the students' experience of how the institution conducts its affairs bears scrutiny. The institution's actions might well belie our fine words about democracy and human rights and the responsibilities of civic engagement – and action speaks louder than words in this matter as in most others. If we do not, as an institution, have properly represented women, minority groups, different cultures and worldviews, what does this convey to our students and staff? If there are only particular people who exercise power and authority how much value can students attach to their university experience? In a world where there is so much to be done before equity can truly be said to have been achieved, it behoves those places where ideals are held up high, not to destroy what precious places still exist for such ideals to flourish.

Elements of globalization pertaining to students' economic life

The forces of globalization are played out in the economies of the world in ways that are beyond the control of the ordinary individual, yet the ordinary individual must conduct his or her economic affairs in this same world. The development of new financial instruments, deregulation of national financial markets, and the growth of international banks and other institutions have created this new system.

Add to this the global regulation of trade by bodies such as the World Trade Organization, GATS, economic trade blocs and geo-economies and one has a mix of factors that act as powerful agents for change – and change which is not always ethical or fair. The world of e-commerce and the protection of electronic money are non-trivial issues in this arena and make the conduct of business of any sort subject to issues unheard of even ten years ago. One cannot be a functioning citizen of this global economy without some basic grasp of these forces. To bring an immediate issue to bear, for example, one questions how the citizens of the UK can vote in a referendum to decide on whether to join the Euro without some basic understanding of some of these forces?

Elements of globalization pertaining to students' physical life

Students' physical life can be stretched to include a range of dimensions but I would like to concentrate first on their natural environment. From the pictures of Earth taken from space to the diseases of rivers, forests and people, we must recognize and bring understanding that each city, however big, and each hamlet, however remote, however poor, will suffer the fate of the whole. We must surely share a vision that derives from the idea that the world will be better off, at best healed, by educational intervention that engages rich and poor, capitalists and subalterns, metropoles and hamlets, nations and united nations; in other words by educational intervention that quite literally shares our common wealth. The task is a massive one and a noble one, if (and I emphasize the proviso) it can overcome the cultural imperialization that characterizes so many initiatives that ride the spirit of globalization.

We know it to be true at the environmental level; and it is true at the human level: we are all interdependent and unless we understand that we are all doomed to a truly awful common fate. Scientists tell us that the world of nature is so small and interdependent that a butterfly flapping its wings in the Amazon rainforest can generate a violent storm on the other side of the Earth. This principle is known as the 'butterfly effect'. The Club of Rome described us in more dramatic terms as a juggernaut out of control. I like the description by Reg Morrison in his *The Spirit in the Gene*. He says: '[w]e have dallied too long at the banquet of natural resources, only to discover that the only way out is past the cashier' (Morrision 1999: 127).

The student's physical environment is also affected by many other manifestations of globalization. These include massive shifts in demography both within nation states and between nation states. Tides of refugees are pushing down national boundaries. They are fleeing in pursuit of a better life. Many are fleeing in pursuit of life itself because they will surely perish if they remain where they are. One of the largest trends in any future study points to massive demographic shifts: shifts in the age profile of first world nations and the ethnic profiles as well. They point to serious changes in the way work is organized and how the sick and elderly are cared for.

Another alarming trend in our new globalized world is the rise of crime and conflict. The expanding reach of organized violence and the global arms market as well as the use of nuclear and biological weapons make us at risk in a way that we have never before experienced in our history. The fact is that the rising tide of globalization erodes barriers to access the keys of mass destruction as modern societies become more dependent on integrated and highly technical infrastructure (see Lake 2001).

Add to this the increase in cybercrime and you begin to understand why people like Kofi Annan urge us to understand that 'taking prevention more seriously will help insure that there are fewer wars and less consequential disasters to cope with' (WFS 2001: 18). Peace-keeping is actually becoming an area of serious study in this new world where many of our well-intentioned efforts have caused more harm than good.

I raise these issues as ones that seriously impact on our lives, and I do so in the belief that if we are to have some understanding of the world we inhabit then we need also to have some understanding of these matters.

Elements of globalization pertaining to students' ethical life

It is interesting and important that we try to understand that while globalization in science and technology, mass communications, trade, finance, tourism, migration, crime and disease are all growing at an unprecedented rate, at the same time the pervasiveness and depth of local identities defined in terms of ethnicity, language, land, religion and traditions have resurged as major forces of our time (Picco et al. 2001: 21). Manuel Castells, a celebrated social theorist, in his powerful work called *The Rise of the Network Society*, tells us in very moving terms that the most striking consequence of this new global network society is its corrosive effect on equality and social justice. In his blunt words: '[e]ntire countries around the world and large segments of the population everywhere are becoming excluded' (quoted in Barber, 1999). This kind of society, he says, is based on a 'systemic disjunction between the local and the global for most individuals and social groups, so denying the future of humans as a humane species'. Castells concludes that the system, over time, is not only economically and technologically unsustainable but also socially and politically unsustainable.

It is quite clear that the great issues of our time, issues involving survival and sustainability, as well as issues about closing the gap between the haves and the have-nots, are going to require choices. These are active choices about sharing; active choices that ought to be made on moral or ethical grounds of one sort or another.

And so the ethics of living and making choices at this time in the history of our world are multiple indeed. They do affect every facet of our lives.

Frederico Mayor (former Director-General of UNESCO), echoing this, has written that there are four unprecedented challenges at the dawn of this new century: the challenge of peace; the challenge of growing and glaring inequality (citing more than half of humanity living on less than $2 a day); the challenge of sustainable development (and reining in North American consumption levels); and (what he calls) the 'drunken boat' syndrome (many states seem to have mislaid their maps and piloting equipment, and even the will to set goals). He believes that rising to these challenges will require four contracts to humanize globalization and form a new international democracy. He calls them the social, natural, cultural and ethical contracts. The essence of the ethical contract is trying to bring the benefits of globalization to everyone, by using the dividends of peace to make a new start (Mayor and Binde 2001).

It is perhaps one of the few comforting aspects of our new world that human rights are being given more and more prominence. If we, as educational institutions, do not give them similar prominence in our curricula and research agendas then we are doing our students a grave injustice. This is also true about the ethical issues raised in virtually every discipline we teach and research.

Elements of globalization pertaining to students' intellectual life

It is perhaps repetitive to identify an intellectual life as separate from the others that have so far been listed. I raise it specifically because of a concern for what has been called the 'anti-intellectualism' of our times. We seem to occupy a world where the word 'intellectual' has even come to have a pejorative meaning. Our media are dominated by stories to do with the rich, the beautiful, the strong and the charismatic – but certainly not the serious and the intellectual. Entertainment is all and we have succumbed, without any noticeable struggle, to a celebrity culture. Susan Sontag comments that 'the undermining of seriousness is almost complete, with the ascendancy of a culture whose most intelligible, persuasive values are drawn from the entertainment industries' (Sontag 2002: 273).

One might imagine that this is of small importance in the face of all the other matters with which we have to contend. The fact is that they are all connected. Many of our problems are problems because we have given them so little thought and public debate. Indeed, public debate is no longer the staple of public life that it once was. Donald Wood believes this is contributing to the decline of democracy, and his excellent analysis captures some of this concern. He writes:

> When times were less complicated, a modicum of reason was good enough to get by. But in today's increasingly complex technological culture – with our information explosion, bewildering scientific environment, shaky economic structures, extended urbanization, ecological complications and suffocating bureaucracies – a modicum of intelligence will no longer suffice. In today's culture we must manifest an even stronger commitment to reason and responsibility. But we fail to do so.
>
> (Wood 1996: 50)

He goes on to an even stronger point: we are opting out of a serious responsibility if we continue along this path, and the very essence of democracy is at risk.

It seems to me that universities have a very special responsibility in this regard – both with respect to their students and to their larger communities. If they do not promote an active intellectual life, promote all the rules of debate that allow disagreeable, controversial and different points of view to be held – and do so in a vigorous and non-partisan way – in the best traditions of free speech in a functioning and lively democracy, then I cannot think who will take on this role.

Conclusion

We know that globalization certainly affects a great many aspects of our lives and we know that it raises many questions. If we understand it to mean that the world is being moulded into shared social space, then we need to ask ourselves what we do in the design of our curricula and research that equips our students to occupy that space responsibly. It raises concerns about human rights, about ethics, about leadership, about how we discharge our democratic rights and responsibilities – and especially those that affect the well-being of the whole, how we preserve our environment, how we act in a global economy and how we look after those who are disaffected in it and by it. We would do well to remember one of the banners in Genoa at a G7 demonstration that declared: 'you are G7, we are 6 billion'. I am astonished, for example, to find how few people in the UK and Europe comprehend that they are living through a time when the greatest catastrophe in human history is taking place – that is HIV/AIDS – and what it means for the future. If we want 'education for citizenship' maybe we should also pause to consider what that means for all of our educational perspectives.

We need to at least give some attention to what it is that we seek from education and what we regard as an educated person. If we divorce these considerations from our concern, we are ourselves failing to acknowledge that education is never value-free and we cannot harness the resources of the world to a common effort while the differences in what we perceive these values to be go unexamined and create ever larger gulfs between us. As we attempt to seek the values that we share (and there are many) we might also in the process find our common humanity (and respond to the HIV/AIDS challenge, for example) and rise above the differences to promote that to which we all subscribe: and that is ever greater access to an appropriate education for our times.

I raise these issues and hope that educators think about them and embark on a process of deep curricula transformation – for indeed that is what is needed in this shared social space. I raise them because I believe they require deep structural change to our present arrangements if we are to be capable of delivery. They most certainly require multi- and inter-disciplinary collaborations. They require cross-institutional collaborations across national boundaries.

I raise these issues also to reassure myself that we are not locked in some tragic struggle where the race between education and disaster has a pre-determined outcome. If we look at the state of the world, we can only conclude that we dare not fail in our task – and I hope that coming together here, as is argued in this book, means that we have accepted that we do indeed have a common responsibility.

10

Higher education and civil society

Maria Slowey

The Universities must play their part in the diffusion of culture through
the whole community. A University like our own situated in the centre
of a great industrial community has an immense opportunity before it, if
it is to make knowledge of these humanistic studies the possession of all
men and women who are faced with the need of it, if all who want a
completer understanding of the ideals and possibilities of our common
life, of economic and political relations, of the laws and the working of
the political and social institutions they are called upon to handle, can
come to the University for help, and look to it for a standard of impartial
and scientific study.
    A.D. Lindsay, founder of the Extra-Mural Education Committee
of the University of Glasgow, subsequently Master of Balliol and Vice
Chancellor of Keele, speaking of Glasgow c. 1923.

(Scott 1971: 102)

Some 80 years on in Glasgow, as elsewhere throughout the Western world,
the great industrial bases are long gone and traditional communities fragmented. Do the dramatic economic, social and political changes over this
period mean that such a vision of the role of the academy in civil society is no
longer relevant? Is the notion that universities might be charged with a particular responsibility for responding to the men and women who are 'faced
with the need' of developing a better understanding of these major forces as
much a feature only of the past as the Clyde shipyards? Or might not contemporary global social and economic conditions mean that the need for
universities to make such a contribution to civil society has never been
greater?

As social institutions, universities engage with civil society in complex ways.
The nature of this interaction not only changes over time and across different nation states, but is also shaped by particular regional and local, social,
economic and demographic circumstances (Barnett 1994; Coffield and
Williamson 1997; Scott 1995, 2001; Thompson 2000). Even considering the

relatively short period of the last century, when for the most part the foundations for modern universities were laid, great changes have taken place in the
interface with civil society: for example, in terms of connections with local
communities, the selection function for certain occupations, the role of
research, the production and dissemination of knowledge, and links with
private and public sector employers and professional bodies.

It is important to maintain a social-historical perspective on change in the
academy, as it is in any social institution. Dramatic as recent changes have
been, Bell and Tight's discussion of *Open Universities* in Britain is a valuable
reminder of the scale of change which had previously taken place in the
nineteenth and early parts of the twentieth century, and which they argue
led in certain respects to a closing rather than an opening of universities
(Bell and Tight 1993).

At the heart of the inter-relationship between universities and society lies a
tension between the autonomy of the academy and the independent pursuit
of knowledge, including that associated with potentially critical perspectives
on its host social formation, and its dependence for its existence on the
latter. Other chapters in this volume have focused on questions about the
relationship between the people and the academy along two axes. Along one
axis, there is the story of the individual over the course of his or her lifetime,
and of particular groups of 'new' learners, moving in, out of and around
higher education. Along the other, there is the dynamic inter-relationship
between higher education and the broader lifewide learning needs and
interests of learners. In this chapter, the focus shifts from the academy and its
relationship with individual learners to that of its relationship with learners
as social actors in civil society and the broader community.

But what society, and whose community? Fragmentation and transience
constituted two of the dominant themes shaping social commentary and
analysis as we moved into a new century. Bauman (2000: 126), for example,
puts forward a strong case that the passage in recent decades from heavy to
light capitalism and from solid to fluid modernity may yet prove to be a
transformation which is 'more radical and seminal' than the advent of capitalism and modernity themselves. Meanwhile, people have to grapple with
changed realities well in advance of recognition, let alone response, by many
social institutions. Thus, in higher education, as Ramsden shows in chapter
one, changes in the student body tend to occur before they are recognized at
official levels by institutions or policy (Schuetze and Slowey 2000: 14).

Over the last two decades universities in the UK have undoubtedly been
subject to accelerating transformations not only in terms of scale, but also in
terms of age, motivation, background of staff and students and curricula,
with consequences for the nature of their connections with civil society (see,
for example, Watson and Taylor 1998; Scott 2000b; Taylor, Barr and Steele
2002). The factors underlying these changes in higher education are, of
course, the same as those impacting on society more broadly: a complex mix
of globalization, technological explosion, growing inequality gaps both
within and between countries, labour market change and volatility,

ecological crises and so on. As the old certainties are challenged, individuals are pushed increasingly onto their own resources.

> Opportunities, dangers, biographical uncertainties that were earlier pre-defined within the family association, the village community, or by recourse to the rules of social states or classes, must now be perceived, interpreted, decided and processed by individuals themselves. The consequences – opportunities and burdens alike – are shifted onto individuals who, naturally, in the face of the complexity of social inter-connections are often unable to take the necessary decisions in a properly founded way, by considering interests, morality and consequences.
>
> (Beck and Gernsheim 2001: 4)

It is desirable from many perspectives for a better balance to be struck between individualization and integration – that is, between the benefits of greater individual autonomy and the contribution to the collective. This represents quite a challenge when in advanced liberal states a form of individualism is the prevailing ideology behind neoliberal reforms (Peters 2001: 124).

> Where the old sociality is 'evaporating' society must be reinvented. Integration therefore becomes possible if no attempt is made to arrest and push back the breakout of individuals. It can happen if we make conscious use of this situation and try to forge new, politically open, creative forms of bond and alliance.
>
> (Beck and Gernsheim 2001: 18)

Beck terms this the 'invention of the political' and regards the question as to whether societies have the strength, imagination and time to do this as being no less than a matter of life and death. Higher education carries great responsibility for these matters, despite the growth of competing providers, despite cut-backs in public investment, despite analyses of crises and ruin (Readings 1996). Barnett's view of a role of higher education is perhaps more pertinent than ever a decade on: '. . . by examining seriously and disinterestedly the concepts available to society, the university opens up and sustains a gap between the civil society and those concepts being examined . . .' (1994: 50).

Delanty (2001: 6) is amongst those making the case for this new role for the academy. Given that the university is no longer the '. . . crucial institution in society for the reproduction of instrumental/technical knowledge and is no longer the codifier of a new fragmented national culture, it can now ally itself with civil society'.

But what might such a new form of alliance between higher education and civil society mean in practice? In the age of fragmentation and growing inequalities, what role might the academy play in supporting and, where necessary assisting in the (re)creation of, civil society and communities? This chapter seeks to throw some light upon this theoretical debate by approaching the question through one particular prism. This concerns the connection between higher education and civil society as operationalized in the form of a current policy focus on the 'third arm' or 'third mission' for higher education, sitting alongside the two core functions of teaching and research. (The terms 'third arm', 'third mission' and 'third leg' tend to be used interchangeably. For ease of presentation the term 'third arm' is used in this chapter.)

In order to explore these issues the views of senior academics from the UK and internationally have been obtained as the first stage of a Delphi study. Participants were selected for their expertise in research and/or engagement with links between higher education and civil society. They are not representative but bring informed perspectives based on their experience and research from different disciplinary backgrounds (see the methodological note at the end of this chapter).

Whose community? Which public? What citizens?

Universities engage with civil society in complex ways, influenced, amongst other factors, by their history, culture, geographical location, resource base, status, leadership and ambitions. One approach to conceptualizing these links is to distinguish between those which are part of 'official business' (whether at the level of the institution, faculty or department) and hence built into strategic, accountability and monitoring arrangements, and those which are at the level of the activities of individual academics where the (still) relatively high degree of autonomy facilitates opportunities for those who choose to engage with the broader community in a wide variety of ways. (The commitment of individuals lies at the heart of many community and outreach initiatives [see Fieldhouse and Associates 1996].)

Such activities include everything from courses and lectures for the public, art galleries, museums, theatres, consultancies, outreach activities, research and development activities (R & D), widening access partnerships, technology transfer, contributions to learned societies, voluntary associations, community development, through to the role played by academics as public intellectuals – including, for an equally envied and despised few, as media stars.

At the risk of oversimplification, it seems useful to make an analytical distinction between three forms of connection between the academy and external communities. First, there are the relationships between universities and the state in terms of government, ministries, semi-state bodies and quangos (quasi-autonomous, non-governmental organizations) of various kinds. Second, universities engage with the private sector as employers of graduates and in a myriad of ways connected with research, consultancy and the like. Third, there are the broader connections with communities and civil society – in the sense used by, for example, Hake (1996) and Paterson (2000). These are represented diagrammatically in figure 10.1. The primary focus of this chapter is on the relationships at the apex of the triangle.

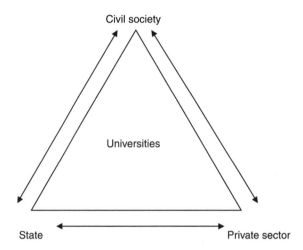

Figure 10.1 Higher education and community connections

Some interpretations of community have followed through into radically orientated approaches to lifelong learning in general and higher education more specifically. Here, community is viewed collectively rather than individually. 'Disadvantaged communities are composed as interlocking collectivities of particular groups, almost always of double disadvantage' (Taylor et al. 2002: 113). Such communities are predominantly working class and also, variously, single parents and particularly women, the unwaged, those on low incomes, with low educational qualifications, of minority ethnic origin and/or elderly. To what extent might work with such groups constitute an appropriate aspect of the third arm of higher education? The answer to this question is important because, as Field puts it, without a democratization of intermediate institutions of which the academy is one '. . . the learning society will continue to generate ever greater inequality and exclusion and become ever more unstable' (Field 2000: 150).

So what is the fit or otherwise between policy statements and perceptions 'on the ground' in relation to third-arm actitivies both in general terms and more specifically in relation to civil and community engagement? In the following section attention is turned to an examination of the implications of several key policy statements and initiatives relevant to third-arm activities, contrasting these with the perceptions of a group of senior academics in the UK and other countries.

Contrasting interpretations of the third-arm functions of higher education

At the outset it is important to note that a majority of the academic respondents indicated that the terms 'third arm' or 'third mission' of higher education were not particularly familiar to them. While all participants proceeded to make educated guesses and informed observations, this initial response from over half of a group of 20 senior academics selected explicitly because of their active engagement in university-community activities is noteworthy.

> I had never envisaged it in this way. The metaphor of third arm is itself odd when one thinks about it. And of course the fact that it is third already symbolizes a hierarchy.
>
> (UK: 7)

> I have never heard of the 'third arm/mission' phrase before, but can get the gist of it from your context.
>
> (Australia: 1)

> These are not terms with which I am familiar.
>
> (UK: 11)

> If I should say what it might be I guess . . .
>
> (UK: 5)

Among a range of possible interpretations for the vague nature of these responses, one is of particular interest for our purposes in this chapter. Could the notion of the third arm reflect a perspective on the academy which has more currency in policy and managerial circles than with some of those engaged with the practice at the level of academic departments? If so, what might the implications be for all concerned?

A number of respondents made explicit reference to the North American land-grant tradition in higher education.

> Community service is an old and important part of the entire higher education system in North America. In some institutions this is *expressis verbis* written into their charter, such as the land-grant universities in the US and the universities in western Canada. But even where this is not part of their explicit mission, most universities have strong (much stronger than in Europe) links with the community. The term 'third' arm is not used here however.
>
> (Canada: 16)

An analysis of national policy perspectives from a variety of sources – government, ministries, funding councils, and representative organizations of higher education institutions (HEIs) – when set against the interpretations of the expert academic group, points to four broad interpretations of the third-arm function of higher education in the UK. There are overlaps between these different conceptions but they carry different and, in some respects potentially competing, implications for both the academy and civil society in practice. They are presented in the form of a typology in figure 10.2.

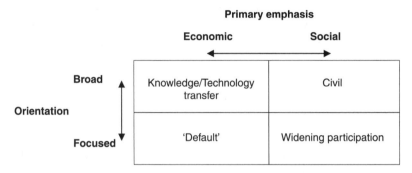

Figure 10.2 Typology of perspectives on the third arm of higher education

One axis relates to the extent to which the priority or emphasis is placed more on the social as opposed to the economic. The other relates to the extent to which the orientation is relatively broad and inclusive or relatively focused. Thus *knowledge transfer* reflects a broad, but predominantly economic, approach to third-arm activities; the *default* approach derives primarily from an accountability perspective, where the third arm is effectively defined in a negative way as everything other than teaching or research; the *widening participation* approach is more socially orientated but focused particularly on individual participation; and the *civil and community* approach reflects a broad and socially orientated perspective of the third arm of the academy emphasizing the public and civil sphere. These four different interpretations are discussed in turn below.

Knowledge and technology transfer

Universities in the UK receive the bulk of their public funding for teaching and research through a formula-driven process tied to measurement in terms of student numbers, research output and associated national assessments of quality. In contrast, public funding for third-arm activities is characterized by being largely initiative based, short term and subject to competitive bidding processes. Examples in recent years have included HEROBAC (Higher Education Reach Out to Business and the Community) from HEFCE, Knowledge Transfer from SHEFC, and the Higher Education Innovation Fund (HEIF) – a cross-departmental initiative.

When we look at how this complex array of initiatives are operationalized in practice, the focus tends to shift in one of two directions – either towards an emphasis on which might be most readily quantified, particularly in economic terms, or alternatively towards the default approach, whereby the third arm includes everything that does not fall conventionally under the heading of either teaching or research. The economic view is illustrated in the comments of respondents from Japan and the UK.

The relationship between university and society, 'service for economy' and 'usefulness to the society' are strongly encouraged by the government and industry in Japan. It is not only applied to the Japanese case but, I believe, to many countries.

(Japan: 2)

'Third arm/mission' of HE I now understand to be the attempt to relate HE to local community imperatives, notably its employment and private sector representatives.

(UK: 10)

I think the notion as used now concerns varied things like 'knowledge transfer', mainly one way, from the university to the community (meaning industry largely) and tied up with notions of the 'knowledge society', knowledge being dispersed etc.

(UK: 14)

One area where the knowledge transfer interpretation of the third arm and the interest in this chapter on the academy and civil society might be expected to come together concerns the role of universities in relation to their region. As an academic from Australia comments:

Across the Australian higher education system, I'd imagine everyone is trying to locate their universities in strategic terms, even regionally, so that (a) they get a greater chance of surviving especially in rural Australia and (b) they carve out a niche identity.

(Australia: 1)

In England and Wales a study was commissioned by HEFCE to develop benchmarks by which the contribution of universities to their regions might be assessed. Six of the seven factors identified in this study point to an emphasis exclusively associated with the economic dimension, the exception being in relation to cultural activities (Charles and Benneworth 2002).

The seven factors suggested for benchmarking the role of universities in their regions are:

(i)   Enhancing regional framework conditions.
(ii)   Human capital development processes.
(iii) Business development processes.
(iv)   Interactive learning and social capital development processes.
(v)   Redistributive processes.
(vi)   Cultural development.
(vii) Promoting sustainability.

(Charles and Benneworth 2002: 10)

Certainly, all of the above may constitute important means by which a university can potentially make a positive contribution to the development of the region in which it is located. The point is not to downplay their significance but rather to highlight the dominance of economic drivers and the relative invisibility of any reference to a broad civil role in relation to the public.

Default

If the above can be seen as an example of an interpretation of the third arm based largely on economic connections at the level of institutions, the 'default model' is one that is essentially dominated by bureaucratic and accountability approaches. Writing about binary systems, Fulton (1996) observes that the most common means of specifying sectoral missions in higher education is through the regulation of staff working conditions in such a way that their role expectations are restricted or shaped. This view is echoed in the observations of a number of respondents.

> . . . the increasing bureaucratisation of higher education, and the regimes of inspection, and the treadmill of the RAE, linked to the 'tyranny' of research criteria in promotions processes, all lead to a significant diminution in the Universities' community approaches, broadly defined.
>
> (UK: 8)

A somewhat different interpretation of the managerial or 'default' approach is provided by a respondent from Japan.

> The first mission is diffusion of knowledge. The second is creation of knowledge. The third is (proper) governance and management. Community service and adult education would be a part of diffusion of knowledge. I see spin-off companies, commercialization and technology transfer as a part of creation of knowledge. . . .
>
> (Japan: 3)

In his analysis of universities and the social agenda Watson distinguishes between two types of activity. The first is about developments where the focus is predominantly internal to the university, associated with issues such as admission, student support and curriculum change. 'The second is significantly outside, where the University recognises that it has an obligation to help to change matters, for example, in schools or in community capability' (Watson 2001: 32). He proceeds to point out that there are risks in the second which not all universities are prepared to take. Some of these risks are associated with the new forms of partnership with which universities need to engage. Here they may not necessarily take the senior determining role to which they are long accustomed. Other risks, however, are associated with the '. . . ambiguities about the bottom line in which a general social good, such as improved staying on rates in schools and further education, may not directly benefit the University which has made the investment to bring it about'.

The categories used in the Transparency Review in the UK offer a good illustration of this 'default' approach to connections between higher education and civil society. In 1998 the Treasury made additional investment in British higher education conditional on providing more open information about the way public funds are spent in higher education.

One of the key requirements of the Transparency Review was that universities should provide detailed information on costs associated with three functions, defined as Teaching (T), Research (R) (distinguishing in both cases between that which is publicly funded and that funded from other, non-public sources) and Other activities (O). An additional element for Support (S) is allocated across these categories.

While it is inevitable that such an exercise has to be conducted at a high level of generality, it is difficult to see how a vibrant, wide-ranging interpretation of the third arm is likely to be signalled and identified though this process. Even more significantly, however, the commonly observed tendency that it is only activities (and outcomes) that can be readily measured which are deemed to be of value seems to apply. This raises legitimate concerns about the potential impact of lumping together a diverse and important range of higher education activities under 'Other' – defined in the guidelines as:

> Consultancy (excluding private) other services rendered, including testing, clinical trials, services provided to the NHS under knock for knock arrangements, residences, catering and conferences, other commercial activities (trading companies), costs of services sold externally by library, estates services etc., outreach.
>
> (Joint Costing and Pricing Steering Group 2000)

This view of the system tends not only to reduce the third arm to 'other' activities, but also to focus attention on those which are predominantly associated with income generation.

Widening participation

Another interpretation of the third arm includes a spectrum of activities with a particular emphasis on issues of widening access so that a larger and a more heterogeneous group of individuals are given the opportunity to participate in higher education. In terms of the typology in figure 10.2, this represents a socially orientated approach, but one which is particularly focused on issues of access for students as individual learners. High-profile policy initiatives in the UK in recent years have addressed strategies to achieve a government target for 50 per cent of the population aged between 18 and 30 to have had the opportunity, by 2010, to benefit from higher education.

This has led, for example, to the setting up of a range of national programmes. One example is 'Partnerships for Progression' with a budget of £60 million between the Higher Education Funding Council for England and the Learning and Skills Council. In Scotland, a similar range of initiatives are supported by the counterpart organizations with a particular focus on regional Widening Access Partnerships.

The widening participation interpretation of third-arm activities is echoed in a number of the comments from the academic respondents. What is evident from their reflections, however, is more of a weighing up of the pros and cons and a recognition of the tensions, if not contradictions, that exist.

Not only is participation in education associated with a range of personal benefits but, as Watson points out in chapter eleven, is also associated with democratic tolerance. While progression rates of school leavers to short- and longer-cycle higher education courses in the UK may have tripled over two decades or so (1980 to 2000), in relation to participation in education and training across the population at large, the story has been characterized as 'two steps forward, one step back' (Aldridge and Tuckett 2002).

> There is something of a paradox here in my view. On the one hand, the massive expansion of higher education and its increasing importance in society has brought at least some of the benefits of HE experience to very greatly increased numbers of learners . . . On the other hand, there are powerful negative factors at work. Amongst these, in my view, are . . . the dominance of an individualistic perspective which effectively ignores or denies the collective in the community.
>
> (UK: 8)

A whole series of reports in recent years, including Moser (1999), have drawn attention to the enormous social deficit in terms of the level of basic skills of adults in the UK. Meanwhile, the figures for Scotland, despite a number of discernible advantages arising from higher staying-on rates, show equally strong influences of social class in relation to adult participation in education and training (Slowey 2003).

In practice, however, the question of widening participation tends to remain focused on issues of progression and access of individual learners – despite persistent and strong evidence about the *social* construction of these opportunities (see, for example, Gorard et al. 1999; Coffield 2000; Hobcraft 2000; Furlong and Forsyth 2003).

Civil and community

A fourth interpretation of the third arm emphasizes civil and community matters. This broader view is reflected in a speech made by the elected president of the representative body of all UK higher education institutions (Universities UK).

> Universities have seen their roles primarily in terms of teaching and research – they educate and train people with the skills they need to

participate fully in society and give them the skills employers need. They enable the UK to punch above its weight in terms of research, not only to support high quality teaching, but also setting up countless spin off companies in areas such as satellite technology, biotechnology and robotics. And this is largely the expectation of the rest of society. But universities are also reaching into their communities, getting their hands dirty by combating social exclusion and improving cultural understanding in their regions.

(Floud 2001)

He proceeds to comment that a major challenge for universities is to make such activities central to their mainstream policies, suggesting that this requires the removal by government of uncertainties concerning resourcing for these areas of work.

This interpretation of the third arm has an explicit connection with the civil and community domain illustrated in the following reflections of respondents.

In the work I do these terms signify linkages with civil society, participation from community groups etc..

(UK: 13)

I would understand this as being directly related to community involvement: for example, by widening access to higher education, and by academic staff using their expertise in non-academic settings, such as participation in issues which interest or are important for the wider public, e.g. through membership of committees.

(UK: 17)

I'd say something like the civil mission to respond to the needs of the various communities served by the university for higher education, but not necessarily as part of structured HE qualifications, around issues of social justice.

(UK: 5)

Some of the respondents made a connection with adult education, continuing education and extra-mural forms of provision.

. . . I am certainly familiar with the idea that universities as (still essentially) public and collectively funded institutions should have a broader 'civil mission'. Traditionally, this has been operationalized particularly, but not exclusively, by university adult education in the form of 'extramural' classes, extension programmes and a broad range of consultancy and community development activities.

(UK: 11)

In Germany, in the last years, the term 'third arm' or 'third mission' of higher education has been often discussed in the meaning of continuing higher education as a new mission of higher education, supplementing teaching and research as the other two functions of higher education. Traditionally, the German university, based on Humboldt's model of higher education, did not embrace any social service function.

(Germany: 19)

There are clearly points of overlap between the four different interpretations of the third arm of higher education outlined here – knowledge transfer, default, widening participation, and civil and community. Furthermore, they are not necessarily mutually exclusive – it is rather a question of degree and emphasis. In the next section I attempt to tease out these issues further by focusing on perceptions of trends over recent years in relation to connections between universities and civil society.

Perceptions of trends

Respondents were invited to comment on their perception of trends both across the system and at the level of their own institution in relation to support for community and civil society involvement. In broad terms three trends were highlighted: first, a growing emphasis by universities on public relations and a rather pragmatic recognition of the potential goodwill value represented by community and civil activities; second, a narrowing of external activities from broader civil engagement to the economic dimensions of third arm activity; and third, more complex patterns were identified, with some areas of activity perceived to be receiving support possibly at the expense of others.

In relation to the first trend some of the comments point to the valuing by universities of civil and community activities as good public relations. In this sense universities may be little different to most large corporations – trying to best position themselves in what Marsden and Andriof term the 'reputation market place' (1998).

I suspect it would make sense for me if it [the third mission] was – to extend the triad – similar to the 'triple bottom line' where the corporate world shows or is meant to show an ethical responsibility/ecological sensitivity as well as its traditional capitalist concerns.

(Australia: 1)

Higher education leaders realize that financial support by the government increasingly depends on the attitudes of the general public. Hence the attempts to become more 'popular' [through increasing involvement in commercial continuing education and co-operation with adult education organisations].

(Austria: 12)

Universities only think about it when they start losing legitimacy.

(New Zealand: 4)

The second trend identified in responses concerned what was perceived to be a narrowing of university-community relations towards the economic knowledge-transfer quadrant of figure 10.2. This tended to be particularly associated with issues of income generation and perceived economic benefit to universities.

> In relation to community and civic society links, I don't think these have received significant support recently because they would often need subsidising – unlike employer links in theory (we assume profit making companies will fund things they see a value in) – and continuity of staffing resource, which they haven't had.
>
> (UK: 14)

> But this [growing commercialisation] has squeezed more traditional views of continuing education as the third activity of universities, which is probably what I would think of first. But then it was always a somewhat withered arm in comparison to its more muscular compatriots of teaching and research.
>
> (UK: 7)

> In relation to community and civic society links, I don't think these have received significant support recently, because they would often need subsidising – unlike employer links in theory (we assume profit making companies will fund things they see a value in) – and continuity of staffing resource, which they haven't had.
>
> (UK: 18)

The broader policy context is highlighted as the main reason for such perceived trends.

> In general terms, I think that in recent years universities have become both more introverted (in how they think about their work and who it's for) and more competitive (in how they relate to the system of higher education as a whole). This trend is, of course, policy-driven, e.g. through the emphasis on research and teaching (no 'third arm' here – unless it can be marketised, in which case it becomes something different).
>
> (UK: 11)

> Overall, therefore, it seems to me that there has been a marked decline in the Universities' commitment to liberal principles and practices overall; this is not to say that such things have disappeared or indeed will disappear. It is, however, the case that such negative trends reflect inevitably the wider social and political context in which they take place.
>
> (UK: 8)

The third trend identified in the responses reflected a more complex pattern whereby some aspects of university-community and civil society connections were perceived as being strengthened while support for others may simultaneously be declining.

It also depends on how you judge university activities. In some ways with some universities having more money coming in from other sources than government, any additional activity – patents, knowledge transfer, etc – is going to constitute an important range of additional activities. In some ways, without commercialisation, universities would have been in a worse state than they are.

(UK: 7)

I am certainly aware of the 'third arm' and its increasing importance . . . Of course there is nothing new about much of this activity. Adult education might be considered as a third arm in its own right. What is perhaps new is the emphasis on business links – possibly in a cynical move to shore up the declining amount of state funding.

(UK: 9)

Supported in general terms by government/SHEFC desires to address social exclusion and injustice and pursue wealth and knowledge creation roles of HE sector; hindered by failure to supply resources to assist.

(UK: 6)

So, on balance, a mixed picture is described by respondents with, at best, perceived policy issues not being followed through in practice. At worst, threats to valuable activities are perceived.

Conclusion: a withered or a muscular arm?

The focus of this chapter has been on the potential contribution which the academy can make to supporting and assisting in (re)creating civil society. The observations of a number of experts working with this agenda suggest something of a paradox. On the one hand the rhetoric of community features high on policy agendas, while at the same time the force of other factors – in particular pressure for research grades, undergraduate and post-graduate teaching, the desire for business and employer connections and the need for income generation – may actually threaten many activities associated with the top right quadrant in figure 10.2.

One of the respondents cited above suggested that the third arm has always tended to be a somewhat 'withered arm' in comparison to its more 'muscular compatriots' of teaching and research. While this may well be the case, the analysis here suggests the need to delve further to explore the relative strengths of different dimensions of the third arm itself – some of which appear to be more muscular than others.

This assessment of the analytic and/or practical value of the concept of the third arm of higher education is thus mixed. It is useful from the perspective of focusing attention outwith the academy to its connections with a wide range of external communities. It has the advantage of being open to flexible interpretation. However, this flexibility also leaves it vulnerable to 'colonization' by stronger elements, specifically the economic interests associated with the market. It is interesting to note that the Chief Executive of the Higher Education Funding Council for England identifies *four* missions for higher education – teaching, research, knowledge transfer and widening participation (Newby 2002). This conception raises the question as to whether it is adequate to leave the civil and community focus as implicit. The views expressed by a selection of experts active in these areas suggest that it may not be.

From the perspective, therefore, of capacity building with disadvantaged sections of society and the civil role of higher education without greater attention to these issues, might universities be in danger of becoming, in Beck's term, 'zombie' institutions (Beck and Gernsheim 2001: 203)? Or might universities have something to learn from one of their weaker partners – adult education – in the world of post-compulsory education and training?

> Adult education, for all its individualism, has retained some uneasy equilibrium between the individual and the civic-political, especially in its international literature. Higher education by contrast has succumbed more fully to fragmentary individualism. Social and civic dimensions feature rather little in mission statements and the curriculum. Seen thus the university appears to reflect the retreat from the collectivity (the 'welfare state') in favour of the same individualistic economic rationalism which characterizes much of its management.
>
> (Duke 2002: 18–19)

If the academy is to make a social contribution to helping to redress Bauman's (1999) unholy trinity of uncertainty, insecurity and unsafety, perhaps we could do worse than return to Robinson's (1968) vision of the 'people's university' . . . or even further back to that expressed by Geddes.

> Education is not merely by and for the sake of thought, it is in a still higher degree by and for the sake of action. Just as the man of science must think and experiment alternately so to must the artist, author and scholar alternate creation or study with participation in the life around them. For it is only by thinking things out as one lives them, and living things out as one thinks them that a man or a society can really be said to think or even live at all (Lecture given by Geddes in Edinburgh at the Ninth Summer School Meeting in August 1895 – which was open to women as well as men).
>
> (Boardman 1994: 159)

Methodological note

The views of 20 UK and international academics expert in the area of higher education – civil society connections were ascertained as the first part of a Delphi study. The relevant questions were: 'What do you understand by the terms "third arm" or "third mission" of higher education?' and 'In relation to community and civil society links, to what extent do you think these have been supported, hindered or otherwise in recent years?' In the latter case they were invited to make a distinction, if they saw one, between trends across the system as a whole and at the level of their own institution. All of the respondents were at the level of professor, reader or equivalent and all were located in academic departments. Some minor editing has been undertaken where the participant's first language was not English. In terms of disciplinary backgrounds, most were from the social sciences and arts – including adult education, cultural studies, economics, education, history, law, philosophy, politics, psychology and urban studies. Almost all had experience of working in more than one institution of higher education, a small number had worked in five or more.

11

The university and life-chances

David Watson

> Universities have a remarkable record of institutional survival. But at times throughout their long history they have lost the plot and the real action has moved elsewhere.
>
> Roger Waterhouse, Vice-Chancellor of the University of Derby,
> in the *Times Higher*, 20 and 27 December 2002, p.14

This chapter is about what Roger Waterhouse would call 'recovering the plot'.

Universities have always changed in response to perceived social and economic needs, and they have always remained the same. There has always been both a worldly, 'instrumental' side to our business and an independent, deeply ethical side. This has meant a permanent ebb and flow between continuity and change in the practice, the self-image, and the external reputation of universities. It has also meant that universities are subject to a peculiar dialectic of 'leadership and lag', admirably captured by Donald Kennedy in his *Academic Duty*.

> Universities are in a dynamic equilibrium with society. On the one hand they appear to lag behind it, acting as conservators of its history and architects of its highest cultural attainments. On the other hand, they are seen as leaders, adventuring into new knowledge domains, developing transforming technologies, and serving as the seedbed for novel and often disturbing ideas.
>
> Both of these roles are part of the university's academic duty.
>
> (Kennedy 1997: 265)

In the twenty-first century a novel combination of external forces appears to bear down on universities. Some of the pressures come from the state, especially as it expects a return from increased investment. More come from the development of a knowledge-based economy, fuelled by developments in information and communications technologies, especially as it draws external interests deeper into the life of the university. 'Knowledge management' and the 'knowledge society' are contested concepts within the academy, along with notions like 'living on thin air' and the 'weightless economy' (Armistead and Meakins 2002). What is not contested is the historical centrality of universities and colleges in the creation and evaluation of socially and economically relevant knowledge. What *has* changed is the size, scope and connectivity of the information and knowledge universe to which academics and their special communities of inquiry contribute. In other words, universities and colleges are necessarily engaged in the evolution of a knowledge society, whether they like it or not.

One of the major concerns, internationally, is with socioeconomic patterns of participation and their relevance for social polarization. The gap between those with access to education and resulting skills, to information, and to influence and those without is widening, not narrowing. Many societies are on their way towards creating what the sociologist Martin Trow called 'universal' systems of higher education (with age participation rates of over 40 per cent), but exclusively for the middle class (Trow 1973).

In the UK, as demonstrated in the editors' introduction as well as chapters one and two, good progress has been made on many aspects of diversity in the student population: gender, age, race and ethnicity, disability and so on. However, in common with most other expanding systems, the question of class has proved particularly intractable. 'Widening' rather than just expanding higher education opportunity has become a political priority, up there with meeting the needs of a knowledge economy. It lies behind one of the New Labour Government's most celebrated second term targets, that 'by the end of the decade, 50 per cent of young people should have the opportunity to benefit from higher education by the time they reach 30 years of age' (Estelle Morris [then Secretary of State for Education and Skills] to David Young [Chair of HEFCE] 29 November 2001). In the 2003 White Paper, *The Future of Higher Education*, while the 50 per cent target appears to have receded a little (the phrase is now 'towards 50 per cent'), the implications of widening and not just increasing participation are frontally addressed (DfES 2003: 57, 67–75).

Detailed analysis of this superficially simple target shows some of the difficulties. As Ramsden and Brown have identified in their study for Universities UK (UUK), not only will demographic change require an additional number of students (estimated at 27,000) for the country (England) to stand still (at 41.5 per cent of 17- to 30-year-olds), but specific hurdles remain. For example, the matriculation 'hinge' at Level 3 (the 'high school graduation' level) is itself hugely skewed: while 61 per cent of 19-year-olds with parents in non-manual occupations have such qualifications, only 37 per cent of children of non-manual workers do so (UUK 2002c).

Fundamentally, of course, the middle-class domination arises because higher education is a positional good. Its benefits are not only economic (as in the so-called 'graduate premium' of lifetime earnings), but also relate to broader aspects of health, happiness, community security and democratic tolerance. These 'wider benefits of learning' have been explored in depth in the British case, as discussed below (HEFCE 2001).

Meanwhile, the resulting apparent 'educational inflation' can lead to some paradoxical outcomes. The authors of *Education and Democratic Citizenship in America* establish that a simple additive model of educational success increases democratic tolerance (as measured through attitude surveys). But it does little for social equality or improving material life-chances. They conclude with a riveting question: 'does competition for educational advantage result in more education than we can afford?' As in a competitive framework for social position educational attainment rates are pressed higher and higher 'in this way, individual rationality may be leading to collective irrationality' (Nie et al. 1996: 194–6).

Participation can also have an effect on public confidence in the value of higher education. In the UK higher education is generally regarded in the popular media with a mixture of envy and contempt. Negative stories – about student behaviour, about novel degrees, about drop-out and the like – can rapidly become moral panics. The contrast with the United States is instructive, where generally university and college stories have an easier ride than they deserve. What is more, this can feed through into positive public attitudes, for example towards science, as shown in figure 11.1 (King 2002).

	% agreement	
	UK 2000[1]	US 2001[2]
S and T make our lives better	67	86
Science makes our lives change too fast	44	38
The benefits of science are greater than harmful effects	43	72
Science research should be supported by the Government (even if no immediate benefits)	72	82
It is important for me to know about science	59	84

[1] Science and the Public 2000
[2] NSF Science and engineering indicators 2002

Figure 11.1   Public attitudes to science and technology (S and T): UK/US comparison

Source: King 2002

There is a powerful demographic base to this divergence. As a recent comparative study from the UK Learning and Skills Research Centre (LSRC) notes, 'most Americans – sooner or later – enrol in College'. Among those who graduated from high school in 1992, 62 per cent had enrolled in some form of tertiary education by 1994 (LSRC 2002: 16). The UK government's 50 per cent target for full or part-time enrolments of under-30s pales into insignificance alongside this achievement, but even here the inexorable penetration of adult life by those with (largely positive) experience of higher education could be predicted to have the same effect.

As for Waterhouse's prediction of the 'action moving elsewhere', universities have for almost the first time in their collective history to deal with the emergence of rival centres of reference. These include corporate universities, commercial accreditation of training courses, and assumption of responsibility for both initial accreditation and continuing professional development by professional and statutory bodies (including in direct competition with higher education institutions). In the UK, both the University for Industry (UfI) and the National Health Service University (NHSU) are examples of officially sponsored entryism. However, such public and private initiatives may find it equally hard to survive and prosper. The UfI has sensibly re-branded itself as an adult advisory service (LearnDirect), and the 'for-profit' sector in the USA has, after an initial boom, fallen upon hard times. During the academic year 2002–03 the *Chronicle of Higher Education* is filled with stories of prestigious American universities cutting their losses on previously hyped for-profit subsidiaries (see stories on Temple [20 July], NYUonline [December 12], and Columbia [7 January], as well as the despairing lead article 'Is Anyone Making Money on Distance Learning?' [16 January 2003]). The latest casualty is the system-wide admissions system's off-shoot: Collegeboard.com (15 January 2003).

Meanwhile, it is tempting (and in some cases easy) for institutional leaders to see such extrinsic influences as their main challenge, to be bought or seen off. The resulting perceived pattern of external forces has had two principal effects on university strategy.

The first is an almost overwhelming fixation on utility, or the instrumentality of the operation. Governments have led the way, by focusing on economic returns as the predominant, if not the sole, justification for expansion and public investment.

A powerful philosophical critique of this development is set out in Richard Taylor et al.'s *For a Radical Higher Education*. For them:

> At present, 'business' in all its many guises has a strong involvement in both the governance and the cultural definition of higher education. Ever since the neo-liberal heyday of Reagan and Thatcher in the 1980s, the governments of the major capitalist nations have sought to involve business and its perspectives in all aspects of public life. Higher education – and education more generally – is no exception. Radical educators should widen community representation and involvement so that the *whole* community is involved in the life, and thus the culture, of institutions.
>
> (Taylor et al. 2002: 161)

Such a diagnosis of the problem (even if it is allied to a dramatically different set of remedies) is strongly supported by Alison Wolf's *Does*

Education Matter? Myths About Education and Economic Growth. In it she puts forward an arresting counter-hypothesis to the official line: 'could it be that growth causes education rather than the other way around?' In practical terms she concludes that 'fine-tuning or kick-starting the economy via state-run vocational education is a misplaced endeavour' (Wolf 2002: 44, 97).

There are some palpable hits in Wolf's analysis. Political, professional and business-led hopes for the kinds of reforms in post-compulsory vocational education and training in the UK since the 1960s can be shown to rest on naïve assumptions: about skills needs; about supply-side reform of courses and curriculum; and about personal and social rates of return to such qualifications. In the course of two decades an approach based upon an admittedly weakening apprenticeship and in-service training model of formation is shown to have been swept away by the full panoply of National Vocational Qualifications (NVQ). Simultaneously, the ineffectiveness of short-term central micro-management is starkly demonstrated.

'Asking business', via such establishment organs as the Confederation of British Industry (CBI), has notably failed, as evidenced by their performance once 'inside' the resulting system. In this sense Wolf's 'silver bullet' alternative to government-supported training seems odd. It is (following Edmund Phelps) 'simply to subsidize jobs' (Wolf 2002: 255). The prospect of the increasing tendency of UK employers to take on 16-year-old school leavers into minimum wage jobs where they offer no training at all being endorsed in this way is breathtaking.

The waste within the vocational qualification bureaucracy has been remarkable: for example, the development and approval of 364 NVQs which have attracted no students at all. Meanwhile, the lack of trust in 'consumers' and a culture of denial of less than satisfactory outcomes have become a consensual and bipartisan feature of political discussion (Wolf 2002: 56, 91, 99, 129, 131). Above all, there has been a consistent failure to understand how students and their families (Wolf speaks of 'the rational teenager') understand only too well how the real progress towards personal prosperity is achieved. This is overwhelmingly via general further and higher education and not through end-stopped, apparently backward-looking vocational routes (79, 87, 177). Nor is this just a feature of UK society, as the case of Germany – often prayed in aid in precisely the opposite direction – shows (88). The charge that vocational further education is 'for other people's children' draws blood.

Does Education Matter? has enjoyed a notable *succès d'estime* (see, for example, the superlatives heaped upon it in *The Economist* [8 June 2002] and the *Times Higher Education Supplement* [13 December 2002]). Calmer and more knowledgeable critics will, however, be more sceptical about this particular prophet crying in the wilderness. The major theoretical plank of the argument – about the personal and collective contradictions of educational inflation – were authoritatively articulated as far back as the 1970s, in work not cited here. For example, in 1972 Lester Thurow identified the role of education as 'a defensive expenditure necessary to protect one's "market share" '. According to his rule, 'the larger the class of educated labor and the more rapidly it grows, the more such defensive expenditures become imperative' (quoted in Nie 1996: 105).

Meanwhile, from the perspective of British higher education, to which Wolf extends her 'slash-and-burn' critique from vocational and further education, there are some serious blind-spots in the book.

First, in contrast to Taylor et al., there is a fatal failure to understand the emancipatory power of higher education. Wolf ignores the work of her colleagues at the Institute of Education on the 'wider benefits' of higher education in improving non-economic personal and social returns to higher education, in areas like, health, crime, and democratic participation. The Wider Benefits of Learning project responsibly corrects for the potential non-educational inputs (such as cognitive ability and family wealth), and shows particularly strong returns for women (HEFCE 2001). The project is also forensically precise about the downsides: like the greater propensity to depressive illness of males who enter higher education and fail to complete than among their lower-achieving peers (ibid.: 37). Internationally, Wolf ignores similar results for the USA from the study by Nie et al. (cited above).

Other relevant research, on the capacity of graduates in work – from all kinds of institutions – to grow their jobs, and make use of occupationally relevant parts of their courses, once established on a career path, is also apparently disregarded. Evidence is only now emerging in the UK of the real effect of the expansion of the late 1980s and 1990s on the careers of graduates. There is new evidence of graduates in work using their skills, growing the job, and continuing to reap significant material benefits. For example, an important survey from Warwick's Institute for Employment Research showed 71 per cent of graduates satisfied with their careers 18 months after graduation. Eighty-nine per cent believe that they are making appropriate use of their graduate skills and knowledge (Purcell et al. 1999).

This has now been invaluably supplemented by the first large-scale study of careers three years after graduation of the class of 1995. *Moving On* shows not only high rates of employment three and a half years after graduation, but also 82 per cent of employed graduates reporting that they were using knowledge and skills developed during their undergraduate courses in their current jobs. Interestingly, only 65 per cent of the jobs held are classed as 'graduate' on traditional criteria. Such results not only begin to confirm the social and economic 'dividend' of investing in higher education (many of these graduates are clearly 'growing' their jobs), but also damaging limitations of analyses that rely on outmoded classifications of what a 'graduate job' really is (Elias et al. 1999). A final source of comfort from *Moving On* is the discovery that the distinction between 'old' and 'new' universities in explaining success in initial employment – and the evidence for perceived institutional status weighing heavily for employers at that stage – dissolves rapidly after three years. The report shows no significant difference between the experience of unemployment of those from 'old' and 'new' universities, and much stronger association of success with the type of course undertaken and the class of degree attained (ibid.: 7). (See also the discussion of these reports in chapter eight.)

The main problem with Wolf's account is thus the failure to take seriously the positive effects of the UK's significant advance in higher education participation. Such outcomes are suppressed in her account in favour of the special problems of elite (and expensive) institutions at one end of the sector, and the small number of cases of market and quality failure at the other. At the top end Wolf is probably at one with Baroness Shirley Williams in her declaration that 'I doubt whether there are any internationally first-rate universities left in Britain: perhaps a few departments here and there' (*Prospect*, January 2003). (Williams was, of course, Secretary of State for Education and Science at precisely the time when, in the 1970s, Wolf sees the Manpower Services Commission as having led us all up the garden path.) As in Williams' intervention, no evidence is cited for this relative decline in the global race except for complaints about the relative levels of academic salaries (Wolf 2002: 221). Counter-evidence, for example about the continuing strength of British research, is buried in footnotes (ibid.: note 22 on p. 286). At the other end of the sector, the very small number of management and institutional failures in higher education (as opposed to further education) are re-hashed. The strong performance of the middle ground (in completion rates, employment destinations, and even in contributing significantly to the overseas earnings which Wolf is keen to maintain) empirically belies the charge of 'across the board second class status' (Wolf 2002: 225, 219; see also Watson 2002, and UUK 2002b: 29).

How could Wolf have reached such persuasive conclusions about vocational and further education, and fall prey to such lazy prejudices about higher education? To take just one example, it is simply not true that the 466 pages of the Dearing Report state and then ignore the question of 'quality of life' or that 'the background papers it commissioned are devoted exclusively to issues of economics and access'. A footnote claims to list the latter but omits at least half of them, covering topics like higher education in other countries, research in the arts and humanities, teaching and support staff surveys, full and part-time student surveys, teacher education, comparative qualification frameworks, and so on (Wolf 2002: 255, 290). The answer might lie in another version of 'other people's children'. There is a powerful sense here of pulling up the ladder; of seeking to maintain an image of elite higher education in which any deviation from the Oxbridge model is just not good enough. This is, of course, in the tradition of a cultural conservatism about higher education with a long and ironically left-wing provenance (see Rustin 1994 and Foster 1994 for examples).

To conclude this discussion of Wolf's book by accentuating the positive, there is another key message in *Does Education Matter?* of critical significance to this volume. Where education *does* matter especially is in the soundness or otherwise of the base in compulsory schooling, 'of providing citizens with a good basic education at primary and secondary level' (Wolf 2002: 256; see also 11, 37 and 159). Much of what has gone wrong here has led to false trails and policy failures, principally through a 'compensatory' approach to training in particular and to vocational further education in general. Much of what has to be put right depends upon a flexible, accessible and democratic system of higher education, not least through its responsibilities to support the other parts of the public service (like school teaching, health and community development).

The second pathology has been to regard almost all of the problems – and hence also their remedies – as originating outside the academy. For example, these are the key predictions made by university leaders, based upon a recent consultation led by the European University Association (EUA) and American Council on Education (ACE). This is what US, Canadian and European leaders said was going to happen to us:

- greater emphasis on the higher education (HE) role in workforce preparation than in social development and cultural identity;
- more 'borderless' provision;
- policy interest in HE as a social investment;
- more partnerships with business and 'non-educational' organizations;
- government insistence on accountability through 'outcome-orientated quality assessments';
- access dependent upon technology because 'traditional modes of instruction cannot fill the need';
- competition and the market will prevent 'brand-name' domination;
- national governments to maintain their influence;
- increase in instruction in English;
- governance and decision-making patterns to inhibit an 'institution's ability to change';
- significant increase in inter-institutional collaboration.

(EUA/ACE 2002: 5)

Fundamentally, these (and other such) witnesses overestimate the extrinsic influences and underestimate the intrinsic influences on the development of the university in the knowledge society. Such a conclusion is consonant with theory about the knowledge society itself. In this field as elsewhere (as discussed in the editors' introduction and for example in chapter seven in relation to the use of information and communication technology [ICT]', the participants out-perform (in the sense of being ahead of) the policymakers in terms of relative influence on the changing shape of the system.

The conceptual framework provided by the discussion of 'life-chances' in this volume requires, however, a different focus, on the more intrinsic pressures brought about by changing interests of the members of the academic community itself: the students, the staff, and their leaders.

First, there is a set of *epistemological* challenges, based in the ways in which teachers and researchers view the world. There have been two influential theoretical interventions on this theme.

The first is the now canonic analysis by Michael Gibbons and his collaborators. They see an inexorable and irreversible shift from 'mode 1' thinking (pure, disciplinary, homogeneous, expert-led, supply-driven, hierarchical, peer-reviewed, and almost exclusively university-based) to 'mode 2' (applied, problem-centred, trans-disciplinary, heterogeneous, hybrid, demand-driven, entrepreneurial, network-embedded etc.) (Gibbons et al. 1994).

The second, more contested, thesis is Ron Barnett's account of 'the death of the university' in the face of 'supercomplexity'. Unlike 'mode 1 to mode 2,' this may be overstated. The key text, *Realizing the University*, starts with a ringing call for a clean break with the past; 'the death is *required*' (emphasis in original). And yet we are constantly reminded that 'the old lives on within the new' (Barnett 1999: 11). How, for example, does the array of new 'values' for the age of super-complexity really differ from those we have been traditionally committed to (at least in theory)?

> What is required is the capacity to tame supercomplexity, to inject a value structure into it even as all value structures are put into the dock. The university has to hold on to the value system that helped to generate supercomplexity – of openness, courage, tolerance and so on – even as supercomplexity puts these same values under the microscope. Super-complexity deprives us of a value anchorage for answering such challenges. The value background that spawned supercomplexity, on the other hand, can help us to just that. The values implicit in rational critical dialogue helped to generate supercomplexity and they can help to keep supercomplexity in its place . . . The ladder of the university's value background has to be kept in place, not kicked away.
>
> (Barnett 1999: 83)

More recently, Barnett has conceded 'that the university is in considerable difficulty but that we may just be able to sustain it' (Barnett 2003: 1). His latest work brings him full circle, back to an image of the university as a community in which the ideals of 'generosity, openness, self-critique, reasonableness, tolerance and imagination' are realised rather than merely latent (ibid.: 178).

Several of these developments have implications for the *curriculum*. First there is the need to adapt to changing patterns of student choice (UUK 2002b: 9). Modern students are canny consumers: remember Wolf's 'rational teenager'. They need to be, especially as an increasing proportion of new workforce entrants are graduates (the latest [2002] DfES figures suggest that 24.6 per cent of the working population have a degree, as opposed to 20.9 per cent in 1997 [*THES* 31 January 2003: 4]). Indeed, they are regularly more effective readers of the emerging employment scene than either the providing institutions or external stakeholders such as government and employers. Nor are they respecters of traditional disciplinary or professional boundaries. The success of 'media studies' in the UK (included in Figure 11.2 within Librarianship and Information Sciences) is probably the most graphic cautionary tale. The rapid growth of such courses led initially to

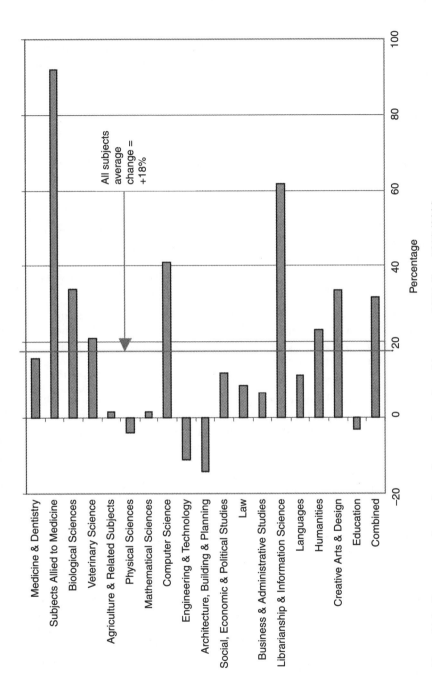

Figure 11.2 Percentage change in student numbers by subject area, 1994/5 to 1999/2000
Source: UUK (2002b)

popular and political outrage; the graduates are now more likely to be employed in occupations related to their degree studies than those who read law.

Providers also have to respond to the effect of revised preparation and expectations of students, not least as a result of their experience of ICT. Jason Frand's seminal essay on 'the information-age mindset' is, I think the most arresting expression of this dilemma. As he writes:

> Most students entering our colleges and universities today are younger than the microcomputer, are more comfortable working on a keyboard than writing in a spiral notebook, and are happier reading from a computer screen than from paper in hand. For them, constant connectivity – being in touch with friends and family at any time and from any place – is of the utmost importance.
>
> (Frand 2000: 15)

He goes on to identify 'ten attributes reflecting values and behaviors' of the resulting mindset, as set out in figure 11.2. The driving concept is borrowed from Alan Kay of Xerox: 'technology is anything that isn't around when you are born'. Many of the other nine are familiar to the parents and teachers of early twenty-first-century teenagers. As Frand observes:

> I can always tell if people are from 'my' generation or the 'Nintendo' generation by how they approach a new software package. Do they check out the menus and the manual first, or do they begin typing and then search for what they want whenever they want it?
>
> (ibid.: 17)

Other attributes are: 'Internet better than TV' (he notes that during 1998, for the first time, American teenagers watched less TV than the previous year, having converted to the web); 'reality no longer real' (as, for example, 'photography can no longer be trusted'); 'doing rather than knowing' ('as our students enter the workplace, the ability to deal with complex and often ambiguous information will be more important than simply knowing a lot of facts'); 'multitasking'; 'typing rather than handwriting'; 'staying connected'; 'zero tolerance for delays'; and 'consumer/creator blurring' (in the world of cut and paste) (ibid.: 16–18).

What is more (and as emphasized in chapter nine), these new students will be global citizens. Too much of the current rhetoric (and of the resulting action) seems to be about global higher education as a simple market, and about the bottom line for institutions.

This avoids having to face up to several things. First there is the damage done by colonial-style intervention which 'substitutes' for traditional university functions in developing countries. An example is in research, where as King (2002) points out, a proper domestic capacity is needed to pull through a properly qualified academic workforce. This connects with the need to bring up to date the historical obligation of more advanced systems of higher education to assist less developed systems to progress.

Meanwhile the development of European and North American models of intellectual property can be seen as a pre-emptive strike (or, even worse, as asset-stripping). As Rajesh Kochhar of the Indian National Institute of Science, Technology and Development writes:

Today when we talk of globally applicable laws, no national laws, least of all American laws, can serve as a role model. This is because so far laws have been made to safeguard national or local interests. Global laws require fresh thinking. When the world was Euro-centric, it was easy to define what was new. If Europe did not know of it, it did not exist before: the 'first European to produce metallic zinc' could be granted a patent (1738), but not the inventor of the telescope 100 years previously, 'on the ground that it is evident that several others have knowledge of its invention.' By the same logic, if the knowledge is available anywhere in the world today, it should not be possible to patent it.

(Kochhar 2002)

Fourth, there is the danger of a kind of reverse saturation of domestic markets by under-priced and sometimes shoddy goods in the form of e-learning (a first world revenge for cheap trainers). The General Agreement of Trade in Services (GATS), now being consulted upon by the World Trade Organization (WTO) opens up the possibility of enforced access to domestic educational markets in precisely this way. Finally and, in the long term perhaps most serious, is the failure adequately to address those parts of the modern university curriculum that should lead to responsible global citizenship. As Stanley Katz has recently inquired, 'do we in the universities believe that we have a mission beyond the functional, that we need to aspire to more than Excellence?' (Katz 2002).

A recent small-scale but conceptually rich study has explored such questions from a student perspective (Ahier et al. 2002). The results are encouraging. John Ahier and his collaborators have tested views of their 'future lives as employees and citizens' held by final year students at one 'old' and one 'new' English university (Cambridge and Anglia Polytechnic University). Despite confirmation of the strong instrumentality in choice of subject and institution alluded to above, such priorities do not seem to have corroded this generation of students' strong sense of a 'social sphere' to which they contribute and of 'sociality' more generally.

In their speech, our respondents recognised four circuits: (i) those of student peers; (ii) the intergenerational; (iii) that of imagined 'abstract others' as recipients of state welfare; (iv) and the formal constitutional dimension of their relationship to state and government. These circuits were governed by principles such as fairness, altruism, reciprocity and responsibility that we will sum up in the more general term, 'mutuality.' . . . The moralising of extended relationships in this manner counters both the fears of those who believe that the absence of a language of formal citizenship indicates privatised withdrawal and those who would wish to celebrate the primacy of calculative individualism.

(Ahier et al.: 141)

In other words, while the current generation of British students – like many elsewhere in the world – have to think long and hard about their economic life-chances, it is crude and inaccurate to typecast them as 'Thatcher's children'. Moreover, this stance is not incompatible with the decline of both interest and confidence in traditional political activity (often previously seen as a proxy for student citizenship). The authors describe their interviewees' 'desire to retain a sense of themselves as moral actors' as well as 'a sense of a civil society beyond the narrowly political that provides the space in which that desire can be lived out' (ibid.: 153). (For a less optimistic prognosis, see Silver and Silver 1997: 147–62.)

As for staff perspectives, there are serious issues about the demography and organization of the academic profession itself. A recent survey by the Higher Education Funding Council for England demonstrates that as it has grown it has become younger and more likely to have experience outside as well as inside the academy (HEFCE 2002: 11). The main message of figure 11.3 is about the combined effects of generational change and of expansion. As a cohort of academics brought into the profession by an earlier spurt of expansion retires at the same time as the system anticipates a new spurt, turnover will be rapid. In these circumstances 'internal' socialization is likely to weaken and new perspectives to gain greater purchase.

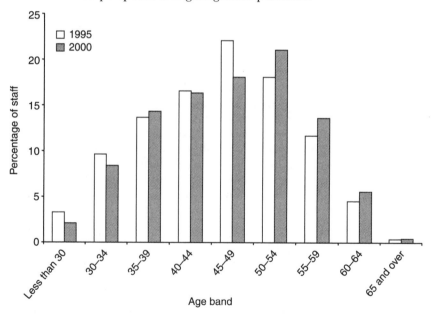

Figure 11.3 Age profile of permanent academic staff: 1995 and 2000

Source: HEFCE (2002)

In a study of the age profile of the academic workforce throughout the English-speaking world, Roderick Floud has demonstrated the global effect of changes like these. Because so many systems experienced a spurt in the 1960s and 1970s, the retirement effect is happening simultaneously. In fact, the UK may be relatively well placed, with 'only 20 per cent over 55, compared with 30 per cent in the USA and Canada. New Zealand and Australia have about 35 per cent aged 50 and over' (Floud 2002). Further plans for expansion, like the UK 50 per cent target, will add additional pressures (the HEFCE calculates the need for another 17,000 teachers to support this target, in addition to the 19,000 replacing retirees in the next decade).

As academics have to cope with a wider range of challenges – in teaching, in research and in support of the 'third-arm' dimension explored in chapter ten – it seems plausible to expect that traditional values and commitments will change. Paul Coaldrake has neatly captured the resulting dilemma:

> In the main, academic work has stretched rather than adapted to meet the challenges posed by transformations of the higher education sector. The preference of many universities and individual academics is to allow accumulation and accretion rather than to undertake the more difficult and threatening task of making strategic choices and reconceptualising what it means to be an effective and productive academic.
>
> (Coaldrake 2000: 16)

In conflict with the mindset described above of many higher education leaders, the 'life-chances' analysis requires response to deep cultural changes embedded within the academic enterprise itself. If correct, this thesis has some important consequences for university leadership, for staff, students, and their sponsors.

To take university leaders as a case in point: dealing successfully with external influences, as it were 'from above,' in the interests of preserving the *status quo* (that is, achieving 'institutional comfort') may turn out to be a Pyrrhic victory, if the internal pressures for change, as it were 'from below', have meanwhile transformed the system. There is something reminiscent here of generals fighting the last war, of industrialists solving yesterday's problems, and of politicians only listening to people over 40.

So what should be done? The main argument advanced here is that a 'life-chances' perspective usefully refreshes the eternal debate about the reinvention of the university. It does so principally by focusing on the needs, capabilities and aspirations of the actual and potential members of the university community. Hence management and leadership must be as much about understanding these forces as about defending the economic interests and the independence of the university at its outer frontiers.

Among the lessons learned are the following:

- the priority of partnership working – with other public services (notably 'compulsory' education), with other higher education institutions (on such underdeveloped national priorities as a mutually respected credit system and qualification framework), and with the wider range of 'users' of the university's services (such as employers and professional services);

- the value of institutional self-study, for example, in really understanding not only the preferences of students and staff but also the impact of changes in their prior and current experience;
- the need to build on these insights through a flexible and responsive curriculum;
- recognition of the impact of success or failure in the university's core mission for other social and economic spheres which rely on it (from such basic matters as the supply of appropriately qualified and confident personnel – such as teachers and health professionals – to the global demands of knowledge-based trade and industry); and
- the importance of 'making the case', of building public and political confidence in a responsible, imaginative and culturally diverse sector.

As indicated in our introduction, UK higher education has made an honourable contribution to the development of lifelong learning. With attention to this agenda, it can also begin to fulfil its obligations to the lifewide dimension.

12

Learning through life – higher education and the lifecourse of individuals

Andrew Pollard

This chapter describes an evolving perspective on lifewide and lifelong dimensions of learner experience, with particular reference to higher education. It starts from a recognition that the growth of student numbers in UK higher education in recent years has produced far more diversity among individual learners. The range of students' *prior* learning experiences has become a significant challenge for teachers and lecturers, and the contribution of higher education to students' *futures* cannot be directly anticipated. However, considering some lifewide and lifelong dimensions of higher education may offer a useful, overarching sense of perspective. It may also contribute to an appreciation of the significance of higher education in people's lives.

I thus want to offer some concepts and ideas as a means of highlighting and interpreting some significant lifewide and lifelong factors, as they affect the progressive development of knowledge, understanding, values and identity by individual learners. Such issues are, of course, 'educational' in the broadest and most profound sense – reaching beyond the specifics of academic subjects or professional capability.

Lifewide analysis of students as learners requires consideration of a wide range of contextual issues and social influences, many of which are addressed in this book. In this chapter, I will draw attention to some concepts which seem to me to be particularly interesting tools for tracing the implications of lifewide factors for individual learners.

Lifelong analysis highlights temporal and developmental factors, and in this respect I will draw on, and extend, a conceptual framework generated from a 12-year longitudinal study of the strategic biographies of school pupils, by Ann Filer and myself.

One way of conceptualizing these issues is offered in figure 12.1 below. In this model, a generic set of lifewide contextualizing factors surrounds the learner and their learning challenges. Most immediately, learners draw on (and face) their family, friends and instructors. Beyond them, lie the broader social context and historical specific location, the cultural environment

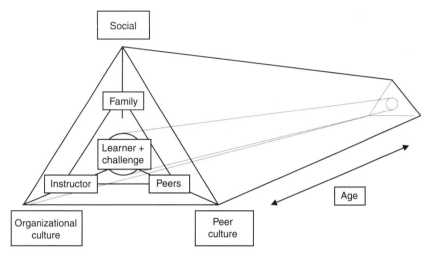

Figure 12.1   The learner through the lifecourse

influencing peers and the organizational culture and imperatives which shape the work of their teachers or superiors. In lifelong terms, at each age and setting through the lifecourse – pre-school, schooling, higher education, employment, retirement, old age – similar factors obtain, moving in or out of prominence but never altogether disappearing.

Such arguments and representations are of interest to me both in terms of contributing to this volume on the changing learning experiences of students in higher education, but also as part of the development of a conceptual framework through which it might be possible, in my role as director, to begin to make sense of ESRC's Teaching and Learning Research Programme as a whole. The Programme's research teams are addressing learning in many educational sectors and the development of ways of theorizing key issues across contexts is thus important. Such issues include, for example, the ways in which social and educational factors constrain or facilitate independent, mastery-oriented dispositions to learn through life; or lead to dependency and low personal esteem.

Lifewide influences on learners and learning

From a sociological perspective, it is impossible to construct a sound analysis of learners and learning without addressing social context. At the start of my longitudinal ethnography, I crystallized these issues around the deceptively simple question: where and when is learning taking place? (see Pollard with Filer 1996).

Descriptive answers to that question can be analysed in various ways, and I identify below three inter-related dimensions:

- Multiple levels of social context – interactional, institutional, local, regional, national, global, and so on.
- Multiple factors structuring social context – geographic, historic, economic, political, ideological, cultural, temporal, and so on.
- Social position, and positioning, of the learner – gender, ethnicity, social class, abilities, and so on.

For example, in this volume Hounsell (chapter five) offers us an interactional analysis of tutor feedback, its effectiveness and changing patterns of use in response to circumstances. As a form of assessment, feedback is also connected to power relationships and social positioning of tutor and student, and thus to institutional practices and national policies. Indeed, Morley (chapter six) shows how students are being reconstructed as consumers by economic and cultural factors around higher education as well as by the restructuring of funding. Such economic factors may gradually come to affect the lived experience of many college and university students, Riddell, Tinklin and Wilson (chapter three) point out that the disabled are a particular, socially positioned group, for whom rights, resources and institutional provision are often imperfectly aligned. Lifewide characteristics of rurality are the focus of Moreland, Chamberlain and Artaraz's chapter four, with particular attention being drawn to the consequences for participation. Finally, we have the broad sweep of Gourley's account of globalization (chapter nine), which demonstrates convincingly the embeddedness of personal student experience within wider social, economic and political factors.

These dimensions – by level, structuring and positioning – provide an analytic device for describing the lifewide contextualization of any learner's experience. In terms of C. Wright Mills' 'sociological imagination' (1959) they constitute the contextualizing 'history' through which 'biography' must be played out.

The conception that influences on learners and learning are 'lifewide' recognizes the significance of social factors on learning, but it is important to avoid any suggestion of social determinism. Indeed, imagination and creativity consistently generates actions which challenge the patterns of behaviour that analysts may predict. Nevertheless, despite these qualifications, there are some ways of conceptualizing patterns of behaviour and making sense of lifewide influences on learning that may be helpful in thinking about the influence of lifewide factors on learners' capacity to interpret experiences and to 'learn'.

In the remainder of this section, I address five such concepts which are of particular interest to me at present. In each case, they reflect a view of learning in terms of the creation and realization of meaning within social, cultural, economic and political contexts. Though this work is clearly incomplete, these concepts provide a contextualizing frame and a tool-kit for use in a developmental model of lifelong identity development.

Significant others

The concept of 'significant others' is long-established as a basic element of symbolic interactionist thought. It reflects the struggle, particularly but not exclusively of the young, to understand oneself (self) in relation to others (society).

Individuals are influenced by those of significance around them. From the reactions of others, they learn about themselves and about expectations and consequences, and they thus come both to distinguish between the 'I' and the 'me', and to build reflexivity and social competence. In the early years, the significance of others may be rooted in physical or emotional dependency or affection – for instance, in relation to parents. During development, the influence of siblings, wider family, peers, teachers, partners, employers, work colleagues, and so on may be seen to significantly increase as the range of social interaction widens. Individual action may also be influenced by remote, or even virtual, culturally significant figures. Through such forms of iterative engagement throughout life, individuals develop a sense of themselves as social actors.

This is a powerful model of socially contextualized learning, but is sometimes interpreted in relatively bounded dyadic ways. For example, a university lecturer may well be regarded as a significant other in relation to a student learner, but the tutor's actual influence is likely to be conditioned by many other factors – not least, by ways in which the student makes sense of and evaluates the knowledge and advice that is offered. Further, if we reflect on the diversity of student backgrounds and experiences, for instance in terms of gender, ethnicity, social class or disability, it is clear that understanding and interpretation is open to a very wide range of other influences.

Networks of meaning

The notion of 'networks of meaning' broadens the interactionist account by conceptualizing human activity and development as a progressive movement between sequential frameworks of understanding. According to Rossetti-Ferreira et al., human 'development occurs by the continuous (re)configuration of nets. In this process, language, knowledge, and the person's subjectivity are being continuously and reciprocally constituted and transformed' (ibid.: 1). The configuration of nets enables, constrains, shapes and mediates thought, action and development.

Cultural resources, reflecting understandings of the past, the present and imagined futures, thus have significant power in the activity and development of a learner. The perspectives and meanings of significant others themselves draw on and reflect available semiotic networks. However, Rossetti-Ferreira and her colleagues suggest that: 'there is no single network. They are always multiple, weaving a mesh, with many intersections. The basic structure of these nets is dialogical, resulting from many interactions with others' (2002: 1). We thus have a concept which locates both the individual and his or her significant others in the context of multiple semiotic networks and diverse frameworks of cultural resource.

The university lecturer may thus offer her disciplinary understanding, as applied to the specific subjects of the department's teaching programme. The student may engage with this directly, but may also be influenced by concepts and experiences from previous learning at home or school, or by ideas and narratives shared between friends and other students in the union bar; including evaluations of lecturers and their credibility. Years later, perhaps in the workplace, the same basic topics may well be revisited, but the framework for interpretation and sense making will have moved on yet again. Engagement with particular networks of meaning thus seems to be associated with particular contexts, relationships and social practices.

Social practices

The significance of social practice has been a prominent interest of socio-cultural analysts in recent years because of the ways in which it grounds and relates culture, learning and identity as manifested in particular contexts. Learning is thus 'situated' and different contexts offer particular types and levels of affordance for learning. Participation in contextually appropriate social practices is seen as being crucial to the development of a learner from peripheral to full membership of the 'community of practice' (Lave and Wenger 1991). In relation to identity, Lave and Wenger conceive of it almost processually – as 'long-term, living relations between persons and their place and participation in communities of practice', so that 'identity, knowing and social membership entail one another' (1991: 53).

This conceptualization of a form of lifewide influence has some interesting applications in relation to higher education's specialist, subject-dominated fields – the 'tribes and territories' of Becher's description (1989). One challenge in England, for instance, is whether students from the diverse backgrounds which 50 per cent participation implies can be inducted into the communities of practice which the academic world presently supports; or whether those communities will themselves need to change. In Lave and Wenger's terms, some students start from more contextually 'peripheral' positions than others, and (irrespective of their intellectual capabilities or potential) may not have the cultural capital to become accomplished participants in the presently legitimated social practices of their academic field. Such ideas have been applied to the higher education experience of student teachers with tracking of their experiences in courses and placement schools (Edwards and Collison 1996). Variations in the latter, of course, their affordance, have crucial consequences for the outcome of student efforts. There are other interesting uses, for instance, in relation to young children and home-school practices (Rogoff et al. 2001) and in relation to workplace learning (Billett 2002).

Dreier (1999) offers an interesting development of these ideas by conceptualizing 'personal trajectories of participation across contexts of social practice'. His concern is to develop a social theory of the developing person. In part, this focuses on the unfolding of experience as individuals progress through successive series of contexts of social practice. However, power relations and other social resources are significant. As he puts it:

> how persons unfold their everyday conduct of life depends on their degree of influence on the social conditions and arrangements they live in and on the way in which they address and realize the challenges and problems of conducting it.
>
> (Dreier 1999: 18)

We thus have a more materially grounded and temporally aware account of personal development and of the influence of lifewide factors. As Dreier puts it: 'the unfolding of a personal trajectory is arranged in historically specific ways' (1999: 19).

Activity systems

Building on the quotation above from Dreier, it is apparent that a framework is required for understanding the relationship between context, action and learning.

Activity theory has a long history and challenging integrative goals. However, even where skilful interpretation is attempted (for example, Daniels 2001), there is undoubtedly a problem in presenting such a complex perspective.

The most significant contemporary exponent of the approach, Engestrom, offers three major characteristics of activity theory. He suggests that it is:

- contextual and oriented at understanding historically specific local practices, their objects, mediating artefacts, and social organization;
- based on a dialectical theory of knowledge and thinking, focused on the creative potential in human cognition; and
- a developmental theory that seeks to explain and influence qualitative changes in human practices over time.

(Engestrom 1999: 381, cited in Daniels 2001)

The enormous value of the approach lies in its holistic ambition to understand mind, learning and action in relation to the multi-dimensional contexts which both shape them and are shaped by them.

We could, for example, consider some of the activity systems which are represented within education, and their effects. For example, Mathematics 'A level' is taught within a particular and historically specific set of constraints and practices – generating recognizable activity systems in schools. In the view of many specialists, there is a disjunction between 'A level' outcomes and the requirements of disciplinary-based university lecturers, who are themselves bound into their own activity systems. In due course, the requirements of workplaces, also embedded in activity systems, introduce further challenges. Cases in each of these settings – school, university, workplace – could be described in terms of their salient 'subjects' (individuals, dyads, groups), 'mediational means' (cultural, conceptual or material tools, signs and forms of expression), 'objects' (motives, goals and outcomes sought), and the social structures, constraints and affordances of their communities. As we know from the furore which regularly surfaces over Maths education, the concerns emanating from schools, universities and workplaces have long histories and reflect established interests and forms of practice. We might say that the activity systems within particular institutions have very strong hinterlands. In the midst of all this, the learner must try to make sense of each setting, by building and applying his or her mathematical understanding as these significant boundaries are crossed.

In a sense, then, what we have here is somewhat similar to the notion of the learner progressing, during the lifecourse, through successive 'frameworks of meaning' (see above). However, activity theory promises a more sophisticated analysis of how such semiotic frameworks are anchored in social systems and social practices and how learners, or actors, accommodate to them. The concept of 'activity system' thus begins to provide a more structurally located account of organizational and interactional context.

Capital

Awareness of individuals' circumstances is crucial to any analysis of learning through the lifecourse, and deploying the concept of 'capital' is an interesting way of approaching this. Of course, the origin of the term lies in Marxist economics, in which it was used to draw attention to significant differences in material resources (such as property) based on inheritance and social class. Such differences still exist, and, despite overall growth, wealth gaps have widened in recent years in many parts of the UK. Poverty remains a significant issue for many. In relation to higher education in England and Wales, many fear that university top-up fees will undermine inclusion and harm the life-chances of young people from less wealthy backgrounds.

Additionally however, other forms of capital have also been identified – in particular, 'cultural' and 'social'. Bourdieu is a key theorist in this context. In his early work (Bourdieu and Passeron 1977) he focused on cultural capital. This denotes high prestige behaviours, understandings, capabilities and habits which may be acquired through socialization, accumulated through education, or purchased and appropriated. Facility with high-brow artistic culture is often cited as an example, but having high levels of cultural capital may also be associated with more routine confidence in dealing with social organizations and situations. It underpins symbolic power. Within student life, some archetypal 'Hooray Henrys and Henriettas' may flaunt a particular form of cultural capital, though there are, of course, others connected to more contemporary forms of lifestyle.

The concept of social capital (Bourdieu 1986) extends this analysis by drawing attention to social resources and networks of influence. For some, such resources are considerable. Multiple layers of family, community and business association may permeate the social field within which an individual lives his or her life. Such networks provide opportunities and offer safety nets for those fortunate enough to benefit from them – though they may also, of course, be limiting in significant ways. Though different in form and power, the social capital of less advantaged groups may well still be highly significant in its own terms and, indeed, be vital in relation to particular circumstances. Moll (1992) coined the concept of 'funds of knowledge' to describe the resources held by disadvantaged communities which, though unrecognized by formal education, remain vital to accomplish everyday life in some settings.

For the individual learner, moving through the lifecourse and perhaps contemplating entry to higher education, these forms of capital are highly significant. Can university be afforded? What will it be like and how will I fit in? What social support will be available?

Summary

I have thus reviewed five concepts providing important insights into the 'lifewide' creating of meaning – significant others, networks of meaning, social practices, activity systems and capital. There are many others too, in what is an amazingly rich and rapidly developing field at the interface of psychology and sociology. The point though, is that, in one way or another, we need to understand learners and the creation of meaning within multiple layers of contextual influence. We now turn from the lifewide, and reach towards the lifelong.

Lifecourse influences on learners and learning

In this section of the chapter, I draw more directly on the theoretical framework generated through the Identity and Learning Programme (Pollard with Filer 1996; Pollard and Filer 1999; Filer and Pollard 2000; Pollard and Filer, forthcoming). In this programme, 18 children from two contrasting primary schools were tracked from the age of 4. Detailed evidence from formal and informal learning contexts was collected until the age of 16. Some of the young people concerned are now experiencing higher education, whilst others are in the workplace or engaging in other forms of training. In drawing on the conceptual outcome of this work, I attempt to provide some illustrations of its possible application to higher education contexts.

Our analytic framework is represented in figure 12.2. It represents a progressive cycle of development in which identity (Who is learning?), meets new challenges (What is to be learned?), in particular circumstances (How supportive is the learning context?), with particular consequences (What are the outcomes?), which roll back to influence the next cycle. And so, we speculate, we can begin to understand the influence of experience on learning through the lifecourse.

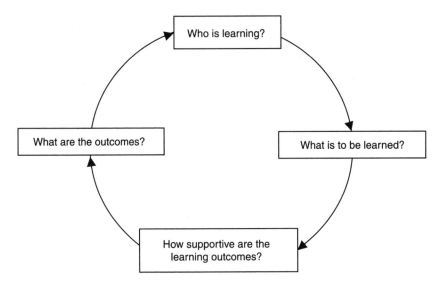

Figure 12.2 A model of learning and identity

I will comment a little on each of these elements in turn, applying them to higher education as I do so.

'Who' is learning?

This element of the model reflects the foundation of the perspective which Ann Filer and I generated through our ethnographic work. As Bruner put it: 'the phenomenon of self is perhaps the single most universal thing about human experience' (Bruner 1996: 35). Humans, of whatever age, are seen as social actors and, building on symbolic interactionist ideas, significant others at successive stages of the lifecourse shape each individual's sense of self; a point of cross-reference with the earlier discussion on lifewide influences on learners.

Identity can be thought of as the way the self is represented and understood within such narratives; both by the individual and by others. There may be some tension between such accounts. There may be multiple manifestations of identity, but there are also likely to be distinctive, underlying continuities. An identity which has been developed in one setting may not be viable given the contextual imperatives of another. This may be manifested at any one time, for instance between formal and informal settings, or over the lifecourse: home to initial school; to later schools; to college; to university; to initial work; to further work; to retirement; to sheltered housing; residential care, and so on. Transitions between settings thus have the potential to challenge established identities and force re-assessment. Social participation thus involves some risk or challenge to self. Strategic biographies are about the management of identity through multiple social contexts. Strategic biographies can be traced over time, trajectories projected and disruptions analysed.

We can apply this perspective to the situation of students engaging with higher education. The transition from school to university has always been recognized as being challenging. For many years in the UK there has been an established pattern of young, middle-class students leaving their families for the first time to attend universities outside their home town. Such students have had to develop new social networks and achieve a degree of self-sufficiency in practical living arrangements as well as meet the new demands of degree-level academic work. Generally, this experience has been regarded as being formative. The personal experience however, is of the students exposing their identity in a number of new and unfamiliar settings. However successful and well-honed that identity may have been at home or school, the first few weeks at university are likely to call for adjustments in response to new social relationships. An early welcome from the Student Union may provide an initial encounter with student culture and, whilst this is likely to be rapidly reinforced in the bar, it may or may not provide continuity with previous practice or expectation. Initial friendships are likely to be formed proximally from the chance allocations of accommodation systems or tutorial groupings. New relationships with teachers or lecturers may seem remote given large group sizes, and the support of family and friends may seem even more distant. The consequential sense of vulnerability is hopefully temporary, as experiences are shared and new relationships form. Over time, old identities are adjusted as new narratives of self are formed. Indeed, the very distance and disconnection from previous social settings makes this possible, and creates opportunity to 'break loose'. Any newly developed identity must be viable in the university setting, must satisfy the significant others and cultural expectations of that setting, and must reflect the realities of each individual's academic and social performance. The student moves into a new phase of life, a key transition from youth to adulthood, and an important stage in a continuous process of personal development. It is a mistake, however, to imagine that past identities can be entirely left behind.

The diversity of our contemporary higher education system reveals some extremes of provision regarding this transitional challenge to identity. The independent school pupil progressing to a 'Russell Group' university has the benefit of a degree of cultural continuity and expectation, and is unlikely to face significant financial hardship. The result is a relatively low drop-out rate among such students. Students at newly established universities serving more diverse social groups face far greater challenges. There may be greater problems of cultural continuity and fewer resources, opportunities and institutionalized structures to shape identification and social relationships. Student financial hardship may be reflected in part-time working and there is a greater likelihood of students being home-based. In relation to identity, the challenges of the new situation are complicated. Previous expectations from significant others and work requirements must be accommodated, but new demands from student and academic life also mount. Maintaining a viable identity in such circumstances is not easy, and this contributes to higher levels of early drop-out from higher education.

A key issue throughout such processes of transition concerns their consequence for each individual's learning disposition, with 'mastery' and 'helplessness' sometime being offered as contrastive extremes. Epistemic identity, which we might view as self-perception as a learner, is a useful concept here. More specifically, it can be defined as a person's view of himself or herself in relation to knowledge, knowing and learning. Epistemic identity reflects cognitive understanding about personal learning strategies, strengths and weaknesses – 'meta-cognition'. However, affective factors are also very important and, for this purpose, may be regarded as the feelings experienced in relation to the self in particular circumstances. For example, 'enjoyment' can be seen as reciprocated self-expression – there is synergy between identity, context and others – and this synergy is an important motivator in learning. Fulfilment and learning flow are experienced, and deep learning may occur. On the other hand, 'anxiety' can be seen as non-reciprocated self-expression – there is tension between identity, context and others – and too much tension can undermine and demotivate learners. Perceived risk is too high and learning may be instrumental.

In the case of higher education, we may aim to support the development of knowledgeable, skilled, confident and independent thinkers. However, such goals cannot be achieved through subject- or course-based structures or experiences alone. The social circumstances which surround and interpolate instructional activities are also crucial to learners' interpretation of content, appropriation of meaning, and thus, deep learning. I will develop this argument below.

What is to be learned?

The second element of the spiralling model developed through the *Identity and Learning Programme* addresses the nature of learning challenges themselves.

Learning challenges may take many forms, from the most informal experiences and relationships, through to those of formal subjects and tasks.

In the context of higher education, we are mainly concerned with the latter. In this respect, we have to acknowledge that all such 'knowledge' is socially produced, socially stratified and socially communicated. So, '*whose* knowledge, skills, attitudes or understanding is on offer, and what are the social implications of its origins?' This takes us directly to the social construction and structuring of knowledge as manifested in the tribes and territories of academe (Becher 1989). There is then a key issue concerning the degree of identification that exists between a learner and the body of knowledge with which they are trying to engage. In my studies of school pupils, this was very apparent in terms of varied engagement with different subjects. For example, one child, Hazel, from an early age developed little understanding and derived no pleasure from Mathematics. She subsequently failed her GCSE and gave up the subject. In the expressive subjects of Art, Drama and English she was far more comfortable and extremely successful. She derived pleasure and fulfilment from them. These subjects became the basis of her higher education studies and her imagined career in teaching. Influences on these patterns of subject engagement could be traced to family and peers, with teacher efforts seeming relatively inconsequential by comparison.

During higher education, with demands of the workplace close-by for most students, both the intrinsic and practical value of different subjects are likely to be continuously evaluated by learners. Their engagement will be influenced by such judgements in relation to their own personal circumstances and identity narratives. How does their programme of study fit in with their situation and aspirations? Of course, a crude pattern may be discerned in which students from more wealthy, middle-class families follow up the intrinsic qualities and deferred rewards of high-status subjects, whilst students in less fortunate circumstances must necessarily pay more attention to short-term conversion of subject study to employment and income. Thus, as institutions struggle towards 50 per cent participation and draw in a wider age-range, we have a rapid expansion of applied and employment-related courses.

Focusing at the individual, psychological level and irrespective of social circumstance, my ethnographic work suggests that the most effective learning occurs when new knowledge, skill or understanding is incorporated into existing schemata in meaningful ways. This must be socially and personally meaningful as well as being conceptually meaningful. Further, it is plausible to suggest that deep, long-term learning of knowledge, skills, attitudes or understanding occurs most effectively when new learning is reinforced by the narratives of personal identity; where it 'makes sense' in terms of the strategic biography of the individual; where it reinforces and enhances the self.

To achieve higher quality learning, the implication in circumstances of widening student participation is that higher education courses have to become more meaningful in terms of students' lives-as-lived and in relation to development through the lifecourse.

How supportive is the learning context?

Learning is an interactive process which takes place in specific contexts of social practice. As we saw earlier, social practices can be seen as being embedded in activity systems, frameworks of cultural expectation and structural imperative.

At the interactional level within higher education, where the student learner and the teacher/tutor/lecturer meet, an intrinsic power differential leaves the student vulnerable. The teacher or lecturer has a formally ascribed position of authority, lays claim to superior subject knowledge, and has significant influence on the assessment of student performance. It is not unknown for teachers and lecturers to use these structural advantages to protect themselves against challenge – though the new era of student consumerism (see Morley, chapter six, again) may eventually undermine this strategy.

In any event, because learning involves some risk taking and personal vulnerability as knowledge and skills are reconstructed, the interpersonal climate within any learning setting (whether home, classroom, lecture theatre, workplace, leisure setting, or residential home) is crucial. I would argue that, where there is an exchange of mutual respect, this increases learner openness and thus 'opportunities to learn'. In the higher education context, this ideal is perhaps most plausibly attainable in personal attention of the higher degree supervision. However, even in large-class situations, a great deal can be conveyed by lecturers through their approach to their teaching. For example, participative activities convey trust and affirm interest in student perspectives irrespective of size of teaching group. A sociological analysis of such teacher-learner relationships represents a mutually respectful accommodation as a 'working consensus'. My view is that such settlement of what is always a potential power struggle between teacher and taught, is normally beneficial for learning.

Addressing more direct psychological factors, we might say that learning takes place when existing knowledge, understanding or skills are extended and meaningfully incorporated into existing schemata. This develops particularly well where there are high levels of subject knowledge and high-quality instruction. In higher education, this is the driver for the aspiration to link research with teaching. In the best situations, lecturers are engaged in research at the cutting edge of their disciplines and are able to share this with their students and support a new generation in original enquiry and knowledge generation. However, it is also possible for expert researchers to miss their audience altogether, and to utterly fail to excite and interest their students. For me, the key issue is that expert teaching requires that teachers offer both cognitive *and* affective support. This requires knowledge of both the subject and the learners. Crucial elements are to assess the existing level of student knowledge and to have some empathic understanding of their frames of reference. It is then more likely that taught input will be matched to pick up on existing knowledge and extend it (utilizing what Vygotsky calls the zone of proximal development) in meaningful ways. Of course, such issues can be addressed in much more depth. For example, the TLRP project led by Hounsell and Entwistle uses Biggs' concept of 'constructive alignment' to study course structure and provision in five subject areas and to measure student learning outcomes (Entwistle et al. 2002). Entwistle's seminal work on 'deep' and 'surface' learning is, of course, of considerable relevance to my argument that sustained learning reflects appropriation within personal identity (Entwistle and Ramsden 1983).

So, if we were to take this argument very seriously in the context of teaching and learning in higher education, we would need to ask not only about the design and organization of courses for the effective delivery of up-to-date subject knowledge, but also about how to connect systematically with student experience and engage with evolving identity narratives. This way, in my view, lies deep, sustainable learning.

What are the learning outcomes?

The conceptual model moves on one more turn and a distinction is drawn between formal and informal learning outcomes.

Formal outcomes may be measures of performance or other records of capabilities. These provide official, categoric certification and records of achievements. In the case of higher education, formal assessment is increasingly broken down into term-by-term testing, thus providing a form of formative feedback. However, the most common and explicit summative outcome is the degree classification. There are many variations in the ways in which this is produced in the UK, with limited standardization. Some professional groups or vocational bodies have consequentially developed their own standards and qualifications. In sociological terms, formal output assessment acts as a differentiation mechanism, providing significant indicators for the consideration of the labour market. There are, of course, patterns in these outputs, based on gender, class, ethnicity, disability, and so on.

In relation to the lifecourse, each student approaches news of his or her final classification with some trepidation, knowing that it has symbolic status and gate-keeping consequences. Some imagined futures, some aspirational identity narratives, will simply become impossible, whilst for others new opportunities may open up. No wonder that for many, as the 'rites of passage' of the degree ceremony are accomplished, there is relief and celebration where a secure foundation has been established for the next transition into the workplace.

Informal learning outcomes can be seen as mediated interpretations of formal outcomes. In other words, they are means by which people make sense of their experiences of feedback about their learning, both during and, in particular, at the conclusion of their course. We can distinguish here between self-esteem and social status.

Self-esteem, or self-confidence, reflects the meaningful incorporation of achievements into epistemic identity and personal narratives. In other words, assessed outcomes are accounted for by the learner. Thus the university or college student reflects on personal progress and takes stock. At best, she reviews and reconstructs her view of herself as a learner in the light of such feedback.

Social status, on the other hand, reflects recognition of achievements that is attributed by others. We might, in particular look for the valuation of significant others here, and it is interesting how prominent parents become once more, when the official ceremonial of the degree ceremony comes round. As messages of attainments and achievements are passed round family and friends, so such recognition increases or undermines the viability of certain personal narratives and identities. Very often, some adjustment is necessary as the graduate begins the next round of the developmental cycle, and progresses to the next stage of his or her lifecourse.

Lifewide and lifelong learning through the lifecourse

We can now start to pull together the strands of the arguments offered in this chapter. First, I have offered a review of some lifewide, contextualizing factors and of concepts which, in my view, offer important insights. These concepts – concerning significant others, networks of meaning, social practices, activity systems and various forms of capital – are offered as useful analytic tools. I have also provided a brief review of some concepts and ideas which represent lifelong learning as a cyclical development of learner identity when new challenges are met during the lifecourse. Although this model was initially generated from a longitudinal study of school pupils, I have tried to illustrate it with examples from higher education and it is also my contention that this may be possible in respect of other phases of the lifecourse.

However, the prominence and significance of particular elements of these frameworks clearly varies at different points. This can be seen if, accepting the risks of oversimplification, we analytically 'freeze' the spiral of development and slice into the model at particular points. In the examples below, it is suggested that key significant others move in and out of focus, along with associated networks of meaning. Particular communities of practice along with their associate activity systems achieve prominence, and then fade to be replaced by others. Forms of economic, cultural and social capital remain crucial – as, of course, do various other forms of social structuring.

Although these models are extremely crude, they make a key point about the changing influence of a variety of social factors through the lifecourse. We draw on and are constrained by various forms of capital and resource, take notice of a succession of significant others, engage with a variety of networks of meaning, formal and informal institutions, social practices and

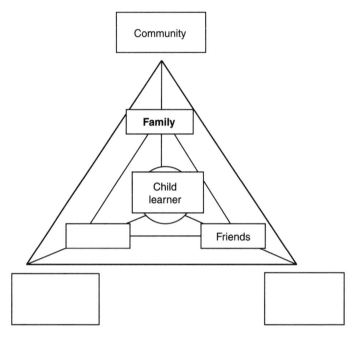

Figure 12.3   Pre-school learning – the influence of family

associated activity systems, and try to enjoy life along the way with friends and family. And all the time, within the limits of our capacities, we adapt, learn, and refine our identities as we work to construct and sustain a meaningful sense of self.

At birth, of course, so much is possible and our parents may play with many imagined futures. However, as institutional engagement starts and various forms of social categorization begin, so our options and expectations begin to narrow. This is true even from the conclusions of the health visitor or play-group organizer, let alone the SAT, GCSE, degree or workplace assessor. We also, progressively of course, have to come to terms with our genetic make up even though we may also work very hard to realize our potential. In this sense, the lifecourse might be seen as a constant conversation between ourselves and our society concerning 'what is' and 'what might be'. The meaning and self-interpretation given to these unfolding lives is represented in the concept of identity, with narratives being constructed to provide explanation of the past and hope or expectation for the future. As we engage with social institutions, we realize, neglect, are thwarted or are otherwise unable to exploit our potential, so options begin to close. Indeed, national policies, organizational cultures and social practices create circumstances for the development of identities and realization of potential, and these can be both enabling and constraining.

Each individual uses strategic negotiation to develop and sustain his or her

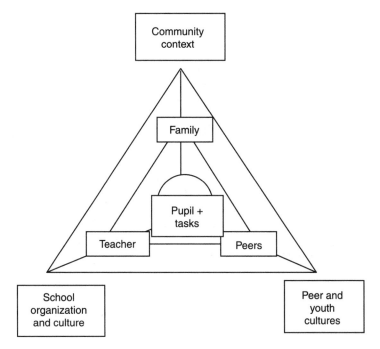

Figure 12.4   Key influences on learning during schooling

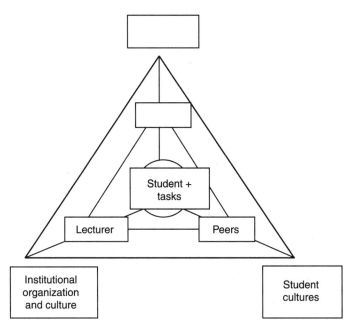

Figure 12.5   Key influences on learning in higher education

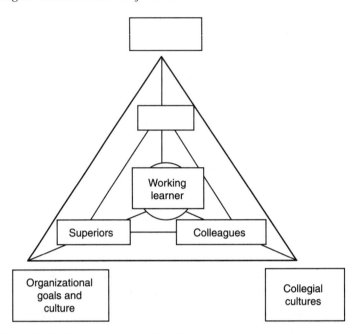

Figure 12.6   Key influences on workplace learning

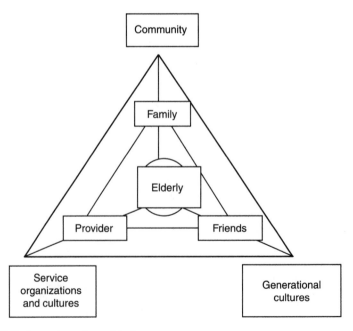

Figure 12.7   Learning when elderly

identity in successive settings – day by day, week by week, year by year. Such strategic biographies may be seen as 'pupil careers', 'student careers' and 'employment careers'. 'Epistemic identities' and learning dispositions are inextricably linked to these developments.

The interpretation of achievements and mediation of official assessments are crucial. Outcomes are likely to be highly differentiated by social factors such as social class, gender and ethnicity. In the cyclical development of learning achievement and disposition, through the various phases and settings of childhood, youth, adulthood, middle-age, retirement and old age, a key factor remains the pattern of reinforcement or discouragement by significant others – and interesting reversals of role also occur, for instance, between parents and children.

At death, the identity narrative faces the challenge of a final transition. For many, self-knowledge, social recognition, spiritual understanding or belief provide contentment, peace and dénouement, but uneasy, unsettled and untimely deaths also occur in which processes of development and narrative construction are disrupted.

In these lifelong, lifewide processes, higher education is a major transitional experience. For many students, it offers a galaxy of opportunities in the best, and widest, educational sense. But it is also one of society's most significant signifying agencies, with a key role in differentiation and the distribution of life-chances. If we are to progress towards a 50 per cent participation target, the realization of the talents, capability and potential of a more diverse student body will be extremely challenging – but the attempt is surely worth it?

Bibliography

Abberley, P. (1987) The concept of oppression and the development of a social theory of disability, *Disability, Handicap and Society*, 2(1): 5–19.

Abbott, D. (2001) Satisfaction Guaranteed (well, almost), *The Independent*, 24 October.

Ahier, J., Beck, J. and Moore, R. (2002) *Graduate Citizens? Issues of Citizenship and Higher Education*. London and New York: Routledge Falmer.

Aittola, T. (1995) Recent changes in student life and study processes, *Scandinavian Journal of Educational Research*, 39(1).

Aldridge, F. and Tuckett, A. (2002) *Two steps forward, one step back: The NIACE survey on adult participation in learning 2002*. Leicester: NIACE.

Alexiadou, N. (2002) Social Inclusion and Social Exclusion in England: Tensions in Education Policy, *Journal of Education Policy*, 17(1): 71–86.

Anderson, C. (1997) Enabling and shaping understanding through tutorials, in F. Marton, D. Hounsell and N. Entwistle (eds) *The Experience of Learning*, 2nd rev. edn. Edinburgh: Scottish Academic Press.

Apple, M. (2000) Between neoliberalism and neoconservatism: education and conservatism in a global context, in N. Burbules and C. Torres (eds) *Globalization and Education: Critical Perspectives*. London and New York: Routledge.

Archer, L. (2003) Social class and higher education, in L. Archer, M. Hutchings and A. Ross (eds) *Higher Education and Social Class: Issues of Exclusion and Inclusion*. London: Routledge.

Armistead, C. and Meakins, M. (2002) A Framework for Practicing Knowledge Management, *Long Range Planning*, 35(1) (February): 49–71.

Association of Commonwealth Universities (ACU) (2001) *Engagement as a Core Value for the University*. London: ACU.

Atkins, M. J. (1999) Oven-ready and self-basting: taking stock of employability skills, *Teaching in Higher Education*, 4(2): 267–80.

Bachirova, T. (2000) How much would love of learning cost? Humanitarian versus pragmatic views on lifelong learning, *Journal of Further and Higher Education*, 24(3): 293–300.

Ball, S., Davies, J., David, M. and Reay, D. (2002) 'Classification' and 'Judgement': social class and the cognitive structures of choice of Higher Education, *British Journal of Sociology of Education*, 23(1): 51–72.

Ball, S., Maguire, M. and Macrae, S. (2000) *Choice, Pathways and Transitions Post-16: New Youth, New Economies in the Global City.* London and New York: Routledge Falmer.

Barber, B. (1999) in *Los Angeles Times*, 23 May.

Barnes, C. (1991) *Disabled People in Britain and Discrimination.* London: Hurst & Co.

Barnes, C. (1999) Disability studies: new or not so new directions? *Disability and Society*, 14(4): 577–81.

Barnes, K. (2001) The introduction of service level agreements for central service and administrative departments in the university of Sheffield, *Perspectives*, 5(2): 38–41.

Barnett, R. (1994) *The Limits of Competence: Knowledge, Higher Education and Society.* Buckingham: SRHE and Open University Press.

Barnett, R. (1990) *The Idea of a University.* Buckingham: SRHE and Open University Press.

Barnett, R. (1999) *Realizing the University in an Age of Supercomplexity.* Buckingham: SRHE and Open University Press.

Barnett, R. (2003) *Beyond All Reason: Living With Ideology in the University.* Buckingham: SRHE and Open University Press.

Baudrillard, J. (1998) *The Consumer Society.* London: Sage.

Bauman, Z. (1997) Universities: old, new and different, in A. Smith and F. Webster (eds) *The Postmodern University? Contested Visions of Higher Education in Society.* Buckingham: SRHE and Open University Press.

Bauman, Z. (2000) *Liquid Modernity.* Cambridge: Polity Press.

Becher, T. (1989) *Academic Tribes and Territories.* Buckingham: Open University Press.

Becher, T. and Trowler, P. (2001) *Academic Tribes and Territories: Intellectual Enquiry and the Cultures of Disciplines.* Buckingham: Open University Press.

Beck, U. (1992) *Risk Society.* London: Sage.

Beck, U. and Gernsheim, E. (2001) *Individualisation: Institutionalized Individualisation and its Social and Political Consequences.* London: Sage Publications.

Bell, R. and Tight, M. (1993) *Open Universities: A British Tradition?* Buckingham: SRHE and Open University Press.

Bennett, N., Dunne, E. and Carre, C. (1999) Patterns of core and generic skills in higher education, *Higher Education*, 37(1): 71–93.

Bensimon, E. (1995) TQM in the Academy: A Rebellious Reading, *Harvard Educational Review*, 4: 593–611.

Bernstein, B. (1996) *Pedagogy, Symbolic Control and Identity.* London: Taylor and Francis.

Biggs, J.B. and Collis, K.F. (1982) *Evaluating the Quality of Learning: The SOLO Taxonomy.* New York: Academic Press.

Billett, S. (2002) Workplace pedagogic practices: co-participation and learning, *British Journal of Educational Studies*, 50(4): 457–81.

Black, P. and Wiliam, D. (1998) Assessment and classroom learning, *Assessment in Education*, 5(1): 7–74.

Blackmore, J. (1999) Localization/Globalization and the midwife state: strategic dilemmas for state feminism in education? *Journal of Education Policy*, 14(1): 33–54.

Blackmore, J. (2000) Globalization: A Useful Concept for Feminists Rethinking Theory and Strategies in Education? in N. Burbules and C. Torres (eds) *Globalization and Education: Critical Perspectives.* London and New York: Routledge.

Blackmore, J. and Sachs, J. (2001) Women leaders in the restructured and internationalised university, in A. Brooks and A. McKinnon (eds) *Gender and the Restructured University: Changing Management and Culture in Higher Education.* Buckingham: Open University Press.

Blight, D., Davis, D. and Olsen, A. (2000) The internationalisation of higher education, in K. Harry (ed.), *Higher Education through Open and Distance Learning.* London: Routledge.

Boardman, P. (1944) *Patrick Geddes: Maker of the Future.* Chapel Hill: University of North Carolina Press.

Bollier, D. (2002) *Rediscovery of the Commons: Managing for the Common Good, Not Just for the Corporate Good.* Available on-line at: http://www.tompaine.com/feature.cfm/ID/6016.

Boud, D. (1995) *Enhancing Learning through Self-Assessment.* London: Kogan Page.

Bourdieu, P. (1986) The forms of capital, in J. Richardson (ed.) *Handbook of Theory and Research for the Sociology of Education.* Westport, Connecticut: Greenwood Press.

Bourdieu, P. (1989) Social space and symbolic power, *Sociological Theory,* 7: 14–25.

Bourdieu, P. (1990) *The Logic of Practice.* Cambridge: Polity Press.

Bourdieu, P. and Passeron, J.C. (1977) *Reproduction in Education, Society and Culture.* London: Sage.

Branthwaite, A., Trueman, M. and Hartley, J. (1980) Writing essays: the actions and strategies of students, in J. Hartley (ed.) *The Psychology of Written Communication.* London: Kogan Page.

Brennan, J., Johnston, B., Little, B., Shah, T. and Woodley, A. (2001) *The Employment of UK Graduates: Comparison with Europe and Japan.* Bristol: HEFCE.

Brew, A. (1999) Towards autonomous assessment: using self-assessment and peer-assessment, in S. Brown and A. Glasner (eds) *Assessment Matters in Higher Education: Choosing and Using Diverse Approaches.* Buckingham: SRHE and Open University Press.

Brooks, A. (2001) Restructuring Bodies of Knowledge, in A. Brooks and A. McKinnon (eds) *Gender and the Restructured University: Changing Management and Culture in Higher Education.* Buckingham: Open University Press.

Brown, G., Bull, J. and Pendlebury, M. (1997) *Assessing Student Learning in Higher Education.* London: Routledge.

Brown, J. S. and Duguid, P. (2000) *The Social Life of Information.* Boston, USA: Harvard Business School.

Brown, P. and Scase, R. (1994) *Higher Education and Corporate Realities: Class Culture and the Decline of Graduate Careers.* London: University College London Press.

Bruner, J. (1996) *Actual Minds: Possible Worlds.* Cambridge, MA: Harvard University Press.

Brynin, M. (2002) Graduate density, gender and employment, *British Journal of Sociology,* 53(3): 363–81.

Burke, P.J. (2002) *Accessing Education: Effectively Widening Participation.* Stoke-on-Trent: Trentham Publications.

Butler, J.P. (1997) *The Psychic Life of Power: Theories in Subjection.* Stanford, California: Stanford University Press.

Campbell, J., Smith, D. and Brooker, R. (1998) From conception to performance: how undergraduate students conceptualize and construct essays, *Higher Education,* 36(4): 449–69.

Candy, P.C. (1991) *Self-direction for lifelong learning: A comprehensive guide to theory and practice.* San Francisco: Jossey Bass.

Candy, P.C. (forthcoming 2003) Linking Thinking: Self-directed learning in the digital age. Final report of National Research Fellowship with the Department of Education, Science and Training. Canberra: Australian Government Publishing Service. [Note: final title of this report not confirmed at time of going to press.]

Candy, P.C., Crebert, R.G. and O'Leary, J. (1994) Developing lifelong learners through undergraduate education. *National Board of Employment Education and Training Commissioned Report Number 28*. Canberra: AGPS.

Castells, M. (2000) *The Rise of the Network Society*. Oxford: Blackwell.

Chanock, K. (2000) Comments on essays: do students understand what tutors write?, *Teaching in Higher Education*, 5(1): 95–105.

Charles, D. and Benneworth, P. (2002) *Evaluating the Regional Contributors on HEI: a Benchmarking Approach*, HEFCE report 02/23. Bristol: HEFCE.

Clegg, S. (1999) Professional education, reflective practice and feminism, *International Journal of Inclusive Education*, 3(2): 167–79.

Clouder, L. (1998) Getting the 'Right Answers': Student Evaluation as a Reflection of Intellectual Development, *Teaching in Higher Education*, 3(2): 185–95.

Coaldrake, P. (2002) Rethinking academic and university work, *Higher Education Management*, 12: 3.

Coffield, F. (ed.) (2000) *What Progress Are We Making With Lifelong Learning?The Evidence From Research*. Newcastle-upon-Tyne: University of Newcastle-upon-Tyne.

Coffield, F. and Williamson, B. (1997) The challenges facing higher education, in F. Coffield and B. Williamson (eds) *Repositioning Higher Education*. Buckingham: Open University Press.

Cohen, R., Boud, D. and Sampson, J. (2001) Dealing with problems encountered in assessment of peer learning, in N. Falchikov (ed.) *Learning Together: Peer Tutoring in Higher Education*. London and New York: Routledge Falmer.

Conlon, G. (2002) *The Financial Returns to HNC/HNDs*. London: Council for Industry and Higher Education.

Connor, H. and Dewson, S. (2001) *Social Class and Higher Education – Issues Affecting Decisions on Participation by Lower Social Class Groups*. Brighton: Institute for Employment Studies.

Crow, L. (1996) Including all of our lives: Renewing the social model of disability, in C. Barnes and G. Mercer (eds) *Exploring the Divide: Illness and Disability*. Leeds: The Disability Press.

Curry, D. (2002) *The Policy Commission on the Future of Farming and Food*. London: DEFRA.

Daniels, H. (2001) *Vygotsky and Pedagogy*. London and New York: Routledge Falmer.

Das, T.K. and Tang, B-S. (2002) Alliance constellations: A Social Exchange Perspective, *Academy of Management Review*, 27(3): 445–56.

Davidson, I. (2002) Rural Society, Social Change and Continuing Education: From Wild Wales to the Aga Saga, in F. Gray (ed.) op. cit.: 19–32.

Delanty, G. (2001) *Challenging Knowledge – the University in the Knowledge Society*. Buckingham: SRHE and Open University Press.

Department for Education and Employment (DfEE) (1997) *Learning Centres: A Guide*. Sheffield: Training Technology Unit.

Department for Education and Employment (DfEE) (1998) *The Learning Age: A Renaissance For a New Britain*. Sheffield: DfEE.

Department for Education and Skills (DfEE) (1999) *Extending Opportunity: A National Framework For Study Support*. London: DfEE.

Department for Education and Skills (DfES) (2000) *National Education and Training*

Targets. London: DfES (Website: DfES www.standards.dfes.gov.uk/other-resources/publications/setting/annex/).

Department for Education and Skills (DfES) (2003) *The Future of Higher Education*. London: HMSO.

Department for Environment, Food and Rural Affairs (DEFRA) (2000) *Our Country-side: the Future. A Fair Deal for Rural England*. London: HMSO. Cm 4909.

Department of Trade and Industry (DTI) (1998) *Competitive Futures: Building the Knowledge Driven Economy*. London: DTI.

DesForges, C. and Kanefsky, J. (2001) Phase Three Research Agenda: priority issues raised in the consultation, *Teaching and Learning Research Programme Newsletter*, October.

Devins, D., Darlow, A. and Smith, V. (2002) Lifelong learning and digital exclusions: Lessons from the evaluation of an ICT learning centre and an emerging research agenda, *Regional Studies*, 36(8): 941–5.

Disability Rights Commission (DRC) (2002) *Code of Practice Post-16: Code of Practice for Providers of Post-16 Education and Related Services*. London: DRC.

Dominelli, L. and Hoogvelt, A. (1996) Globalization, contract government and the Taylorization of intellectual labour in academia, *Studies in Political Economy*, 49: 71–100.

Dreier, O. (1999) Personal trajectories of participation across contexts of social practice, *Outlines*, 1(1): 5–32.

Duke, C. (2002) *Managing the Learning University*. Buckingham: Open University Press.

Dunne, N., Bennet, E. and Carre, J. (1997) Higher education: Core skills in a learning society, *Journal of Education Policy*, 12(6): 511–25.

Edwards, A. and Collison, J. (1996) *Mentoring and Developing Practice in Primary Schools*. Buckingham: Open University Press.

Edwards, R. (1997) *Changing Places? Flexibility, Lifelong Learning and a Learning Society*. London: Routledge.

Elias, P., McKnight, A., Pitcher, J., Purcell, K. and Simm, C. (1999). *Moving On: Graduate Careers Three Years After Graduation*. Short report for the DfES, Higher Education Careers Service Unit (CSU), Association of Graduate Careers Advisory Services (AGAS) and the Institute of Employment Research (IER). Manchester: CSU.

Engestrom, Y., Miettinen, R. and Punamaki, R. J. (1999) *Perspectives on Activity Theory*. Cambridge: Cambridge University Press.

Enterprise and Lifelong Learning Committee (ELLC) of the Scottish Parliament (2002) *Report on Lifelong Learning*. Edinburgh: The Stationery Office.

Entwistle, N. and Ramsden, P. (1983) *Understanding Student Learning*. London: Croom Helm.

Entwistle, N., McCune, V. and Hounsell, D. (2002) *Approaches to Studying and Perceptions of University Teaching-Learning Environments*. ETL Project Occasional Report, No. 1.

European Commission (2001) *Making a European Area of Lifelong Learning a Reality*. Luxembourg: Office for Official Publications.

European University Association/American Council on Education (EUA/ACE) (2002) *The Brave (and Smaller) New World of Higher Education: a transatlantic view*. Washington: ACE.

Falchikov, N. (1995) Peer feedback marking: developing peer assessment, *Innovations in Education and Training International*, 32(2): 175–87.

Falchikov, N. (2001) *Learning Together: Peer Tutoring in Higher Education.* London and New York: Routledge Falmer.

Falchikov, N. and Boud, D. (1989) Student self-assessment in higher education: a meta-analysis, *Review of Educational Research,* 59(4): 395–430.

Falchikov, N. and Goldfinch, J. (2000) Student peer assessment in higher education: a meta-analysis comparing peer and teacher marks, *Review of Educational Research,* 7(3): 287–322.

Falk, I. (ed.) (2001) *Learning to Manage Change: Developing Regional Communities for a Local-Global Millenium.* Tasmania: Council for Rural Learning and Rural Affairs.

Falk, I. and Kilpatrick, S. (2000) What is Social Capital? A Study of Interaction in a Rural Community, *Sociologica Ruralis,* 40(1): 87–110.

Farmer, J.C., Baird, A.G. and Iversen, L. (2001) Rural deprivation: reflecting reality, *British Journal of General Practice,* 51(467): 486–91.

Field, J. (2000) *Lifelong Learning and the New Educational Order.* London: Trentham Books.

Field, J. (2002) Further and Higher Education Links in England, pp. 59–67 in M. Osborne, J. Gallacher and M. Murphy (eds) *A Research Review of FE/HE Links: a report to the Scottish Executive.* Glasgow/Stirling: Centre for Research in Lifelong Learning.

Field, J. and Leicester, M. (eds) (2000) *Lifelong Learning: Education Across the Lifespan.* London and New York: Routledge Falmer.

Fieldhouse, R. and Associates (1996) *A History of Modern British Adult Education.* Leicester: NIACE.

Filer, A. and Pollard, A. (2000) *The Social World of Pupil Assessment: Processes and Contexts of Primary Education.* London: Continuum.

Floud, R. (2001) Delivering the third mission: does one size fit all? Paper presented to the HERDA-SW Conference, 15–16 November. www.universitiesuk.ac.uk/speeches (accessed 3 January 2003).

Floud, R. (2002) Age of Wisdom, *The Guardian,* 1 October.

Forsyth, A. and Furlong, A. (2000) *Socio-economic Disadvantage and Access to Higher Education.* Bristol: Policy Press.

Foster, C. (1994) The Closed University, *Living Marxism,* 24–28 October.

Frand, J.L. (2000) The Information Age Mindset: changes in students and implications for higher education, *Educause Review,* 35(5): 14–24.

Freedman, S. (1999) *A Critical Review of the Concept of Equality in British Anti-Discrimination Legislation.* Cambridge: University of Cambridge Centre for Public Law.

Frouws, J. (1998) The Contested Redefinition of the Countryside: An Analysis of Rural Discourses in the Netherlands, *Sociologica Ruralis,* 38(1): 54–68.

Fulton, O. (1996) Which academic profession are you in? in R. Cuthbert (ed.) *Working in Higher Education.* Buckingham: SRHE and Open University Press, 157–69.

Furlong, A. and Forsyth, N. (2003) *Losing Out: Access from Disadvantaged Backgrounds.* Glasgow: University of Glasgow, Department of Sociology.

Gallacher, J. (2002) Articulation links between further education colleges and higher education institutions in Scotland, in M. Osborne, J. Gallacher and M. Murphy (eds) *A Research Review of FE/HE Links.* Edinburgh: Scottish Executive, in press.

Gallacher, J. (2002) Parallel lines? Higher education in Scotland's colleges and higher education institutions, *Scottish Affairs,* 40 (Summer): 123–39.

Gallacher, J., Leahy, J. and MacFarlane, K. (1997) *The FE/HE Route: New Pathways into*

Higher Education. Research Report for SOEID. Glasgow: Glasgow Caledonian University.

Gardner, H. (1999) Assessment in context, in P. Murphy (ed.) *Learners, Learning and Assessment.* London: Paul Chapman. [Reprinted, in abridged form, from H. Gardner (1992) Assessment in context: the alternative to standardized testing, in B.R. Gifford and M.C. O'Connor (eds) *Changing Assessments: Alternative Views of Aptitude, Achievement and Instruction.* Dordrecht: Kluwer.]

Gibbons, M., Limoges, C., Nowotny, H., Schwarzman, S., Scott, P. and Trow, M. (1994) *The New Production of Knowledge: The Dynamics of Science and Research in Contemporary Societies.* London: Sage.

Gibbs, G. (1995) *Assessing Student-Centred Courses.* Oxford: Oxford Centre for Staff Development.

Gibbs, G. (1999) Using assessment strategically to change the way students learn, in S. Brown and A. Glasner (eds) *Assessment Matters in Higher Education: Choosing and Using Diverse Approaches.* Buckingham: SRHE and Open University Press.

Gilchrist, R., Phillips, D. and Ross, A. (2003) Participation and potential participation in UK higher education, in L. Archer, M. Hutchings and A. Ross (eds) *Higher Education and Social Class: Issues of Exclusion and Inclusion.* London and New York: Routledge Falmer.

Godfrey, C., Hutton, S., Bradshaw, J., Coles, B., Craig, G. and Johnson, J. (2002) *Estimating the Cost of Being 'Not in Education, Employment or Training' at age 16–18.* Research Report RR346. London: DfES.

Golden, S., Spielhofer, T., Sims, D., Asiton, S. and O'Donnell, L. (2002) *Re-engaging the Hardest to Help Young People: The Role of the Neighbourhood Support Fund.* Research Report RR366. London: DfES.

Gooding, C. (2000) Disability Discrimination Act: From statute to practice, *Critical Social Policy,* 20(4): 533–49.

Goodyear, P., Salmon, G., Spector, M., Steeples, C. and Tickner, S. (2001) Competences for on-line teaching: A special report, *Educational Technology Research and Development,* 49(1): 65–72.

Gooler, D.D. (1986) *The Education Utility: The Power to Revitalize Education and Society.* Englewood Cliffs, New Jersey: Educational Technology Publications.

Gorard, S., Rees, G. and Fevre, R. (1999) Patterns of Participation in Lifelong Learning: Do families make a difference? *British Educational Research Journal,* 25: 517–32.

Gorbachev, M. (1999) *On my Country and the World.* New York: Columbia University Press.

Gould, S.J. (1997) The exaptive excellence of spandrels as a term and prototype, *Proceedings of the National Academy of Sciences of the USA,* 94 (Sept): 10750–5. [http://www.pnas.org/content/vol94/issue20/#EVOLUTION].

Gray, F. (ed.) (2002) *Landscapes of Learning.* Leicester: NIACE.

Griffiths, M. (2000) Collaboration and Partnership in Question: Knowledge, Politics and Practice, *Journal of Education Policy,* 15(4): 383–95.

Grimes, S. (2000) Rural areas in the Information Society: Diminishing distance or increasing learning capacity? *Journal of Rural Studies,* 16: 13–21.

Guile, D. (2001) Seminar on the MA in Higher and Professional Education, University of London Institute of Education, London, March.

Habermas, J. (1971) The university in a democracy: democratization of the university. *Toward a Rational Society.* London: Heinemann.

Hake, B.J. (1996) The University-Community Interface in Europe, in J. Elliott,

H. Francis, R. Humphreys and D. Istance (eds) *Communities and their Universities: The Challenge of Lifelong Learning.* London: Lawrence and Wishart: 48–61.

Halsey, A.H. (1995) *Decline of Donnish Dominion: The British Academic Professions in the Twentieth Century.* Oxford: Oxford University Press.

Hargreaves, D.H. (1999) The knowledge-creating school, *British Journal of Educational Studies*, 47(2): 122–44.

Hauden, J.A. and MacLean, D. (2002) 'E' is for Engagement. Transforming your Business by Transforming your People, *Journal of Change Management*, 2(3): 255–65.

Henkel, M. (2000) *Academic Identities and Policy Changes in Higher Education.* London: Jessica Kingsley Publishers.

Hey, V. (2001) The Construction of Academic Time: sub-contracting academic labour in research, *Journal of Education Policy*, 16(1): 67–84.

Higgins, R., Hartley, P. and Skelton, A. (2002) The conscientious consumer: reconsidering the role of assessment feedback in student learning, *Studies in Higher Education*, 27(1): 53–64.

Higher Education Funding Council for England (HEFCE) (2001) *Performance Indicators in Higher Education.* HEFCE report 01/69. Bristol: HEFCE.

Higher Education Funding Council for England (HEFCE) (2002) *The Wider Benefits of Higher Education: Report by the Institute of Education.* Report 01/46, July.

Higher Education Funding Council for England (HEFCE) (2002) *Academic Staff: Trends and Projections.* Issues Paper, 2002/43, September.

Higher Education Statistics Agency (HESA) (1999) *Insight 2000, A Statistical Guide to Undergraduate Study.* Cheltenham: HESA.

Higher Education Statistics Agency (HESA) (2002a) *Reference Volume: Students in Higher Education Institutions, 2000–2001.* Cheltenham: HESA.

Higher Education Statistics Agency (HESA) (2002b) *Higher Education Management Statistics – Institution-level.* Cheltenham: HESA.

Hobcraft, J. (2000) *The Roles of Schooling and Educational Qualifications in the Emergence of Adult Social Exclusion.* CASE Paper 43, London: London School of Economics.

Hochschul-Informations-System (HIS) (2002) *Euro Student: Social and Economic Conditions of Student Life in Europe 2000.* W.Bertelsmann Verlag GmbH, and http://www.his.de/Abt2/Auslandsstudium/Eurostudent/index_html

Hodge, M. (2002) Parliamentary reply in *Hansard*, 8 July: col. 722W. London: The Stationery Office.

Hodge, M. (2003) Higher education's contribution to changing society, in *Higher Education Digest*, Issue 44.

Hornby, G. (1999) Inclusion or Delusion: Can one size fit all? *Support for Learning*, 14(4): 152–7.

Hounsell, D. (1987) Essay-writing and the quality of feedback, in J.T.E. Richardson et al. (eds) *Student Learning: Research in Education and Cognitive Psychology.* Milton Keynes: SRHE and Open University Press.

Hounsell, D. (1997) Contrasting conceptions of essay-writing, in F. Marton, D. Hounsell and N. Entwistle (eds) *The Experience of Learning.* Edinburgh: Scottish Academic Press. [Orig publ. in the 1984 edition under the title 'Learning and essay-writing'.]

Hounsell, D. (1998) Learning, assignments and assessment, in C. Rust (ed.) *Improving Students as Learners*, Proceedings of the Fifth International Symposium on Improving Student Learning, University of Strathclyde, 8–10 September 1997. Oxford: Oxford Centre for Staff and Learning Development.

Hounsell, D. (2000) Reappraising and recasting the history essay, in A. Booth and P. Hyland (eds) *The Practice of University History Teaching*. Manchester: Manchester University Press.

Hounsell, D. and McCune, V. (in press) Students' experiences of learning to present, in C. Rust (ed.) Proceedings of the Tenth International Improving Learning Symposium, Brussels, 4–6 September 2002. Oxford: Oxford Centre for Staff and Learning Development.

Hounsell, D. and Murray, R. (1992) *Essay-Writing for Active Learning*. Sheffield: CVCP Universities' Staff Development Unit.

Hounsell, D., McCulloch, M. and Scott, M. (1996) *The ASSHE Inventory: Changing Assessment Practices in Scottish Higher Education*. Edinburgh and Sheffield: University of Edinburgh and Napier University, Edinburgh in association with the Universities' and Colleges' Staff Development Agency (UCoSDA). http://www.ltsn.ac.uk/genericcentre/projects/assessment/asshe/default.asp

House of Commons (2001) *Sixth Report of the Select Committee on Education and Employment – Higher Education: Student Retention*. London: House of Commons.

Howie, G. (2002) A Reflection of Quality: instrumental reason, quality audits and the knowledge economy, *Critical Quarterly*, 44(4): 140–7.

Hung, D. (2001) Theories of Learning and Computer Mediated Leaning Technologies, *Educational Media International*, 38(4): 281–7.

Hyland, P. (2000) Learning from feedback on assessment, in A. Booth and P. Hyland (eds) *The Practice of University History Teaching*. Manchester: Manchester University Press.

Hyland, T. (2001) Third Way Values and Post-school Education Policy, *Journal of Education Policy*, 17(2): 245–58.

Ikeda, D. (1996) *A New Humanism*. New York: Weatherhill.

Istance, D., Schuetze, H.G. and Schuller, T. (2002) *International Perspectives on Lifelong Learning: From Recurrent Education to the Knowledge Society*. Buckingham: SRHE and Open University Press.

Ivanic, R., Clark, R. and Rimmershaw, R. (2000) What am I supposed to make of this? The messages conveyed to students by tutors' written comments, in M.R. Lea and B. Stierer (eds) *Student Writing in Higher Education: New Contexts*. Buckingham: SRHE and Open University Press.

Jackman, A. (1846) Advocating an Atlantic Telegraph, in the *Vermont Mercury* in August 1846. Cited in Standage, T. (1998) *The Victorian Internet: The remarkable story of the telegraph and the Nineteenth Century's online pioneers*. London: Phoenix, 136.

James, D. (2000) Making the graduate: perspectives on student experience of assessment in higher education, in A. Filer (ed.) *Assessment: Social Practice and Social Product*. London and New York: Routledge Falmer.

Jaques, D. (2000) *Learning in Groups*, 3rd edn. London: Kogan Page.

Jarvis, P. (2000) The corporate university, in J. Field and M. Leicester (eds) *Lifelong Learning: Education Across the Lifespan*. London and New York: Routledge Falmer.

Johnson, R. and Deem, R. (2003) Talking of Students: Tensions and Contradictions for the Manager-Academic and the University in Contemporary Higher Education (in press), *Higher Education*.

Johnson, S. (2002) Lifelong Learning and SMEs: Issues for Research and Policy, *Journal of Small Business and Enterprise Development*, 9(3): 285–95.

Joint Costing and Pricing Steering Group (JCPSG) (2000) *Transparency Review of Research*, www.jcpsg.ac.uk.

Jung, A. (2002) Wa(h)re Bildung, *Der Spiegel special*, 3/2002: 140–44.

Kasl, E. (2001) Groups that learn and how they do it, in I. Falk (ed.) op. cit.: 91–9.

Kasl, E., Marsick, V. and Dechant, K. (1997) Teams as Learners: A Research Based Model of Team Learning, *Journal of Applied Behavioural Science*, 33(2): 227–46.

Katz, S.N. (2002) Choosing Justice Over Excellence, *Chronicle of Higher Education*, 17 May.

Kennedy, D. (1997) *Academic Duty*. Cambridge and London: Harvard University Press.

Kenway, J. and Langmead, D. (1998) Governmentality, the 'now' university and the future of knowledge work, *Australian Universities' Review*, 41(2): 28–31.

King, D. (2002) Science Policy in Government, Marie Jahoda Lecture, University of Sussex, 9 October.

Kochhar, R. (2002) International Research Collaboration in a Changing World. Presentation to the EU-India seminar, University of Brighton, 13 September.

Konu, A. and Rimpela, M. (2002) Well-being in schools: A Conceptual Model, *Health Promotion International*, 17(1): 79–87.

Lake, A. (2001) *Six Nightmares*. New York: Little, Brown & Co.

Laurillard, D. (1997) Learning formal representations through multimedia, in F. Marton, D. Hounsell and N. Entwistle (ed.) *The Experience of Learning*, 2nd rev. edn. Edinburgh: Scottish Academic Press.

Laurillard, D. (2002) *Rethinking University Teaching: A Conversational Framework for the Effective Use of Learning Technologies*, 2nd edn. London and New York: Routledge Falmer.

Lave, J. and Wenger, E. (1991) *Situated Learning: Legitimate Peripheral Participation*. Cambridge: Cambridge University Press.

Lea, M.R. and Stierer, B. (eds) (2000) *Student Writing in Higher Education: New Contexts*. Buckingham: SRHE and Open University Press.

Lea, M.R. and Street, B.V. (2000) Student writing and staff feedback in higher education: an academic literacies approach, in M.R. Lea and B. Stierer (eds) *Student Writing in Higher Education: New Contexts*. Buckingham: SRHE and Open University Press.

Learning and Skills Research Centre (LSRC) (2002) *Saving for Learning Strand 2: an international comparison*. Taunton: LSRC.

Lillis, T. and Turner, J. (2001) Student writing in higher education: contemporary confusion, traditional concerns, *Teaching in Higher Education*, 6(1): 57–68.

Lonsdale, M. (2002) *Global Gateways: A Guide to Online Knowledge Networks*. Melbourne: Australian Council for Educational Research. Available on-line at http://www.educationau.edu.au/research/globalgateways.pdf

Luke, C. (2001) *Globalization and Women in Academia: North/West – South/East*. Mahwah, New Jersey: Lawrence Erlbaum Publishers.

Lynch, K. and O'Riordan, C. (1998) Inequality in Higher Education: a study of class barriers, *British Journal of Sociology of Education*, 19(4): 445–78.

Lyotard, J. (1984) *The Postmodern Condition*. Manchester: Manchester University Press.

Major, L.E. (2001) A watchdog bitten, *The Guardian*, 27 March.

Marceau, J. (2000) Australian universities: a contestable future, in T. Coady (ed.) *Why Universities Matter: A Conversation About Values, Means and Directions*. Sydney: Allen and Unwin.

Marcuse, H. (1969) *An Essay on Liberation*. Boston, USA: Beacon Press.

Marginson, S. (1997) Competition and Contestability in Australian Higher Education, *Australian Universities Review*, 40(1): 5–14.

Margolis, E. (ed.) (2001) *The Hidden Curriculum in Higher Education.* London and New York: Routledge.

Marsden, C. and Andriof, J. (1998) Understanding corporate citizenship and how to influence it, *Journal of Citizenship Studies,* 2(2): 329–52.

Marsden, T. (1999) Rural Futures: The Consumption Countryside and its Regulation, *Sociologica Ruralis,* 39(4): 501–20.

Marton, F., Hounsell, D. and Entwistle, N. (eds) (1997) *The Experience of Learning,* 2nd rev. edn. Edinburgh: Scottish Academic Press.

Mason, R. (1998) *Globalising Education.* London: Routledge.

Mason, R. and Williams, G. (2002) How Much Does Higher Education Enhance the Employability of Graduates? Paper presented to a HEFCE/LTSN seminar at the Royal Society, London, September.

Mayor, F. and Bindé, J. (2001) *The World Ahead: Our Future in the Making.* London: Zed Books.

McDonough, P. M., Antonio, A.L., Walpole, M. and Perez, L. (1997) College Rankings: who uses them and with what impact? American Educational Research Association Annual Meeting, Chicago, April.

McDowell, L. and Sambell, K. (1999) Fitness for purpose in the assessment of learning: students as stakeholders, *Quality in Higher Education,* 5(2): 107–23.

McWilliam, E., Hatcher, C. and Meadmore, D. (1999) Developing professional identities: remaking the academic for corporate times, *Pedagogy, Culture and Society,* 7(1): 55–72.

Meadmore, D. (1998) Changing the Culture: The Governance of the Australian pre-millennial university, *International Studies in Sociology of Education,* 8: 27–45.

Meager, N., Doyle, B., Evans, C. et al. (1999) *Monitoring the Disability Discrimination Act 1995.* London: DfEE.

Meert, H. (2000) Rural Community Life and the Importance of Reciprocal Survival Strategies, *Sociologica Ruralis,* 40(1): 319–39.

Mills, C.W. (1959) *The Sociological Imagination.* New York: Oxford University Press.

Mohr, J. (2002) Alles top, einfach traumhaft, *Der Spiegel special,* 3/2002: 150–54.

Moll, L. (ed.) (1992) *Vygotsky and Education.* Cambridge: Cambridge University Press.

Moore, R. and Muller, J. (1999) The Discourse of 'Voice' and the Problem of Knowledge and Identity in the Sociology of Education, *British Journal of Sociology of Education,* 20(2): 189–205.

Moreland, N., Artaraz, K., Smith, M. and Lavelle, J. (forthcoming) Grass Roots and Suits: Working With Educational Institutions in Collaborative Projects. Submitted to *Research in Post-Compulsory Education and Training.*

Moreland, N., Lavelle, J. and Hunt, A. (2002) (Re) Searching for Learners: Learner Defined Needs in a Rural Collaborative Project involving ICT. In E. Wagner and A. Szucs (eds) *Open and Distance Learning in Europe and Beyond: Rethinking International Co-operation.* Granada: EDEN.

Morley, L. (2003) *Quality and Power in Higher Education.* Buckingham: Open University Press.

Morris, L. (1979) *Elusive Equality: The Status of Black Americans in Higher Education.* Washington, DC: Howard University Press.

Morrison, R. (1999) *The Spirit in the Gene.* New York: Cornell University Press.

Moser, C. (1999) *Improving Literacy and Numeracy: A Fresh Start.* Report of the Working Group on post-school basic skills. London: DfEE.

Mulraney, J. and Turner, P. (2001) A Regional Approach to Youth Employment: The role of young people in renewing regional communities, in I. Falk (ed.) op. cit.: 149–62.

National Audit Office (2002) *Improving Student Achievement in the English Higher Education Sector.* London: The Stationery Office.

National Committee of Inquiry into Higher Education (NCIHE) (1997), *Report of the Scottish Committee,* http://www.leeds.ac.uk/educol/ncihe/scottish.htm (accessed 6 March 2002).

National Committee of Inquiry into Higher Education (NCIHE) (1997) *Higher education in the learning society.* (The Dearing Report). London: NCIHE.

Naylor, R., Smith, J. and McKnight, A. (2002) Sheer Class? The Extent and Sources of Variation in the UK Graduate Earnings Premium. Mimeo, Department of Economics, University of Warwick.

Nettles, M. (1988) *Toward Black Undergraduate Student Equality in American Higher Education.* Westport Connecticut: Greenwood Press.

Newby, H. (2002) Keynote Address to the UACE Annual Conference, University of Bath.

Nie, N., Junn, J. and Stehlik-Barry, K. (1996) *Education and Democratic Citizenship in America.* Chicago: University of Chicago Press.

Nightingale, P., Te Wiata, I., Toohey, S., Ryan, G., Hughes, C. and Magin, D. (1996) *Assessing Learning in Universities.* Kensington, NSW: University of New South Wales Press.

Norton, L.S. (1990) Essay-writing: what really counts?, *Higher Education,* 20(4): 411–42.

Office for National Statistics (ONS) (2000) *Standard Occupational Classification 2000.* London: The Stationery Office.

Office of Training and Further Education (OFTE) (1998) TAFE teachers online: Professional development for online delivery. Melbourne: Office of Training and Further Education and Australian National Training Authority.

Oliver, M. (1990) *The Politics of Disablement.* Basingstoke: Macmillan.

Oliver, R. and Towers, S. (2000) *Uptime: Students, Learning and Computers. A Study of ICT Literacy and Access Among Australian Tertiary Students.* Canberra: Australian Department of Education, Training and Youth Affairs.

Organisation for Economic Co-operation and Development (OECD) (1996) *Employment and Growth in the Knowledge-Based Economy.* Paris: OECD.

Pannelli, R. (2002) Young Rural Lives: strategies beyond diversity, *Journal of Rural Studies,* 18: 113–22.

Panelli, R., Nairn, K. and McCormack, J. (2002) 'We Make Our Own Fun': Reading the Politics of Youth with(in) Community, *Sociologica Ruralis,* 42(2): 106–30.

Parry, G. and Thompson, A. (2001) *Higher Education in FE Colleges.* London: LSDA.

Paterson, L. (2000) Civil Society and Democratic Renewal, in S. Baron, J. Field and T. Schuller (eds) *Social Capital: Critical Perspectives.* Oxford: Oxford University Press.

Patten, J. (1993) Only quality can save universities, *The Times,* 6 December.

Pengelly, R. (2002a) *How to Work with Micro-Businesses.* London: LSDA.

Pengelly, R. (2002b) *How to Work with Small Businesses.* London: LSDA.

Perry, M. (2000) Migration to and from HE study: an investigation using distances travelled, *Statistics Focus,* 1(2).

Peters, M.A. (2001) *Poststructuralism, Marxism and Neoliberalism: Between Theory and Politics.* Lanham: Rowman and Littlefield.

Phillips, M., Fish, R. and Agg, J. (2001) Putting together ruralities: towards a symbolic analysis of rurality in the British mass media, *Journal of Rural Studies,* 17(1): 1–27.

Picco, G. et al. (2001) Crossing the Divide: Dialogue among Civilizations, *Seton Hall Journal of Diplomacy & International Relations*, 2(1): 5–10.

Pollard, A. with Filer, A. (1996) *The Social World of Children's Learning: Case-studies of Pupils from Four to Seven*. London: Cassell.

Pollard, A. and Filer, A. (1999) *The Social World of Pupil Career: Strategic Biographies Through Primary School*. London: Continuum.

Pollard, A. and Filer, A. (forthcoming) *Learning Differently: The Social World of Secondary Schooling*. London: Continuum.

Prosser, M. and Webb, C. (1994) Relating the process of undergraduate essay-writing to the finished product, *Studies in Higher Education*, 19(2): 125–38.

Pugsley, L. (1998) Throwing Your Brains At It: Higher Education, Markets and Choice, *International Studies in Sociology of Education*, 8: 71–90.

Purcell, K. and Hogarth, T. (1999) *Graduate Opportunities, Social Class and Age: Employers' Recruitment Strategies in the New Graduate Labour Market*. London: Council for Industry and Higher Education/Institute for Employment Research.

Purcell, K., Pitcher, J. and Simm, C. (1999). *Working out? Graduates' Early Experience of the Labour Market*. Report for DfES, CSU, AGAS and IER. Manchester: CSU.

Quality Assurance Agency (QAA) (2000) *Handbook for Academic Review*. Gloucester: Quality Assurance Agency for Higher Education.

Raab, G. (1998) *Participation in Higher Education in Scotland*. Edinburgh: SHEFC.

Raab, G. and Davidson, K. (1999) *Distribution of FE Provision in Scotland*. Edinburgh: Scottish Office Education and Industry Department.

Ramaprasad, A. (1983) On the definition of feedback, *Behavioral Science*, 28: 4–13.

Ramsden, B. (2001) *Patterns of Higher Education Institutions in the United Kingdom*. London: Universities UK and SCOP.

Ramsden, P. (1998) Out of the Wilderness, *The Australian*, 29 April: 39–41.

Ray, C. (1998) Culture, Intellectual Property and Territorial Rural Development, *Sociological Ruralis*, 38(1): 3–20.

Ray, C. (1999) Towards a Meta-Framework of Endogenous Development: Repertoires, Paths, Democracy and Rights, *Sociologica Ruralis*, 39(4): 521–37.

Readings, B. (1996) *The University in Ruins*. Cambridge, MA: Harvard University Press.

Reay, D., Davies, J., David, M. and Ball, S. (2001) Choices of Degree or Degrees of Choice? Class, 'Race' and the Higher Education Choice Process, *Sociology*, 35(4): 855–74.

Resnick, L.B. (1987) Learning in school and out, *Educational Researcher*, 16(9): 13–20.

Richardson, T. (2000) Discourses of rurality in EU spatial policy: The European spatial development perspective, *Sociologica Ruralis*, 40(1): 53–74.

Riddell, S. and Banks, P. (2001) *Disability in Scotland: A Baseline Study*. Edinburgh: Disability Rights Commission.

Riddell, S., Wilson, A. and Tinklin, T. (2002) Disability and the wider access agenda: supporting disabled students in different institutional contexts, *Widening Participation and Lifelong Learning*, 4(3): 13–26.

Riesman, D. (1998) *On Higher Education: The Academic Enterprise in an Era of Rising Student Consumerism*. New Brunswick: Transaction Publishers.

Robbins, L. (1963) *Higher Education: Report of the Committee Appointed by the Prime Minister Under the Chairmanship of Lord Robbins 1961–63*, Cm 2154. London: HMSO.

Robinson, E. (1968) *The New Polytechnics*. Harmondsworth: Penguin.

Rogoff, B., Turkanis, C.G. and Bartlett, L. (2001) *Learning Together: Children and Adults in a School Community*. Oxford: Oxford University Press.

Rommetveit, R. (1974) *On Message Structure*. Chichester: Wiley.

Rommetveit, R. (1979) On the architecture of intersubjectivity, in R. Rommetveit and R.M. Blakar (eds) *Studies of Language, Thought and Communication.* London: Academic Press.

Rossetti-Ferreira, M.C., Amorim, K.S. and Silva, A.P.S. (2002) The network of meanings perspective: basic concepts and theoretical assumptions. Paper given at the 5th Congress of the International Society for Cultural Research and Activity Theory, Amsterdam, June.

Rowntree Foundation (2000) Exclusive Countryside? Social Inclusion and Regeneration in Rural Areas, *Foundations,* 760: 1.

Russell, C. (1993) *Academic Freedom.* London: Routledge.

Rustin, M. (1994) Flexibility in Higher Education, in R. Burrows and B. Loader (eds) *Towards a Post-Fordist Welfare State?* London: Routledge.

Ryley, P. (2002) Social exclusion and lifelong learning in rural areas, in F. Gray (ed.) op. cit.: 33–47.

Sadler, D.R. (1989) Formative assessment and the design of instructional systems, *Instructional Science,* (18): 119–44.

Sadler, D.R. (1998) Formative assessment: revisiting the territory, *Assessment in Education,* 5(1): 77–84.

Said, E. (1994) *Representations of the Intellectual: The 1993 Reith Lectures.* London: Vintage.

Scholte, J.A. (2000) *Globalization: A Critical Introduction.* London: St Martin's Press.

Schuetze, H.G. and Slowey, M. (eds) (2000) *Higher Education and Lifelong Learners: International Perspectives on Change.* London and New York: Routledge Falmer.

Scott, D. (1971) *A.D. Lindsay.* Oxford: Oxford University Press.

Scott, P. (1995) *The Meanings of Mass Higher Education.* Buckingham: SRHE and Open University Press.

Scott, P. (2000a) The death of mass higher education and the birth of lifelong learning, in J. Field and M. Leicester (eds) *Lifelong Learning: Education Across the Lifespan.* London and New York: Routledge Falmer.

Scott, P. (ed.) (2000b) *Higher Education Re-formed.* London: Falmer Press.

Scott, P. (2001) Higher Education: an Overview, in UACE Occasional Paper No. 26, *Lifelong Learning and Higher Education: The Next Phase.* Cambridge: UACE, 15–23.

Scott, P. (2002) Partnerships for Progression: evolution or transformation? *Educational Developments,* 3(3): 1–3.

Scottish Executive (2002) *Students in Higher Education in Scotland: 2000–01.* Edinburgh: Scottish Executive Information Directorate.

Scottish Executive (2003a) *Life through Learning through Life.* Glasgow: Scottish Executive Enterprise and Lifelong Learning Department.

Scottish Executive (2003b) *A Framework for Higher Education in Scotland.* Edinburgh: The Stationery Office.

Segal Quince and Wicksteed Limited (1999) *Providing public information on the quality and standards of higher education courses: Report to DENI, HEFCE, HEFCW, QAA, SHEFC.* Cambridge: Segal Quince and Wicksteed.

Sen, A. (1999) *Development as Freedom.* Oxford: Oxford University Press.

Sennett, R. (1998) *The Corrosion of Character: The Personal Consequences of Work in the New Capitalism.* New York: Norton.

Sennett, R. (2001) Street and Office: Two Sources of Identity, in W. Hutton and A. Giddens (eds) *On the Edge, Living with Global Capitalism.* London: Vintage.

Shakespeare, T. and Watson, N. (1997) Defending the social model, *Disability and Society,* 12(2): 293–301.

Shaw, J. (1995) *Education, Gender and Anxiety*. London: Taylor and Francis.

Shiner, M. and Modood, T. (2002) Help or Hindrance? Higher Education and the Route to Ethnic Equality, *British Journal of Sociology of Education*, 23(2): 209–32.

Shore, C. and Selwyn, T. (1998) The Marketisation of Higher Education: Management, Discourse and the Politics of Performance, pp. 153–71, in D. Jary and M. Parker (eds) *The New Higher Education*. Stoke-on-Trent: Staffordshire University Press.

Shore, C. and Wright, S. (1999) Audit culture and anthropology: neo-liberalism in British higher education, *Journal of the Royal Anthropological Institute*, 5(4): 557–75.

Shucksmith, M. (2000) Endogenous Development, Social Capital and Social Inclusion: Perspectives from LEADER in the UK, *Sociologica Ruralis*, 40(2): 208–18.

Shucksmith, M. and Chapman, P. (1998) Rural Development and Social Exclusion, *Sociologica Ruralis*, 38(2): 225–42.

Silver, H. and Silver, P. (1997) *Students: Changing Roles, Changing Lives*. Buckingham: SRHE and Open University Press.

Simpson, D. and Cieslik, M. (2000) Expanding Study Support Nationally: implications from an evaluation of the East Middlesborough Education Action Zone's programme, *Educational Studies*, 26(4): 503–15.

Skinner, B.F. (1954) The science of learning and the art of teaching, *Harvard Educational Review*, 24: 88–97.

Slowey, M. (2003, forthcoming) Changing and persisting patterns: the public and lifelong learning in Scotland, in N. Sargant and F. Aldridge (eds) *Adult Learning and social division: a persistent pattern*, Vol. 2. Leicester: NIACE.

Smith, D., Campbell, J., and Brooker, R. (1999) The impact of students' approaches to essay writing on the quality of their essays, *Assessment and Evaluation in Higher Education*, 24(3): 327–38.

Smith, J., McKnight, A. and Naylor, R. (2000) Graduate employability: Policy and Performance in HE in the UK, *Economic Journal*, 110: F382–F411.

Sontag, S. (2002) *Where the Stress Falls*. London: Jonathan Cape.

Spivak, G.C. (1988) 'Can the Subaltern Speak', in C. Nelson and L. Grossberg (eds) *Marxism and the Interpretation of Culture*. Urbana: University of Illinois Press.

Strathern, M. (2000) The Tyranny of Transparency, *British Educational Research Journal*, 26(3): 309–21.

Taylor, R., Barr, J. and Steele, T. (2002) *For a Radical Higher Education: after postmodernism*. Buckingham: SRHE and Open University Press.

Teaching and Learning Research Programme (TLRP) (2001), *Focus Group Report*, unpublished paper, July.

Thomas, C. (1999) *Female Forms: Experiencing and Understanding Disability*. Buckingham: Open University Press.

Thompson, E.P. (1970) *Warwick University Ltd*. Harmondsworth: Penguin.

Thompson, J. (ed.) (2000) *Stretching the Academy: The Politics and Practice of Widening Participation in Higher Education*. Leicester: NIACE.

Tough, A.M. (1966) The assistance obtained by adult self-teachers, *Adult Education*, 17: 30–7.

Tough, A.M. (1971) *The Adult's Learning Projects*. Toronto: Ontario Institute for Studies in Education.

Touraine, A. (1971) *The May Movement: Revolt and Reform*. New York: Random House.

Trow, M. (1973) *Problems in the Transition from Elite to Mass Higher Education*. Berkeley: Carnegie Commission on Higher Education.

UNITE (2003) *Student Living Report 2003*. Bristol: UNITE.

United Nations Educational Cultural and Social Organization (UNESCO) (1997) ISCED definitions, http://www.uis.unesco.org/en/pub/pub0.htm.

United Nations Educational Scientific and Cultural Organization (UNESCO) (2002) *Universal Declaration of Cultural Diversity*. Geneva: UNESCO.

Universities UK (UUK) (2002a) *Patterns of Higher Education Institutions in the UK: second report* (September). London: UUK.

Universities UK (UUK) (2002b) *The Internal Economy of UK Higher Education Institutions, 1994–2002* (September). London: UUK.

Universities UK (UUK) (2002c) *The 50 per cent target for participation in higher education – background information*, UUK Information Note 1/02/160, 11 December.

Ward, N. (2002) Representing rurality? New Labour and the electoral geography of rural Britain, *AREA*, 34(2): 171–81.

Warwick (2002) Baroness Warwick of Undercliffe, speech in the House of Lords reported in House of Lords, in *Hansard* 27 Nov 2002: col 758. London: The Stationery Office.

Waterhouse, R., in the *Times Higher*, 20 and 27 December, 2002, p.14.

Watson, D. (2001) UK Universities and the social agenda, in R.A. Thomson, A.M. Fleming and I. Ground (eds) *People or Profit: Social Inclusion Versus Vocational Relevance*. Glasgow: University of Strathclyde and UACE, 26–38.

Watson, D. (2002) Can We All Do It All? Tensions in the mission and structure of UK higher education, *Higher Education Quarterly*, 56(2): 143–55.

Watson, D. and Taylor, R. (1998) *Lifelong Learning and the University: a Post-Dearing Agenda*. London: Falmer Press.

Wiener, N. (1961) *Cybernetics, or Control and Communication in the Animal World*, 2nd edn. New York: Wiley.

Wolf, A. (2002) *Does Education Matter? Myths About Education and Economic Growth*. London: Penguin.

Wolfendale, S. and Corbett, J. (eds) (1996) *Opening Doors: Learning Support in Higher Education*. London: Cassell.

Wood, D.N. (1996) *Post-Intellectualism and the Decline of Democracy*. New York: Praeger.

Woodward, W. (2001) Ex-polytechnics failing to recruit state school students, *Education Guardian*, 19 December.

World Future Survey (WFS) (2001) *WFS/GBN Globalization Guide*, October.

Yeatman, A. (1995) Interpreting contemporary contractualism, in J. Boston (ed.) *The State Under Contract*. Wellington: Bridge Williams Books.

Yorke, M. (2001a) Formative assessment and its relevance to retention, *Higher Education Research and Development*, 20(2): 115–26.

Yorke, M. (2001b) Outside benchmark expectations? Variation in non-completion rates in English higher education, *Journal of Higher Education Policy and Management*, 23(2): 147–58.

Yorke, M. (2002) *Improving student achievement in the English higher education sector*. Report by the National Audit Office. London: The Stationery Office.

Index

The Society for Research into Higher Education

The Society for Research into Higher Education (SRHE), an international body, exists to stimulate and coordinate research into all aspects of higher education. It aims to improve the quality of higher education through the encouragement of debate and publication on issues of policy, on the organization and management of higher education institutions, and on the curriculum, teaching and learning methods.

The Society is entirely independent and receives no subsidies, although individual events often receive sponsorship from business or industry. The Society is financed through corporate and individual subscriptions and has members from many parts of the world. It is an NGO of UNESCO.

Under the imprint *SRHE & Open University Press*, the Society is a specialist publisher of research, having over 80 titles in print. In addition to *SRHE News*, the Society's newsletter, the Society publishes three journals: *Studies in Higher Education* (three issues a year), *Higher Education Quarterly* and *Research into Higher Education Abstracts* (three issues a year).

The Society runs frequent conferences, consultations, seminars and other events. The annual conference in December is organized at and with a higher education institution. There are a growing number of networks which focus on particular areas of interest, including:

Access	Learning Environment
Assessment	Legal Education
Consultants	Managing Innovation
Curriculum Development	New Technology for Learning
Eastern European	Postgraduate Issues
Educational Development Research	Quantitative Studies
FE/HE	Student Development
Funding	Vocational Qualifications
Graduate Employment	

Benefits to members

Individual

- The opportunity to participate in the Society's networks
- Reduced rates for the annual conferences
- Free copies of *Research into Higher Education Abstracts*

- Reduced rates for *Studies in Higher Education*
- Reduced rates for *Higher Education Quarterly*
- Free copy of *Register of Members' Research Interests* – includes valuable reference material on research being pursued by the Society's members
- Free copy of occasional in-house publications, e.g. *The Thirtieth Anniversary Seminars Presented by the Vice-Presidents*
- Free copies of *SRHE News* which informs members of the Society's activities and provides a calendar of events, with additional material provided in regular mailings
- A 35 per cent discount on all SRHE/Open University Press books
- The opportunity for you to apply for the annual research grants
- Inclusion of your research in the *Register of Members' Research Interests*

Corporate

- Reduced rates for the annual conference
- The opportunity for members of the Institution to attend SRHE's network events at reduced rates
- Free copies of *Research into Higher Education Abstracts*
- Free copies of *Studies in Higher Education*
- Free copies of *Register of Members' Research Interests* – includes valuable reference material on research being pursued by the Society's members
- Free copy of occasional in-house publications
- Free copies of *SRHE News*
- A 35 per cent discount on all SRHE/Open University Press books
- The opportunity for members of the Institution to submit applications for the Society's research grants
- The opportunity to work with the Society and co-host conferences
- The opportunity to include in the *Register of Members' Research Interests* your Institution's research into aspects of higher education

Membership details: SRHE, 76 Portland Place, London W1B 1NT, UK Tel: 020 7637 2766. Fax: 020 7637 2781. email: srhe@mailbox.ulcc.ac.uk
world wide web: http://www.srhe.ac.uk./srhe/
Catalogue: SRHE & Open University Press, McGraw-Hill Education, McGraw-Hill House, Shoppenhangers Road, Maidenhead,
Berkshire SL6 2QL. Tel: 01628 502500. Fax: 01628 770224. email: enquiries@openup.co.uk – web: www.openup.co.uk

QUALITY AND POWER IN HIGHER EDUCATION

Louise Morley

This book examines the power relations that organize and facilitate quality assurance in higher education. It interrogates power in terms of macro systems of accountability, surveillance and regulation, and uncovers the ways in which quality is experienced by academics and managers in higher education. Louise Morley reveals some of the hidden transcripts behind quality assurance and poses significant questions:

- What signs of quality in higher education are being performed and valued?
- What losses, gains, fears and anxieties are activated by the procedures?
- Is the culture of excellence resulting in mediocrity?

Quality and Power in Higher Education covers a wide range of issues including the policy contexts, new managerialism, the costs of quality assurance, collegiality, peer review, gender and equity implications, occupational stress, commodification and consumer values in higher education, performativity, league tables, benchmarking, increasing workloads and the long-term effects on the academy. It draws upon Morley's empirical work in the UK, on international studies and on literature from sociology, higher education studies, organization studies and feminist theory. It is important reading for students and scholars of higher education policy and practice and for university managers and policy-makers.

Contents
Introduction – The policy context of quality in higher education – How quality is assessed – Managing quality – The psychic economy of quality – Changing employment regimes – The micropolitics of quality – Reconstructing students as consumers – (E)quality – Desiring changes – References – Index.

208pp   0 335 21226 3 (Paperback)   0 335 21227 1 (Hardback)

FOR A RADICAL HIGHER EDUCATION
AFTER POSTMODERNISM

Richard Taylor, Jean Barr and Tom Steele

This is a timely and a challenging work. The contemporary debate about the purposes of higher education needs to be refocused: on the transmission of values as well as the utility of skills; on its emancipatory as well as its instrumental roles in modern society. This book should be read by students and their teachers, as well as by policy-makers and their pay-masters.

David Watson, Director, University of Brighton

This is a forceful restatement of the classic 'Left' analysis of both the shortcomings, and radical potential, of higher education. In an age of soft-focus sound-bite New Labour politics such a restatement is badly needed. The authors take no prisoners in their critique of postmodernism as an empty and conformist discourse that inhibits radical action. Not everyone will agree with this book, but everyone should read it.

Peter Scott, Vice-Chancellor, Kingston University

Higher education is being transformed, not least because of its rapid expansion. What should be the priorities, objectives and purposes of this new higher education? Much current policy development for universities and colleges is implicitly based on postmodernist ideas. *For a Radical Higher Education* explores these postmodernist approaches through social and political theory, philosophy, cultural studies and feminism, and proposes radical alternatives. It argues that, although postmodernism has provided useful insights and corrections to other frames of reference, it leads often to a reactionary and conformist position. Its emphases on relativism, consensus and apolitical cynicism in relation to all progressive perspectives, effectively gives support to those who see higher education increasingly incorporated into technicism and free market cultures. In contrast, this book argues for a revitalized and radical university, characterized by critical, sceptical enquiry, tolerance, and a commitment to humanistic, egalitarian politics.

Contents

Introduction – The postmodernist position on higher education – Contexts – Postmodernism and politics – Revaluing the Enlightenment: the university and the educated public – Universities as epistemological communities – Policy development in higher education – The policy context – Contested concepts of lifelong learning – Community, globalization and learner autonomy – Professionalism and vocationalism – Conclusion – Radical perspectives for the new higher education – References – Index.

192pp   0 335 20868 1 (Paperback)   0 335 20869 X (Hardback)

openup
ideas and understanding
in social science

www.**openup**.co.uk

 **Browse, search and
order online**

 **Download detailed
title information and
sample chapters***

*for selected titles

www.**openup**.co.uk